Schweser Video Class Workbook

2013 CFA Level I

Volume 2

SCHWESER VIDEO CLASS WORKBOOK, VOLUME 2 (2013 CFA LEVEL I)

Published in November 2012 by Kaplan Schweser.
Printed in the United States of America.

ISBN: 978-1-4277-4254-4 / 1-4277-4254-5

PPN: 3200-2889

Contents

Study Session 9

Financial Reporting and Analysis: Inventories, Long-Lived Assets, Income Taxes, and Non-Current Liabilities

LOS 29.a Distinguish
CFAI p. 374, Schweser p. 182

Inventories

Inventory Equation

Beg. Inv + Purchases – COGS = End Inv

or

Beg. Inv + Purchases – End Inv = COGS

Beginning inventory (BI)	X
Purchases (P)	X
Available for sale	X
Ending inventory (EI)	(X)
Cost of goods sold (COGS)	X

Matching Concept

2

LOS 29.a Distinguish
CFAI p. 374, Schweser p. 182 Inventories

Inventory Costs

- Product costs are capitalized as inventory
  - Purchase cost less discounts and rebates
  - Conversion costs including labor and overhead
  - Other costs necessary to bring the inventory to its present location
- Period costs are expensed when incurred
  - Abnormal waste
  - Storage costs (unless a required production cost)
  - Selling and administrative costs

 3

LOS 29.a Distinguish
CFAI p. 374, Schweser p. 182 Inventories

Capitalization of Inventory Cost – Example

Units produced	1,500,000
Raw materials	$10,000,000
Direct labor	$5,300,000
Manufacturing overhead	$2,700,000
Freight-in to plant	$150,000
Storage cost of finished goods	$375,000
Abnormal waste	$200,000
Administrative costs	$190,000

Assuming no abnormal waste is included in labor or overhead, calculate the capitalized cost of one unit.

 4

LOS 29.a Distinguish
CFAI p. 374, Schweser p. 182
Inventories

Capitalization of Inventory – Example

Materials	$10,000,000	
Labor cost	$5,300,000	Conversion Cost
Manufacturing overhead	$2,700,000	
Freight-in to plant	$150,000	
Total capitalized cost	$18,150,000	
Units produced	1,500,000	
Cost per unit	$12.10	

 5

LOS 29.b Describe
CFAI p. 375, Schweser p. 184
Inventories

Inventory Costing Methods

There is a short video in the Schweser Library covering the computation of COGS and ending inventory balances under FIFO, LIFO, and weighted average cost methods.

 6

LOS 29.b Describe
CFAI p. 375, Schweser p. 184 Inventories

Inventory Cost Flow Methods

4 Methods	Description	Ending Inventory	COGS
FIFO	EI most recent purchases	Highest	Lowest
LIFO (No IFRS)	EI oldest purchases	Lowest	Highest
AVCO	Average cost of units available	Middle	Middle
Specific Identification	EI actual cost of specific items included in EI		

Note: Assuming rising prices and constant or increasing inventory levels

 7

LOS 29.c Calculate/Explain
CFAI p. 377, Schweser p. 185 Inventories

Example – Inventory Cost Flow

Assume beginning inventory consisted of one unit costing $10. During the current period, two more units were purchased, the first at $12 and the second at $14. One unit was sold for $17.

Calculate COGS, gross profit, and ending inventory using FIFO, LIFO, and average cost.

 8

LOS 29.c Calculate/Explain
CFAI p. 377, Schweser p. 185

Inventories

Example – Inventory Cost Flow

	FIFO	Avg. Cost	LIFO
Revenue	$17	$17	$17
COGS	10[a]	12[c]	14[e]
Gross Profit	$7	$5	$3
End Inventory	$26[b]	$24[d]	$22[f]

[a] First unit purchased

[b] Most recent purchases = $12 + $14

[c] Average cost per unit = ($10 + $12 + $14) / 3

[d] Average cost of units remaining = 2 units × $12

[e] Last unit purchased

[f] Earliest purchases = $10 + $12

9 - 3

LOS 29.c Calculate/Explain
CFAI p. 377, Schweser p. 185

Inventories

Inventory Cost Flow and Price Changes

- When prices are **rising** (as in the example):
  1. FIFO provides an artificially **low value of COGS** while LIFO is more useful (reflects current costs)
  2. LIFO provides an artificially **low value of ending inventory** while FIFO is more useful (reflects current costs)
- When prices are declining, the reverse is true
- With stable prices, all methods result in the same COGS and ending inventory

10

LOS 29.d Calculate/Compare
CFAI p. 379, Schweser p. 188 Inventories

Inventory Systems

- Periodic System
  - Inventory and COGS are determined at the end of the period
  - Beg Inv + Purchases – End Inv = COGS
- Perpetual System
  - Inventory and COGS are continuously updated as each sale occurs
  - No purchases account needed

 11

LOS 29.d Calculate/Compare
CFAI p. 379, Schweser p. 188 Inventories

Example – Inventory Systems

Use the following to calculate COGS and ending inventory under FIFO and LIFO for the month of March using a periodic and perpetual inventory system:

Mar 1 (beg. inventory)	4 units @ $3.00 per unit
Mar 14 sale	3 units
Mar 25 purchase	10 units @ $3.70 per unit
Mar 28 sale	8 units

 12 - 1

LOS 29.d Calculate/Compare
CFAI p. 379, Schweser p. 188 — Inventories

Example – Inventory Systems

FIFO Periodic

Beg Inv.	$12.00 (4 units × $3.00)
+ Purchases	37.00 (10 units × $3.70)
– End Inv.	11.10 (3 units × $3.70)
= COGS	$37.90

Same Results!

FIFO Perpetual

Mar 14 sale	$9.00 (3 units × $3.00)
Mar 28 sale	28.90 (1 unit × $3.00) + (7 units × $3.70)
COGS	$37.90
End Inv.	$11.10 (3 units × $3.70)

 13 - 1

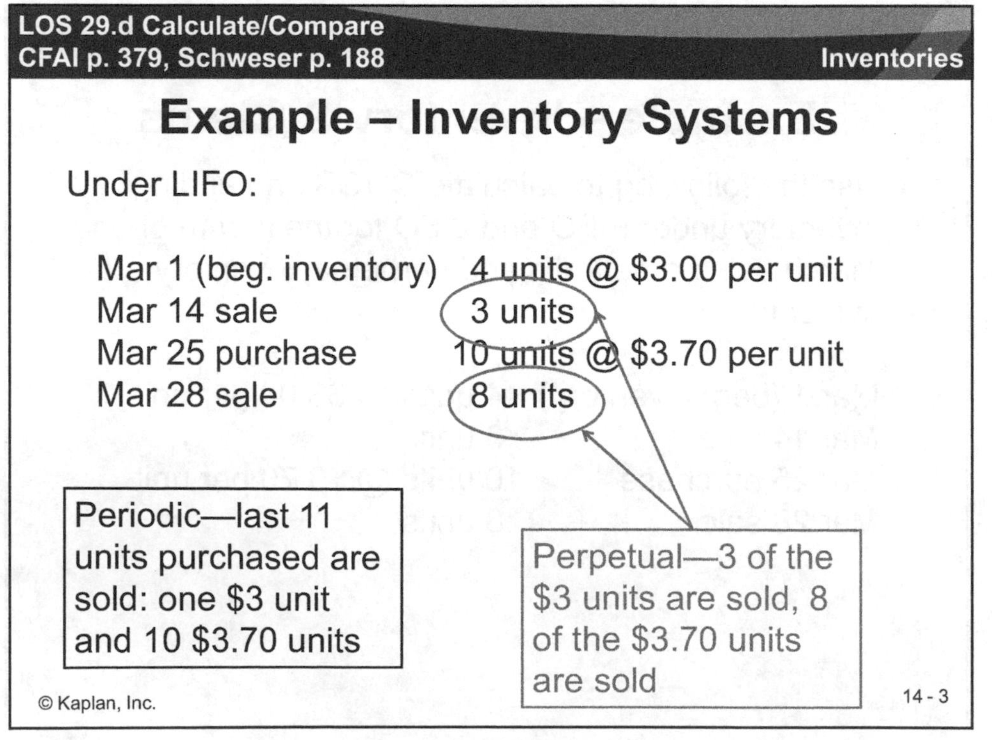

LOS 29.d Calculate/Compare
CFAI p. 379, Schweser p. 188
Inventories

Example – Inventory Systems

LIFO Periodic

Beg Inventory	\$12.00 (4 units × \$3.00)
+ Purchases	37.00 (10 units × \$3.70)
– End Inventory	9.00 (3 units × \$3.00)
= COGS	\$40.00

Different Results!

LIFO Perpetual

Mar 14 sale	\$9.00 (3 units × \$3.00)
Mar 28 sale	29.60 (8 units × \$3.70)
COGS	\$38.60
End Inventory	\$10.40 (1 unit × \$3.00) + (2 units × \$3.70)

15 - 1

LOS 29.d Calculate/Compare
CFAI p. 379, Schweser p. 188
Inventories

Example – Inventory Systems

Summary

Inventory System	FIFO COGS	LIFO COGS	FIFO Inventory	LIFO Inventory
Periodic	\$37.90	\$40.00	\$11.10	\$9.00
Perpetual	\$37.90	\$38.60	\$11.10	\$10.40

- The inventory system only affects the LIFO and average cost flow methods
- FIFO and specific identification are unaffected
- FIFO and LIFO relationships remain!

16

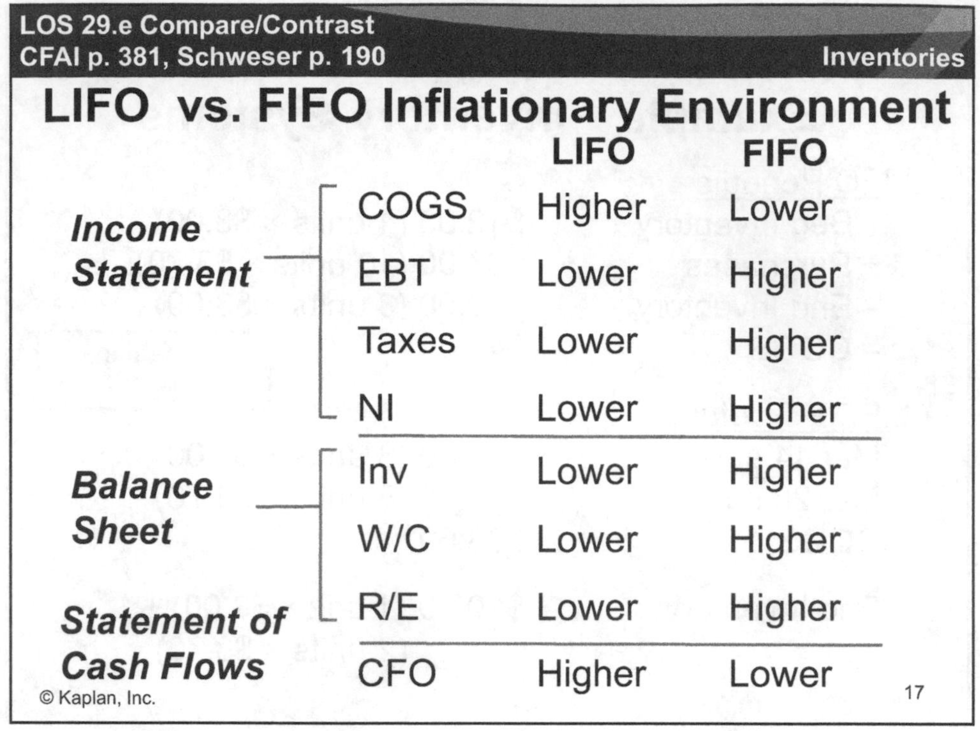
LOS 29.e Compare/Contrast
CFAI p. 381, Schweser p. 190
Inventories
LIFO vs. FIFO Inflationary Environment
LIFO
FIFO
Income Statement
COGS Higher Lower
EBT Lower Higher
Taxes Lower Higher
NI Lower Higher
Balance Sheet
Inv Lower Higher
W/C Lower Higher
R/E Lower Higher
Statement of Cash Flows
CFO Higher Lower
© Kaplan, Inc.
17

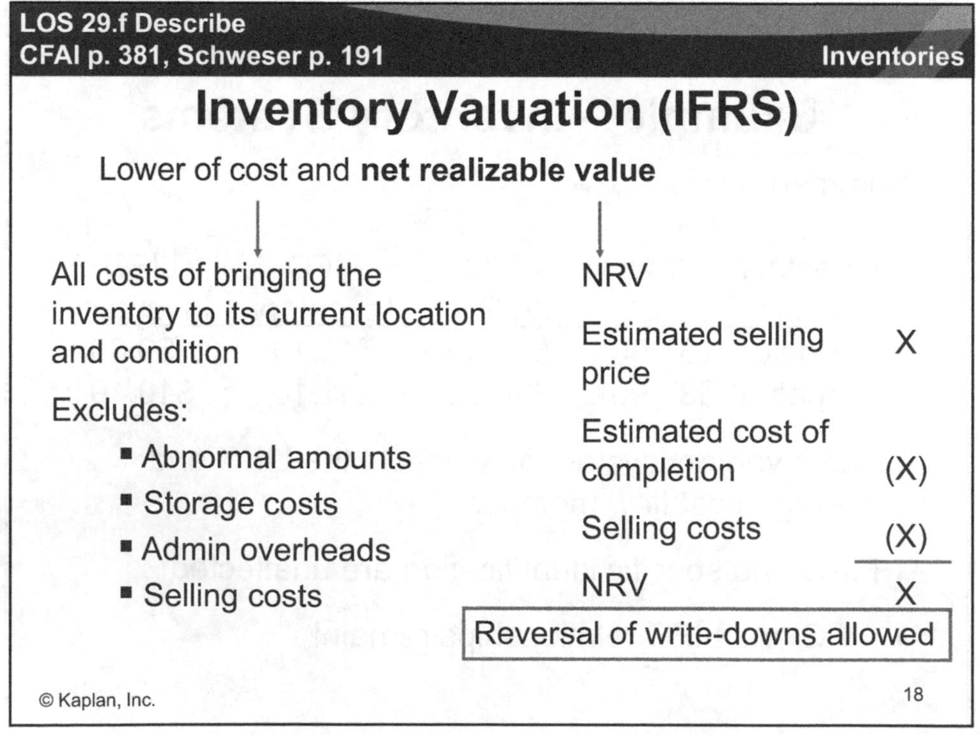
LOS 29.f Describe
CFAI p. 381, Schweser p. 191
Inventories
Inventory Valuation (IFRS)
Lower of cost and net realizable value
All costs of bringing the inventory to its current location and condition
Excludes:
Abnormal amounts
Storage costs
Admin overheads
Selling costs
NRV
Estimated selling price X
Estimated cost of completion (X)
Selling costs (X)
NRV X
Reversal of write-downs allowed
© Kaplan, Inc.
18

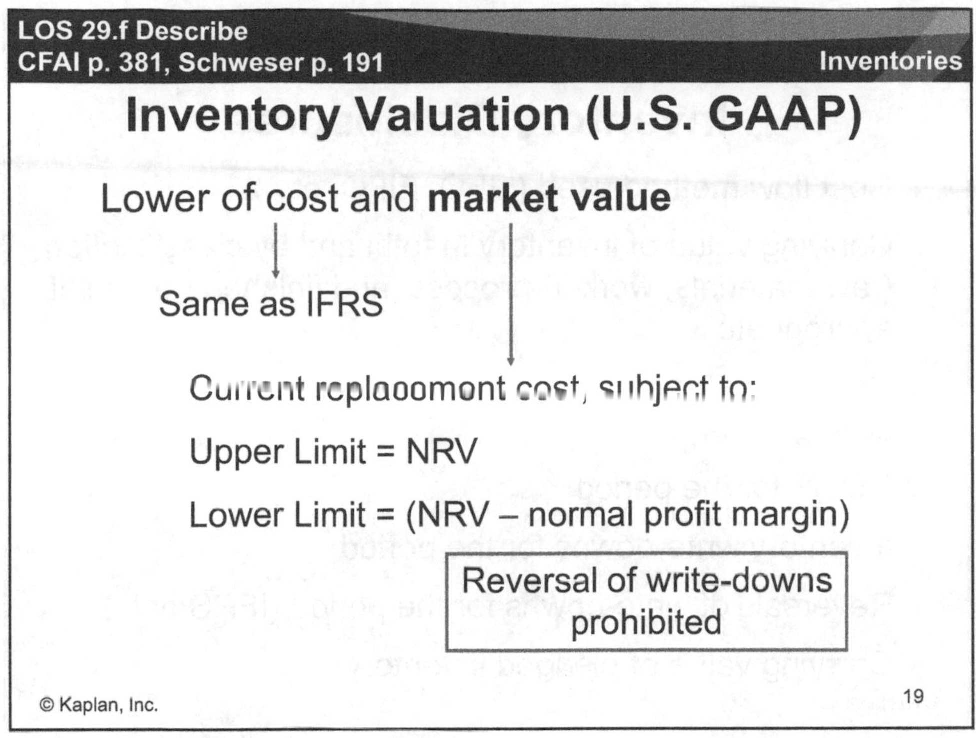

LOS 29.f Describe
CFAI p. 381, Schweser p. 191 Inventories

Inventory Valuation

- Under IFRS and U.S. GAAP, reporting inventory above cost is permitted in some industries, primarily producers and dealers of commodity-like products
  - Reported on the balance sheet at net realizable value
  - If active market exists, quoted market price is used; otherwise, recent market transactions are used
  - Unrealized gains/losses recognized in the income statement

20

LOS 29.g Describe
CFAI p. 383, Schweser p. 194 Inventories

Inventory Disclosures

- Cost flow method used (LIFO, FIFO, etc.)
- Carrying value of inventory in total and by classification (raw materials, work-in-process, and finished goods), if appropriate
- Carrying value of inventory reported at fair value less selling costs
- COGS for the period
- Inventory write-downs for the period
- Reversals of write-downs for the period (IFRS only)
- Carrying value of pledged inventory

 21

LOS 29.h Calculate/Interpret
CFAI p. 384, Schweser p. 194 Inventories

Profitability Ratios and Inventory Method

- As compared to FIFO, LIFO is a better measure of economic cost in the income statement (COGS based on recent prices)
- Assuming inflation, LIFO produces:
  - Higher COGS
  - Lower gross profit
  - Lower operating profit
  - Lower net profit

Lower Margins

 22

LOS 29.h Calculate/Interpret
CFAI p. 384, Schweser p. 194 Inventories

Liquidity Ratios and Inventory Method

- As compared to LIFO, FIFO is a better representation of economic cost on the balance sheet (inventory based on recent prices)
- Assuming inflation, FIFO produces:
    - Higher inventory balances
    - Higher current ratio
    - Higher working capital

Higher Current Assets

 23

LOS 29.h Calculate/Interpret
CFAI p. 384, Schweser p. 194 Inventories

Activity Ratios and Inventory Method

- LIFO COGS is based on recent prices and LIFO ending inventory is based on historical prices
- Assuming inflation, LIFO produces:
    - Higher inventory turnover (COGS / Avg. Inventory) because of the higher numerator and lower denominator
    - Lower days inventory on hand (365 / inventory turnover) because of the higher denominator

 24

LOS 29.h Calculate/Interpret
CFAI p. 384, Schweser p. 194

Inventories

Leverage Ratios and Inventory Method

- Assuming inflation, FIFO results in higher assets (inventory reported at recent prices) and higher equity (higher net income from lower COGS) as compared to LIFO
- Assuming inflation, FIFO produces lower leverage:

Lower debt-to-assets ratio
Lower debt-to-equity ratio

Higher Denominators

25

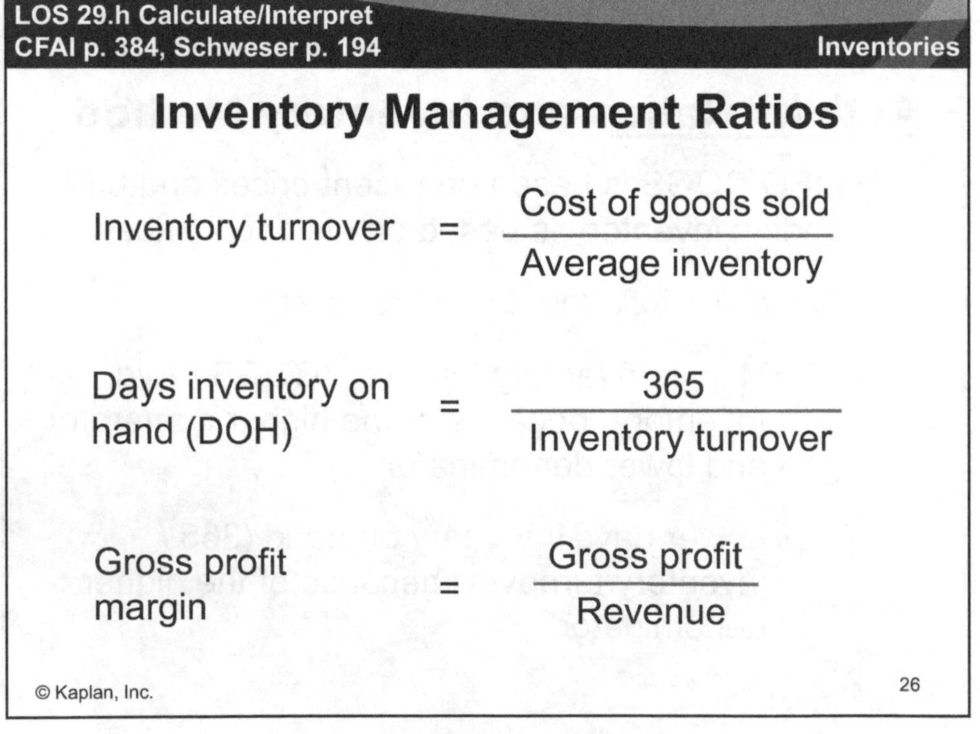

LOS 29.h Calculate/Interpret
CFAI p. 384, Schweser p. 194

Inventories

Inventory Management

Condition	Possible Interpretation
Low turnover (high DOH)	Slow-moving or obsolete inventory
High turnover (low DOH) with low sales growth relative to industry	May be losing sales from insufficient inventory levels
High turnover (low DOH) with sales growth at or above industry average	Efficient inventory management

27

Inventories

Inventory Methods – Problem

For analytical purposes an analyst would prefer to use:

A. LIFO COGS and FIFO inventory.

B. FIFO COGS and FIFO inventory.

C. FIFO COGS and LIFO inventory.

28 - 1

Inventories, Long-Lived Assets, Income Taxes, and Non-Current Liabilities

30. Long-Lived Assets

Financial Reporting and Analysis

LOS 30.a Distinguish
CFAI p. 404, Schweser p. 204

Long-Lived Assets

Capitalizing vs. Expensing: An Overview

- Costs can either be capitalized as an asset on the balance sheet or immediately expensed in the income statement
  - Capitalizing involves depreciating or amortizing the asset's cost over its useful life
  - Expensing results in an immediate reduction of net income
- General rule:
  - Capitalize if there is a future economic benefit
  - Immediately expense if the future benefit is unlikely or highly uncertain

30

LOS 30.a Distinguish
CFAI p. 404, Schweser p. 204 Long-Lived Assets

Capitalizing vs. Expensing: An Overview

- Capitalized cost includes expenditures necessary to prepare the asset for use (e.g., freight, installation, taxes)
- Subsequent related expenditures that provide more benefits are capitalized (e.g., replacing the roof on a building)
- Costs that merely sustain the asset's usefulness are immediately expensed (e.g., repair and maintenance)

 31

LOS 30.a Distinguish
CFAI p. 404, Schweser p. 204 Long-Lived Assets

Capitalizing vs. Expensing: Financial Statement Effects

	Capitalize	Expense
Assets & Equity	Higher	Lower
Net income (first year)	Higher	Lower
Net income (other years)	Lower	Higher
Income variability	Lower	Higher
ROA & ROE (first year)	Higher	Lower
ROA & ROE (other years)	Lower	Higher
Debt ratio & Debt-to-equity	Lower	Higher
CFO	Higher	Lower
CFI	Lower	Higher

 32

LOS 30.a Distinguish
CFAI p. 404, Schweser p. 204 Long-Lived Assets

Capitalizing Interest Costs

- Interest incurred during construction is capitalized ("held-for-use" assets and discrete projects)
- Objective is to accurately measure the asset's cost and better match cost with revenues
- The interest rate is based (in order) on:
    1. Project-specific debt
    2. Unrelated debt
- Interest expense on debt in excess of construction costs is immediately expensed

 33

LOS 30.a Distinguish
CFAI p. 404, Schweser p. 204 Long-Lived Assets

Capitalizing Interest Costs

- Capitalized interest is reduced by income earned from temporarily investing the debt proceeds (IFRS only)
- Once construction is complete, capitalized interest is depreciated in the income statement
- **Capitalizing interest costs results in higher interest coverage ratio (lower denominator)**
    - Many analysts add capitalized interest to interest expense before calculating interest coverage
    - The result is a reduction in interest coverage (higher denominator)

 34

LOS 30.a Distinguish
CFAI p. 404, Schweser p. 204

Long-Lived Assets

Capitalization of Interest – Example

A company is constructing a machine that it will use in its production facility. The average cost of the machine in process is $2m. The company has borrowed $1m at 5% interest to finance the construction. The company has $6m of 10% debentures.

Calculate the interest to be included as a cost of the machine and the interest expense that would appear in the income statement.

LOS 30.a Distinguish
CFAI p. 404, Schweser p. 204

Long-Lived Assets

Capitalization of Interest – Example

Interest capitalized		$
Interest on construction debt	($1m × 0.05)	50,000
Interest on debentures	($1m × 0.10)	100,000
		150,000

Interest expense		$
Interest on construction debt	($1m × 0.05)	50,000
Interest on debentures	($6m × 0.10)	600,000
Less: Interest capitalized		(150,000)
		500,000

Long-Lived Assets

Capitalizing Expenses – Problem

Firm Aggressive capitalizes certain expenses that Firm Conservative does not in year 20X0. In year 20X0, compared to Firm Aggressive, Firm Conservative will *most likely* have:

A. higher assets.

B. lower leverage ratios.

C. lower ROE.

37 - 2

LOS 30.b Compare
CFAI p. 408, Schweser p. 208

Long-Lived Assets

Intangible Assets

- **Intangible assets lack physical substance**
- Identifiable intangibles
  - Can be separated from, and controlled by, the firm
  - Expected to provide future benefits that are probable and whose cost can be reliably measured
- Unidentifiable intangibles cannot be separated from the firm (e.g., goodwill)
- Finite-lived intangibles are amortized over their useful lives
- Indefinite-lived intangibles are not amortized but tested for impairment

38

LOS 30.b Compare
CFAI p. 408, Schweser p. 208 Long-Lived Assets

Intangible Assets

Internally developed intangibles expensed as incurred

Exception: R&D, software development costs

- Research costs involve the discovery of new knowledge and understanding
- Development costs involve the translation of research findings into a plan

IFRS: Research costs are expensed as incurred, but development costs are capitalized

U.S. GAAP: Research and development costs are expensed as incurred

 39

LOS 30.b Compare
CFAI p. 408, Schweser p. 208 Long-Lived Assets

Intangible Assets

Software Development Costs

- Software developed for sale
  - **IFRS & U.S. GAAP:** Expensed as incurred until technological feasibility is reached

    Issue: Determining feasibility requires judgment
- Software developed for internal use
  - **IFRS:** Same as software developed for sale
  - **U.S. GAAP:** Capitalize all software development costs

 40

LOS 30.b Compare
CFAI p. 408, Schweser p. 208

Long-Lived Assets

Intangible Assets

Purchased Intangibles

- Recorded at cost
- When purchased as part of a group, price paid is allocated based on fair value of each asset

  Issue: Analyst usually more interested in type of asset than value assigned (e.g., franchise rights may provide insight into future performance)

Intangibles obtained in a business acquisition

- Identifiable net assets recorded at fair value
- Difference in purchase price and fair value of identifiable net assets reported as **goodwill**

41

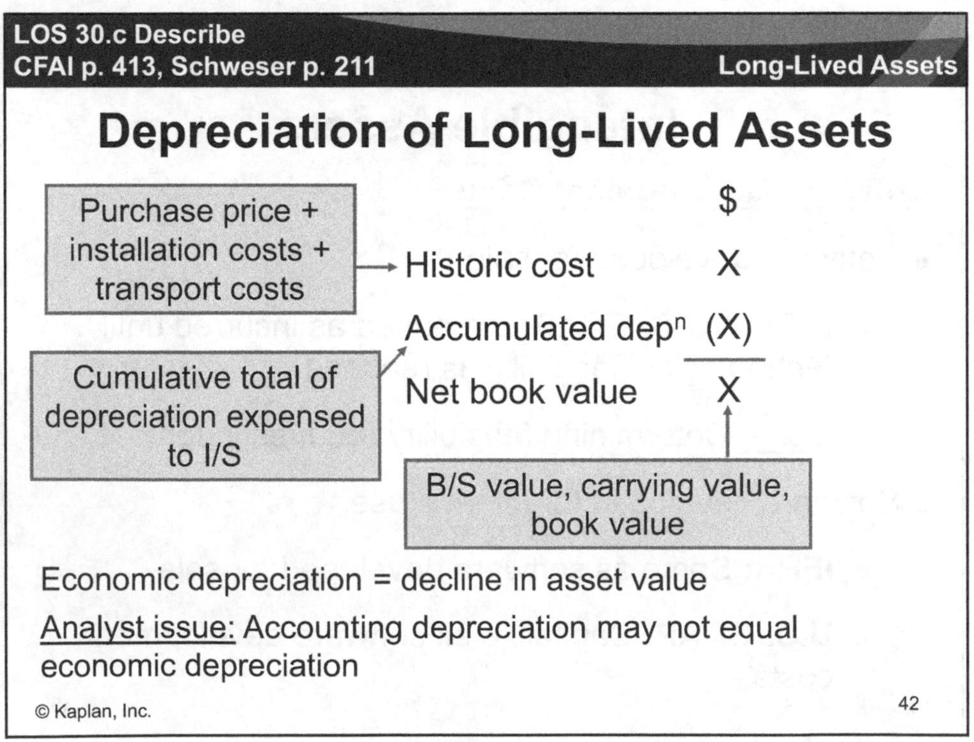

LOS 30.c Describe
CFAI p. 413, Schweser p. 211 Long-Lived Assets

Depreciation Methods

Straight-Line

- Equal amount of expense each period
- Often used for financial reporting purposes

Accelerated (Double-declining balance)

- Higher expense in the early years and lower expense in the later years

Units-of-production

- Expense is based on usage rather than time

Total depreciation expense is the same under all methods; timing is the only difference!

 43

LOS 30.d Calculate
CFAI p. 413, Schweser p. 211 Long-Lived Assets

Depreciation Methods

Straight-line

SL = (Cost – Salvage Value) / Useful Life

Double-declining balance

$DDB = \underbrace{(\text{Cost} - \text{Acc Dep}^{n})}_{\text{NBV}} \times (2/_{\text{Useful Economic Life}})$

Do not depreciate below salvage value!

Units-of-production

$UOP = (\text{Cost} - \text{Salvage Value}) \times (^{\text{Units used}}/_{\text{Total capacity}})$

 44

LOS 30.d Calculate
CFAI p. 413, Schweser p. 211 Long-Lived Assets

Depreciation – Example

At the beginning of Year 1, a firm purchased a new machine for £4,000. The machine has an estimated life of four years or 1,000 units of production. The salvage value is estimated at £500.

Assuming the firm produces 400 units in Year 2, calculate depreciation expense for Year 2 using the following methods:

1. Straight-line
2. Double-declining balance
3. Units-of-production

 45

LOS 30.d Calculate
CFAI p. 413, Schweser p. 211 Long-Lived Assets

Depreciation – Example

Straight-line

(£4,000 cost – 500 salvage) / 4 years = £875

Double-declining balance

Year 1 = (£4,000 cost – 0 Acc Dep) × 2/4 = £2,000
Year 2 = (£4,000 cost – 2,000 Acc Dep) × 2/4 = £1,000

Units-of-production

(£4,000 cost – 500 salvage) × 400 units produced / 1,000 total units = £1,400

 46

LOS 30.c,d Describe/Calculate
CFAI p. 413, Schweser p. 211

Long-Lived Assets

Impact of Depreciation Method on Financial Statements

	Straight-Line	Accelerated
Depreciation expense	Lower	Higher*
Net income	Higher	Lower*
Assets	Higher	Lower
Equity	Higher	Lower
Return on assets	Higher	Lower*
Return on equity	Higher	Lower*
Turnover ratios	Lower	Higher
Cash flow	Same	Same

* **Early years** or **growing firm**

47

LOS 30.c Describe
CFAI p. 413, Schweser p. 211

Long-Lived Assets

Estimates in Depreciation Calculations

Changes in salvage value and useful life both represent changes in accounting estimates, not changes in accounting principle

- Firm does not restate past income; change disclosed in notes
- Given longer useful life or higher salvage value, depreciation is less, leading to increased EBIT, net income, and ROE
- Shorter life or lower salvage value has opposite effects

48

LOS 30.c Describe
CFAI p. 413, Schweser p. 211

Long-Lived Assets

Component Depreciation

Component depreciation involves depreciating an asset based on the separate useful lives of the asset's individual components

- Required under IFRS
- Permitted under U.S. GAAP but seldom used

Example: An office building consists of a roof, walls, elevator, HVAC, carpeting, furniture, fixtures, etc.

Issue: The firm must estimate the useful lives of each component and depreciate each separately

49

Long-Lived Assets

Depreciation Methods – Problem

Accelerated depreciation methods:

A. lead to higher book values than does the straight-line method.

B. result in lower net income in early years, higher net income in later years.

C. allocate larger portions of cost to later accounting periods.

50 - 1

LOS 30.e,f Describe/Calculate
CFAI p. 420, Schweser p. 216 Long-Lived Assets

Amortizing Intangibles

- Process is identical to depreciation except estimating useful lives is more complicated because of legal, regulatory, and economic factors
- Intangibles with finite lives
  - Amortize over useful life
  - Pattern should match consumption of benefits (use straight-line, accelerated, or units-of-production)
- Intangibles with indefinite lives
  - No amortization
  - Periodic impairment review

 51

LOS 30.g Describe
CFAI p. 422, Schweser p. 218 Long-Lived Assets

Asset Revaluation

- U.S. GAAP: Depreciated historic cost
- IFRS choice: Depreciated historic cost or fair value
- **Revaluation below historic cost**
  - B/S asset reduced to fair market value
  - Loss taken to income statement
  - Subsequent reversals of value recognized in income statement up to original loss
  - Increase in value above original cost taken to equity
- **Revaluation above original cost**
  - B/S asset increased to fair market value
  - Gain taken directly to equity

 52

LOS 30.h Explain
CFAI p. 425, Schweser p. 218 Long-Lived Assets

Impairment of Long-Lived Assets

IFRS

- Annually assess indications of impairment (e.g., decline in market value or physical condition)
- Asset is impaired when book value (historical cost – acc. depreciation) > recoverable amount
- Recoverable amount is greater of "fair value less selling costs" and "value in use" (present value of future cash flows)
- If impaired, write down asset to recoverable amount and recognize loss in the income statement
- Loss reversal is allowed up to original loss

 53

LOS 30.h Explain
CFAI p. 425, Schweser p. 218 Long-Lived Assets

Impairment of Long-Lived Assets

U.S. GAAP (2-step process)

Assess only when indication that book value may not be recoverable through future use

1. Identification of impairment: Asset is impaired when book value > asset's estimated future undiscounted cash flows
2. Loss recognition: If impaired, write down asset to fair value (or discounted value of future cash flows if fair value unknown), recognize loss in I/S

   Loss reversal prohibited for assets "held for use"

 54

LOS 30.h Explain
CFAI p. 425, Schweser p. 218 Long-Lived Assets

Impairment of Long-Lived Assets

Assets Held for Sale (IFRS & U.S. GAAP)

- Asset is tested for impairment when transferred from "held for use" to "held for sale"
- Depreciation expense no longer recognized
- Asset is impaired if book value > net realizable value (fair value – selling costs)
- If impaired, write down asset to NRV
- Loss reversals are allowed up to the original loss under IFRS and U.S. GAAP

 55

LOS 30.h Explain
CFAI p. 425, Schweser p. 218 Long-Lived Assets

Impairment – Example

Information related to machinery owned by Milano Company follows:

	€
Original cost	500,000
Accumulated depreciation	350,000
Expected future cash flows	145,000
Fair value	140,000
Value in use	130,000
Selling costs	20,000

Assuming Milano continues to use the machinery in the future, calculate the impairment loss, if any, under both IFRS and U.S. GAAP.

 56

LOS 30.h Explain
CFAI p. 425, Schweser p. 218

Long-Lived Assets

Impairment – Example

IFRS

Book value	150,000	(500,000 – 350,000)
– Recoverable amount	130,000	← Greater of "value in use" and "fair value less selling costs"
Impairment loss	€20,000	

U.S. GAAP

1. Impairment identification

   150 book value > 145 expected future cash flows

2. Loss measurement

Book value	150,000
– Fair value	140,000
Impairment loss	€10,000

57- 6

LOS 30.h Explain
CFAI p. 425, Schweser p. 218

Long-Lived Assets

Impact of Impairment on Financial Statements

- Balance sheet: Reduces assets, liabilities (deferred taxes), and stockholders' equity
- Income statement: The loss **decreases current period income** from continuing operations; in future years, reduced depreciation results in higher net income (potential earnings management)
- Cash flow: Unaffected because the impairment is not deductible for tax purposes—impairments are non-cash charges
- Disclosure: MD&A, footnotes

58

LOS 30.h Explain
CFAI p. 425, Schweser p. 218 Long-Lived Assets

Impact of Impairment on Ratios

- **Fixed asset and total asset turnover ratios** increase due to reduced assets
- **Debt-to-equity ratio** increases due to reduced equity
- **Current year ROA and ROE** decrease →% reduction in net income > % reduction in assets/equity
- **Future ROA and ROE** increase due to lower assets and equity, higher net income with lower depreciation

 59

LOS 30.h Explain
CFAI p. 425, Schweser p. 218 Long-Lived Assets

Impairment of Long-Lived Assets

Analysts should recognize that:

- Past earnings have been overstated due to insufficient depreciation
- **Management has some control** over the timing of impairment recognition and size of impairment losses
- Impairments involve judgment—potential earnings management
- Consider revising earnings and cash flow forecasts

 60

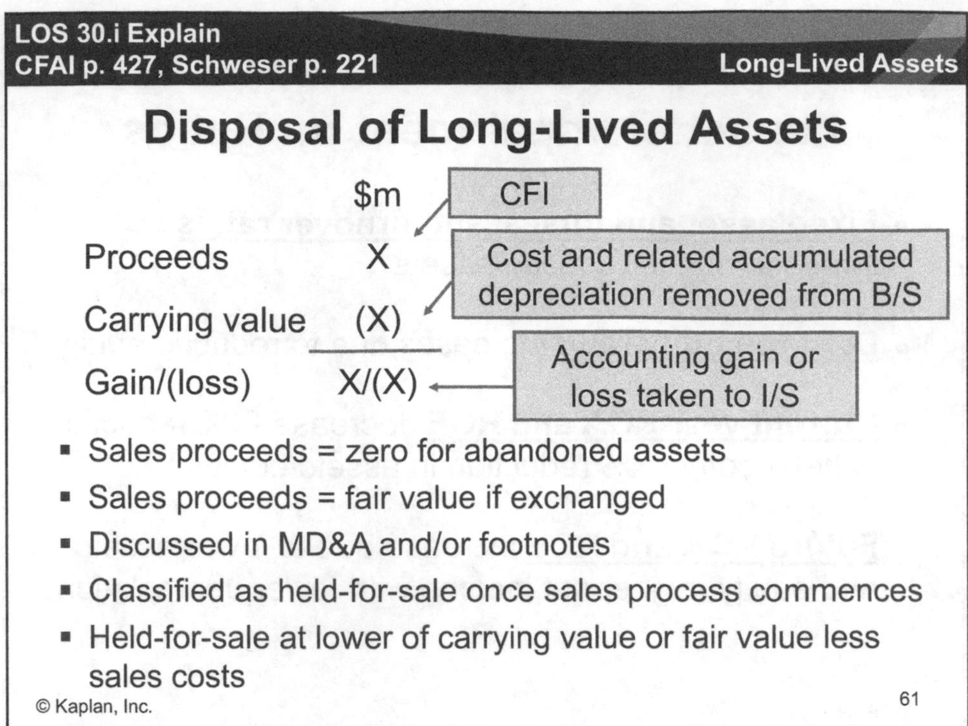

LOS 30.j Describe
CFAI p. 429, Schweser p. 221
Long-Lived Assets

Disclosure Requirements

<u>Tangible and Intangible Assets</u>

- Carrying value for each class of asset
- Accumulated depreciation and amortization
- Title restrictions and assets pledged as collateral
- For impaired assets, the loss amount and the circumstances that caused the loss
- For revalued assets (IFRS only), the revaluation date, how fair value was determined, and carrying value using historical cost model

62

LOS 30.k Compare
CFAI p. 435, Schweser p. 222 Long-Lived Assets

Investment Property

- IFRS only
- Owned for the purpose of earning rental income and/or capital appreciation
- Valued at cost or fair value
  - Cost model same as PP&E (i.e., depreciated cost)
  - Fair value model—changes in value taken to income statement, not comprehensive income
- Disclose: Fair value model or cost model
  - Fair value model: Determination of fair value
  - Cost model: Depreciation method, useful lives, fair value

 63

Inventories, Long-Lived Assets, Income Taxes, and Non-Current Liabilities

31. Income Taxes

Financial Reporting and Analysis

LOS 31.a Describe/Define
CFAI p. 450, Schweser p. 230

Income Taxes

Income Tax Accounting

Tax Reporting	**$**
Revenue	10,000
Tax allowable costs	(8,000)
Taxable income	2,000
Tax payable @ 30%	(600)
	1,400

Financial Accounting	**$**
Revenue	10,000
Accrual based costs	(5,000)
Pre-tax income	5,000
Tax @ 30%	(1,500)
	3,500

Sources of Differences

- Timing differences
- Permanent differences

Sources of Timing Differences

- Accrual vs. modified cash accounting
- Differences in reporting methods and estimates

$$\text{Income tax expense} = \text{Taxes Payable} + \Delta\ \text{Deferred Tax}$$

65

LOS 31.a Describe/Define
CFAI p. 450, Schweser p. 230

Income Taxes

Tax Terms From the Tax Return

- **Taxable income**: Amount of income subject to taxes
- **Taxes payable**: Actual tax liability for the current period (based on taxable income)
- **Income tax paid**: Actual cash flow for taxes
- **Tax loss carryforward**: Current net taxable loss available to reduce taxes in future years; can result in deferred tax assets
- **Tax base**: Net amount of asset or liability used for tax reporting purposes

66

LOS 31.a Describe/Define
CFAI p. 450, Schweser p. 230

Income Taxes

Tax Terms for Financial Reporting

Accounting profit: Pre-tax financial income, earnings before tax

Income tax expense: Tax on the income statement (includes cash taxes and deferred taxes)

Tax payable + Δ DTL – Δ DTA

Deferred tax liability (DTL): Balance sheet item created when taxes payable < income tax expense, due to temporary differences

Deferred tax asset (DTA): Balance sheet item created when taxes payable > income tax expense, due to temporary differences

67

LOS 31.a Describe/Define
CFAI p. 450, Schweser p. 230 Income Taxes

Tax Terms for Financial Reporting (continued)

Valuation allowance: Reserve against deferred tax assets that may not reverse in the future

Carrying value: Balance sheet value of an asset or liability

Note that both DTLs and DTAs are presented on the balance sheet, not netted

IFRS: DTL and DTA always non-current

U.S. GAAP: DTL and DTA current and non-current depending on reversal

 68

LOS 31.b Explain
CFAI p. 452, Schweser p. 231 Income Taxes

Differences: Accounting vs. Taxable Profits

- Revenues and expenses recognised in different periods for accounts and tax (e.g., warranty expenses)
- Carrying values of assets and liabilities may differ (e.g., depreciation)
- Specific revenues and expenses not recognized for tax or accounting purposes
- Tax loss carryforwards
- Gains and losses from asset disposals calculated differently for tax and financial statements

 69

LOS 31.b Explain
CFAI p. 452, Schweser p. 231

Income Taxes

Deferred Tax

Deferred Tax Liability

Tax Deduction > Accounting Expense

The result is that taxable income is smaller than profit before tax and hence we pay less tax today and more tax in the future

Deferred Tax Asset

Tax Deduction < Accounting Expense

The result is that taxable income is greater than profit before tax and hence we pay more tax today but will pay less tax in the future

LOS 31.b Explain
CFAI p. 452, Schweser p. 231

Income Taxes

Deferred Tax Liabilities

Example of a deferred tax liability caused by using different depreciation methods for taxes and for financial reporting

Tax Reporting		**Financial Reporting**	
	Yr 1		Yr 1
Revenue	150	Revenue	150
Depreciation	(100)	Depreciation	(50)
Taxable income	50	Pre-tax income	100
Taxes payable	(20)	Tax expense	(40)

LOS 31.b Explain
CFAI p. 452, Schweser p. 231

Income Taxes

Deferred Tax Liabilities (continued)

- Tax expense ($40 on income statement) is greater than taxes payable ($20 on tax return)
- The $20 **difference** is a deferred tax liability that is **added to the DTL** on the balance sheet
- Under the liability method, the DTL is the tax due in the future (based on enacted tax rates) when/if the cumulative difference between taxable and pre-tax income **reverses**

72

LOS 31.c Determine
CFAI p. 455, Schweser p. 232

Income Taxes

Tax Bases

- **Tax Base of Asset** = amount deductible for tax purposes in future periods as economic benefits are realized
- Tax base may not equal accounting carrying value due to cumulative differences
- Differences = temporary timing differences
- Difference between carrying value × tax rate = DTA or DTL
- Non-taxable benefits: tax base and carrying value will be the same (permanent differences)

73

LOS 31.c Determine
CFAI p. 455, Schweser p. 232

Income Taxes

Tax Bases

- **A liability's tax base** = the carrying value of the liability minus any amounts that will be deductible on the tax return in the future
- Differences = temporary timing differences
- The tax base of revenue received in advance is the carrying value minus the amount of revenue that will *not* be taxed in the future

74

LOS 31.d Calculate/Interpret
CFAI p. 455, Schweser p. 234

Income Taxes

Deferred Tax Liability – Example

A firm acquires an asset for $21,000 with a 3-year useful life and no salvage value. The asset will generate $16,000 of annual revenue for three years. The tax rate is 30% and the firm is allowed to depreciate the asset using DDB for tax purposes but uses straight line in the accounts.

Compute the tax implications.

75

LOS 31.d Calculate/Interpret
CFAI p. 455, Schweser p. 234

Income Taxes

Deferred Tax Liability Solution

Tax Reporting

Year	1	2	3
	$	$	$
Revenue	16,000	16,000	16,000
Depreciation	(14,000)	(4,667)	(2,333)
Taxable income	2,000	11,333	13,667
Tax payable @ 30%	(600)	(3,400)	(4,100)
	1,400	7,933	9,567

76 - 4

LOS 31.d Calculate/Interpret
CFAI p. 455, Schweser p. 234

Income Taxes

Deferred Tax Liability Solution

Financial Accounts

	1	2	3
	$	$	$
Revenue	16,000	16,000	16,000
Depreciation	(7,000)	(7,000)	(7,000)
Pre-tax income	9,000	9,000	9,000
Tax expense @ 30%	(2,700)	(2,700)	(2,700)
Net income	6,300	6,300	6,300
B/S DTL	2,100	1,400	0

77 - 5

LOS 31.d Calculate/Interpret
CFAI p. 455, Schweser p. 234

Income Taxes

Deferred Tax Liability Solution

	1	2	3
	$	$	$
Accounting Dep^n	7,000	7,000	7,000
Tax Return Dep^n	(14,000)	(4,667)	(2,333)
Difference	(7,000)	2,333	4,667
Tax Rate	30%	30%	30%
Δ DTL	(2,100)	700	1,400
Tax Payable	(600)	(3,400)	(4,100)
Δ DTL	(2,100)	700	1,400
Tax Expense	(2,700)	(2,700)	(2,700)

78 - 6

LOS 31.d Calculate/Interpret
CFAI p. 455, Schweser p. 234

Income Taxes

Deferred Tax Liability Alternative

	1	2	3
	$	$	$
Tax base	7,000	2,333	0
Carrying value	(14,000)	(7,000)	(0)
Difference	(7,000)	(4,667)	0
Tax Rate	30%	30%	30%
DTL	(2,100)	(1,400)	0
Tax Payable	(600)	(3,400)	(4,100)
Δ DTL	(2,100)	700	1,400
Tax Expense	(2,700)	(2,700)	(2,700)

79

LOS 31.d Calculate/Interpret
CFAI p. 455, Schweser p. 234
Income Taxes

Deferred Tax Asset – Example

A firm has revenues of $8,000 for each of three years. The firm estimates the warranty expense to be 12.5% of revenues each year. The actual expenditure of $3,000 to meet warranty claims was not made until the third year.

Tax Reporting	1 $	2 $	3 $
Revenue	8,000	8,000	8,000
Repairs	-	-	(3,000)
Taxable income	8,000	8,000	5,000
Tax payable @ 30%	(2,400)	(2,400)	(1,500)
	5,600	5,600	3,500

 80-2

LOS 31.d Calculate/Interpret
CFAI p. 455, Schweser p. 234
Income Taxes

Deferred Tax Asset Solution

Financial Accounts	1 $	2 $	3 $
Revenue	8,000	8,000	8,000
Warranty Expense	(1,000)	(1,000)	(1,000)
Pre-tax income	7,000	7,000	7,000
Tax Expense@ 30%	(2,100)	(2,100)	(2,100)
PAT	4,900	4,900	4,900
B/S DTA	300	600	0

 81-5

LOS 31.d Calculate/Interpret
CFAI p. 455, Schweser p. 234
Income Taxes

Deferred Tax Asset Solution

	1 $	2 $	3 $
Accounting Expense	1,000	1,000	1,000
Tax Return Expense	0	0	(3,000)
Difference	1,000	1,000	(2,000)
Tax Rate	30%	30%	30%
Δ DTA	300	300	(600)
Tax Payable	(2,400)	(2,400)	(1,500)
Δ DTA	300	300	(600)
Tax Expense	(2,100)	(2,100)	(2,100)

82

LOS 31.d Calculate/Interpret
CFAI p. 455, Schweser p. 234
Income Taxes

Deferred Tax Asset Alternative

	1 $	2 $	3 $
Carrying value	1,000	2,000	0
Tax base	(0)	(0)	(0)
Difference	1,000	2,000	(0)
Tax Rate	30%	30%	30%
DTA	300	600	0
Tax Payable	(2,400)	(2,400)	(1,500)
Δ DTA	300	300	(600)
Tax Expense	(2,100)	(2,100)	(2,100)

83

LOS 31.e Evaluate
CFAI p. 460, Schweser p. 238 Income Taxes

Liability Method for Deferred Taxes

- DTAs and DTLs are based on differences that are **expected to reverse**
- DTA and DTL values are adjusted for changes in **tax rates** for the period when differences are expected to reverse
- DTA adjusted with **valuation allowance** to reflect probability that DTA will not be realized in future periods

 84

LOS 31.d,e Calculate/Interpret/Evaluate
CFAI p. 460, Schweser p. 238 Income Taxes

Effect of a Change in Tax Rate

When the ***tax rate <u>decreases</u>***:

Deferred tax *liability* ↓ Income tax expense ↓

Deferred tax *asset* ↓ Income tax expense ↑

When the ***tax rate <u>increases</u>***:

Deferred tax *liability* ↑ Income tax expense ↑

Deferred tax *asset* ↑ Income tax expense ↓

tax expense = tax payable +ΔDTL – ΔDTA

Net effect depends on relative sizes of DTL and DTA

 85

LOS 31.d,e Calculate/Interpret/Evaluate
CFAI p. 460, Schweser p. 238 Income Taxes

Effects of Tax Rate Change – Example

A firm acquires an asset for $24,000 with a 3-year useful life and no salvage value. The asset will generate $20,000 of annual revenue for three years. The firm is allowed to depreciate the asset using DDB for tax purposes and straight line in the accounts.

During Year 1 the tax rate is 40% but it will fall to 35% in Year 2.

 86

LOS 31.d,e Calculate/Interpret/Evaluate
CFAI p. 460, Schweser p. 238 Income Taxes

Deferred Tax – Tax Rate Change

Tax Reporting

Year	1	2	3
	$	$	$
Revenue	20,000	20,000	20,000
Depreciation	(16,000)	(5,333)	(2,667)
Taxable income	4,000	14,667	17,333
Tax payable	(1,600)	(5,133)	(6,067)
	2,400	9,534	11,266

 87

LOS 31.d,e Calculate/Interpret/Evaluate
CFAI p. 460, Schweser p. 238

Income Taxes

Deferred Tax – Tax Rate Change

Financial Accounts

	1	2	3
	$	$	$
Revenue	20,000	20,000	20,000
Depreciation	(8,000)	(8,000)	(8,000)
Pre-tax income	12,000	12,000	12,000
Tax Expense	(4,800)	(3,800)	(4,200)
PAT	7,200	8,200	7,800
B/S DTL	3,200	1,867	0

88

LOS 31.d,e Calculate/Interpret/Evaluate
CFAI p. 460, Schweser p. 238

Income Taxes

Deferred Tax – Tax Rate Change

	1	2	3
Accounting Dep^n	8,000	8,000	8,000
Tax Return Dep^n	(16,000)	(5,333)	(2,667)
Difference	(8,000)	2,667	5,333
Tax Rate	40%	35%	35%
Deferred Tax	(3,200)	933	1,867
Tax Payable	(1,600)	(5,133)	(6,067)
Correction		400	
Deferred Tax	(3,200)	933	1,867
Tax Expense	(4,800)	(3,800)	(4,200)

Issue: Year 1 liability created at 40% but reverses at 35%

(8,000) × 40% = (3,200)

(8,000) × 35% = (2,800)

Difference = (400)

89

LOS 31.d,e Calculate/Interpret/Evaluate
CFAI p. 460, Schweser p. 238 — Income Taxes

Tax Rate Change Alternative

	1	2	3
Tax base	8,000	2,667	0
Carrying value	(16,000)	(8,000)	(0)
Difference	(8,000)	(5,333)	0
Tax Rate	10%	35%	35%
DTL	(3,200)	(1,867)	0
Tax Payable	(1,600)	(5,133)	(6,067)
Δ DTL	(3,200)	1,333	1,867
Tax Expense	(4,800)	(3,800)	(4,200)

 90

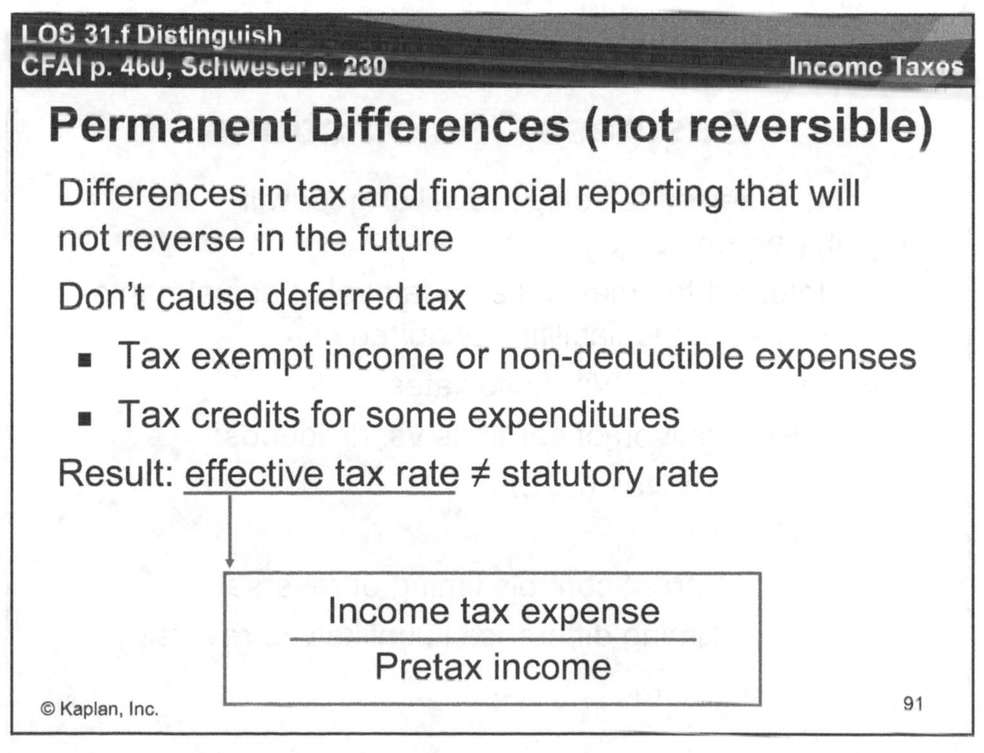

LOS 31.f Distinguish
CFAI p. 460, Schweser p. 239

Income Taxes

Temporary Differences – Initial Recognition

- Carrying amount ≠ tax base at initial recognition
- May be due to government grants for asset purchases
- Grants ↓ carrying value
- No deferred tax (no DTA)
- Rule: No deferred tax accounted for if there is no impact on accounting or taxable profit at the time of the transaction

92

LOS 31.f Distinguish
CFAI p. 460, Schweser p. 239

Income Taxes

Business Combinations

- No deferred tax on goodwill or goodwill impairments
- Deferred tax may arise on fair value adjustments of assets and liabilities acquired
- Subsidiaries, JVs, Associates
  - Recognition of earnings vs. dividends
  - Deferred tax (DTL)
  - Unless:
    - Parent controls timing of reversal
    - Timing difference is unlikely to reverse

93

LOS 31.g Describe
CFAI p. 465, Schweser p. 241 Income Taxes

Valuation Allowance

- A **valuation allowance** reduces a deferred tax asset
- Is based on the likelihood that the asset will not be realized (e.g., no taxable income expected)
- Can be used to manipulate income: increasing the valuation allowance will decrease income, decreasing the allowance will increase income
- May affect analysts' assumptions regarding future earnings (earnings prospects)

 94

LOS 31.h Compare
CFAI p. 460, Schweser p. 242 Income Taxes

Comparison of Deferred Tax Items

Analyst should examine disclosures showing:

- Change in DTLs by source/category (e.g., excess of tax over book depreciation)
- Change in DTAs by source/category (e.g., writedown of inventory)
- Change in valuation allowance

 95

LOS 31.i Analyze/Explain
CFAI p. 469, Schweser p. 244

Income Taxes

Required Deferred Tax Disclosures

- Deferred **tax liabilities / assets**, any valuation allowance, and net change in valuation allowance
- Unrecognized deferred tax liability for **undistributed earnings of subsidiaries** and joint ventures
- **Current-year tax effect** of each type of temporary difference
- Components of income tax expense
- Tax loss **carryforwards and credits**
- **Reconciliation of difference between income tax expense as a % of pre-tax and statutory tax rate**

96

LOS 31.i Analyze/Explain
CFAI p. 469, Schweser p. 244

Income Taxes

Disclosures About Deferred Tax Items

- Be aware of **differences** in tax reconciliation **between periods**
- Consider the firm's **growth rate and capital spending levels** when determining whether temporary differences due to accelerated depreciation will reverse
- Look for **cumulative differences** due to **asset impairments and post-retirement benefits**
- **Restructuring charges** can create a deferred tax asset

97

LOS 31.i Analyze/Explain
CFAI p. 469, Schweser p. 244

Income Taxes

Analyst Treatment of Deferred Tax Liabilities

- When differences are expected to reverse and result in future tax payments, **treat DTL as debt** in calculating leverage ratios
- When differences are not expected to reverse and result in future tax payments, **treat DTL as equity** in calculating leverage ratios
- When the amount and timing of future tax payments from reversal is uncertain, **exclude from both debt and equity**

98

LOS 31.j Identify
CFAI p. 474, Schweser p. 240

Income Taxes

Key Differences IFRS and U.S. GAAP

Deferred tax differences

- IFRS revaluation of PP&E and intangibles
- Undistributed profits from subsidiaries, associates, joint ventures
- Deferred tax assets
  - IFRS recognized if probable recovery
  - U.S. GAAP full recognition reduced by valuation allowance
- Presentation
  - U.S. GAAP current and non-current
  - IFRS non-current

99

Income Taxes

Deferred Taxes – Problem

A deferred tax asset would *most likely* be created by:

A. using straight line depreciation for financial reporting and using an accelerated method for tax returns.

B. differing treatment of warranty expenses for taxes and for financial reporting.

C. utilizing an existing tax loss carryforward to reduce a given year's taxes payable.

100 - 1

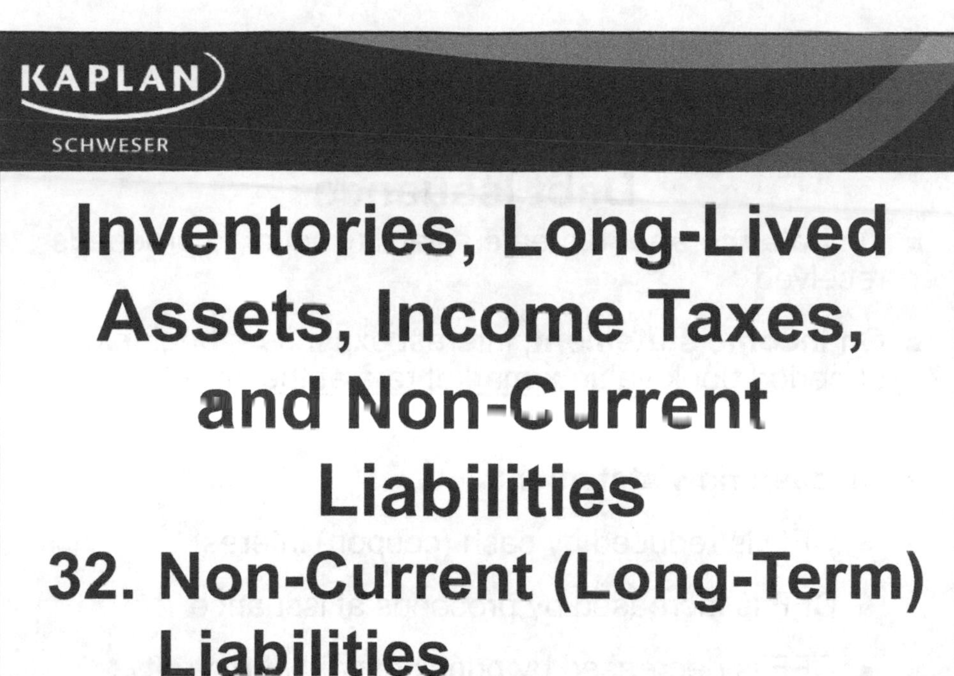

LOS 32.a Determine
CFAI p. 488, Schweser p. 257

Non-current (Long-Term) Liabilities

Bond Terminology

Par value → The face value to be paid at maturity

Coupon rate → Stated rate used to calculate the coupon payment

Initial liability → Issue price (PV of future cash flows discounted at the market rate of interest at issuance)

Effective Interest Rate → The discount rate (IRR) that equates PV of future cash flows (coupon payments and par value) with the issue price

Interest Expense → Book value × Effective interest rate

102

LOS 32.a Determine
CFAI p. 488, Schweser p. 257

Non-current (Long-Term) Liabilities

Financial Statement Effects of Debt Issuance

- On **balance sheet**, create a liability equal to proceeds received
- On **income statement**, interest expense = beginning of period book value × market rate at the time of issuance
- On **cash flow statement**
  - CFO is reduced by cash (coupon) interest
  - CFF is increased by proceeds at issuance
  - CFF is decreased by principal paid at maturity

103

LOS 32.a Determine
CFAI p. 488, Schweser p. 257

Non-current (Long-Term) Liabilities

Bonds Issued at Face Value

Market rate = Coupon rate

Balance sheet

- Initial liability is equal to issue price, which is face value
- Liability remains at face value over bond term (no amortization required)
- Face amount is repaid at maturity

Income statement

- Interest expense = Book value × Market rate at issuance
- Since market rate and coupon rate are the same, expense is equal to the coupon payment

104

LOS 32.a Determine
CFAI p. 488, Schweser p. 257

Non-current (Long-Term) Liabilities

Bonds Issued at a Discount
Market rate > Coupon rate

Balance sheet

- Initial liability equal to issue price, which is *less* than face
- Liability *increases* over time as the discount is amortized
- Book value is equal to PV of remaining cash flows discounted at the market rate at issuance
- Face amount (including discount) is repaid at maturity

Income statement

- Interest expense = Book value × market rate at issuance
- Expense *increases* over time as BV increases to face

 105

LOS 32.a Determine
CFAI p. 488, Schweser p. 257

Non-current (Long-Term) Liabilities

Bonds Issued at a Premium
Coupon rate > Market rate

Balance sheet

- Initial liability equal to issue price which is *higher* than face
- Liability *decreases* over time as the premium is amortized
- Book value is equal to PV of remaining cash flows discounted at the market rate at issuance
- Face amount is repaid at maturity (borrower keeps premium)

Income statement

- Interest expense = Book value × market rate at issuance
- Expense *decreases* over time as BV declines to face

 106

LOS 32.a Determine
CFAI p. 488, Schweser p. 257

Non-current (Long-Term) Liabilities

Bonds Issued at a Premium
Coupon rate > Market rate

Effective Interest Method of Amortization of Premium/Discount

- Interest expense = YTM at issuance times beginning balance sheet liability
- Difference between coupon interest and interest expense is amortization of premium of discount
- Required under IFRS, preferred under U.S. GAAP

Straight-line Amortization of Premium/Discount

- Annual amortization is discount/years or premium/years
- Interest expense is coupon +/- amortization
- Permitted under U.S. GAAP

 107

LOS 32.b Discuss
CFAI p. 492, Schweser p. 258

Non-current (Long-Term) Liabilities

Accounting for Bonds Issued at a Discount

Leeds Corp. issues a 3-year, $1,000 par value bond with an annual coupon of 10% at $951.96. The market interest rate is 12%. Using **effective interest** amortization method:

	Liability on Balance Sheet	Interest Expense	Coupon Int. Paid	Discount Amortization
Year 1	951.96	114.24	100	14.24
Year 2	966.20	115.94	100	15.94
Year 3	982.14	117.86	100	17.86
Bond redemption	1,000			

 108

LOS 32.b Discuss
CFAI p. 492, Schweser p. 258

Non-current (Long-Term) Liabilities

Accounting for Bonds Issued at a Discount

Leeds Corp. issues a 3-year, $1,000 par value bond with an annual coupon of 10% at $951.96. The market interest rate is 12%. Using **straight-line** amortization of discount:

	Liability on Balance Sheet	Interest Expense	Coupon Int. Paid	Discount Amortization
Year 1	951.96	116.01	100	16.01
Year 2	967.97	116.01	100	16.01
Year 3	983.98	116.02	100	16.02
Bond redemption	1,000			

 109

LOS 32.b Discuss
CFAI p. 492, Schweser p. 258

Non-current (Long-Term) Liabilities

Accounting for Zero Coupon Bonds

Vine Corp. issues a 3-year, zero coupon bond with a par value of $1,000 for $711.78. The market interest rate is 12%. Using the **effective interest** method:

	Balance Sheet Liability	Interest Expense	Coupon Int. Paid	Discount Amortization
Year 1	711.78	85.41	0	85.41
Year 2	797.19	95.66	0	95.66
Year 3	892.85	107.14	0	107.14
Bond redemption	1,000			

 110

LOS 32.b Discuss
CFAI p. 492, Schweser p. 258

Non-current (Long-Term) Liabilities

Accounting for Premium Bonds

Illiquid Corporation issues a 3-year, $1,000 par value bond with an annual coupon of 20% at $1,130.88. The market interest rate is 14.33%. Using the **effective interest** method:

	Balance Sheet Liability	Interest Expense	Coupon Int. Paid	Premium Amortization
Year 1	1,130.88	162.06	200	–37.94
Year 2	1,092.94	156.62	200	–43.38
Year 3	1,049.56	150.40	200	–49.60
Bond redemption	1,000			

LOS 32.b Discuss
CFAI p. 492, Schweser p. 258

Non-current (Long-Term) Liabilities

Accounting for Premium Bonds

Illiquid Corporation issues a 3-year, $1,000 par value bond with an annual coupon of 20% at $1,130.88. The market interest rate is 14.33%. Using **straight-line** amortization:

	Balance Sheet Liability	Interest Expense	Coupon Int. Paid	Premium Amortization
Year 1	1,130.88	156.37	200	–43.63
Year 2	1,087.25	156.37	200	–43.63
Year 3	1,043.62	156.38	200	–43.62
Bond redemption	1,000			

LOS 32.b Discuss
CFAI p. 492, Schweser p. 258

Non-current (Long-Term) Liabilities

Issuance Costs

Costs incurred at time of issuance for legal fees, commissions, printing, etc.

IFRS

- Deducted from initial bond liability
- Result is higher effective interest rate

U.S. GAAP

- Shown on balance sheet as a prepaid expense (deferred charge)
- Controversial treatment because asset does not provide future economic benefits
- Amortized over the bond's life

113

Non-current (Long-Term) Liabilities

Bond Issuance – Problem

Acme issues an 8%, 10-year annual-pay bond when market yield is 7.5% for $1,034.32.

Impact of the bond on net income in the first year is:

A. –$80.00, and NI is less than with equal proceeds from par debt

B. –$77.57, and NI is more than with equal proceeds from par debt

C. –$77.57, and NI is the same as with equal proceeds from par debt

114 - 2

LOS 32.b Discuss
CFAI p. 492, Schweser p. 258

Non-current (Long-Term) Liabilities

Effect of Changing Interest Rates

- Inverse relationship between the **market value** (fair value) of debt and interest rates
- Once debt is issued, firms report the book value (not market value) of debt; **changes in interest rates do not affect balance sheet or income statement**

Δ interest rate: carrying value ≠ fair value

- Exception: liabilities hedged with derivatives "fair value hedges"

115

LOS 32.b Discuss
CFAI p. 492, Schweser p. 258

Non-current (Long-Term) Liabilities

Effect of Changing Interest Rates

For analysis, market value is more relevant than book value

- Market value reflects the cost to buy back the debt and cancel the liability
- Lower market values reflect stronger solvency positions

IFRS and U.S. GAAP give firms irrevocable option to report debt at fair value

116

LOS 32.c Discuss
CFAI p. 498, Schweser p. 263

Non-current (Long-Term) Liabilities

Debt Extinguishment

	$
B/S carrying value	X
Repurchase price	(X)
Gain/(Loss)	X/(X)
Unamortized issuance costs	(X)
Gain/(Loss) on repurchase	X/(X)

U.S. GAAP only

I/S continuing operations

No gain/loss at maturity

Gain or loss if repurchased prior to maturity

Repurchase > carrying value = loss

Repurchase < carrying value = gain

Detail in MD&A, footnotes

117

LOS 32.d Explain
CFAI p. 500, Schweser p. 264

Non-current (Long-Term) Liabilities

Covenants

Restrictions placed on borrower to protect lender

Violation = technical default (lender can demand payment)

Affirmative covenants – borrower agrees to:

- Make timely payment of principal and interest
- Maintain certain ratios (current ratio, D/E, coverage, etc.)
- Maintain collateral and pay taxes

Negative covenants – borrower will refrain from:

- Paying dividends and repurchasing shares
- Engaging in mergers and acquisitions
- Issuing more debt

118

LOS 32.e Discuss
CFAI p. 501, Schweser p. 264

Non-current (Long-Term) Liabilities

Disclosure of Long-Term Debt

B/S split between:

Current liabilities

- Long-term liabilities

Footnotes

- Nature of the liabilities
- Maturity dates
- Stated and effective interest rates
- Call provisions and conversion privileges
- Restrictions imposed by creditors
- Assets pledged as security
- Amount of debt maturing in each of the next five years

 119

LOS 32.f Discuss
CFAI p. 504, Schweser p. 265

Non-current (Long-Term) Liabilities

Reasons to Lease

Alternative to borrowing and purchasing asset

Advantages:

1. Short period of use
2. Cheaper financing (potentially)
3. No down payment
4. Fixed rates
5. May have fewer covenants
6. Less risk of obsolescence
7. Potential financial reporting adv (op lease)
8. Tax advantages—synthetic leases

 120

LOS 32.g Distinguish
CFAI p. 505, Schweser p. 266

Non-current (Long-Term) Liabilities

Finance (Capital) vs. Operating Lease

U.S. GAAP: Treat **as capital lease** if **any** of the following criteria are met:

1. Title to the leased asset is transferred to the lessee at the end of the lease
2. A bargain purchase option exists
3. The lease period is at least 75% of the asset's economic life
4. The PV of the lease payments ≥ 90% of the leased asset's fair value

IFRS: Treat as **finance lease** if substantially all rights and risks of ownership are transferred (no quantitative criteria)

121

LOS 32.h Determine
CFAI p. 506, Schweser p. 267

Non-current (Long-Term) Liabilities

Treatment of Finance Lease

Treat **as if leased asset were purchased** with debt

- Lower of fair value or PV of future lease payments is reported as a **balance sheet asset and liability**
- Asset is **depreciated** over time
- Interest expense on liability is recognized
- Lease payments treated like amortizing debt — each payment is **part interest and part principal**

122

LOS 32.h Determine
CFAI p. 506, Schweser p. 267

Non-current (Long-Term) Liabilities

Finance Lease Example

Firm leases asset for 3 years

Payments = $10,000 year

Straight-line depreciation, no salvage value

Fair market value = $27,000 ← Use lower of:

Lease discount rate = 7%

Balance Sheet Effects:

Asset = PV lease payments

Liability = PV lease payments

I/Y = 7
N = 3
PMT = $10,000
} $26,243

123

LOS 32.h Determine
CFAI p. 506, Schweser p. 267

Non-current (Long-Term) Liabilities

Finance Lease Example (continued)

Year	Beg. value	Interest expense @7%	Payment	Year-end lease value	Book value asset
1	26,243	1,837	10,000	18,080	17,495
2	18,080	1,266	10,000	9,346	8,747
3	9,346	654	10,000	0	0

Principal payment = $10,000 – interest

Depreciation = $26,243 ÷ 3 = $8,748/yr.

$18,080 long term, $8,163 current, Total $26,243

124

LOS 32.h Determine
CFAI p. 506, Schweser p. 267

Non-current (Long-Term) Liabilities

Finance Lease Example (continued)

	CFO (Interest)	*CFF (Principal)*
1	**1,837**	10,000 – 1,837 = **8,163**
2	**1,266**	10,000 – 1,266 = **8,734**
3	**654**	10,000 – 654 = **9,346**

Operating lease CFO = $10,000 annual outflow
Rent expense = $10,000/year

Finance lease expense = interest + depreciation
Net income in early years lower for finance lease
CFO higher, CFF lower for finance lease

LOS 32.h Determine
CFAI p. 506, Schweser p. 267

Non-current (Long-Term) Liabilities

Income Statement Effects

Year	Finance (Capital) Lease			Operating Lease
	Interest	Dep^n	Total	Rental Expense
1	$1,837	$8,748	$10,585	$10,000
2	$1,266	$8,748	$10,014	$10,000
3	$654	$8,747	$9,401	$10,000
Total	$3,757	$26,243	$30,000	$30,000

Early years: higher expenses → lower NI with finance lease
Later years: lower expenses → higher NI with finance lease

LOS 32.h Determine
CFAI p. 506, Schweser p. 267

Non-current (Long-Term) Liabilities

Finance vs. Operating Lease

Financial Statement Totals	Finance	Operating
Assets	Higher	Lower
Liabilities	Higher	Lower
Net income (early years)	Lower	Higher
Net income (later years)	Higher	Lower
Total Net Income	Same	Same
Cash flow from operations	Higher	Lower
Cash flow from financing	Lower	Higher
Total cash flow	Same	Same

 127

Non-current (Long-Term) Liabilities

Leases – Problem

If Acme reports its lease of equipment as an operating lease rather than as a capital lease the effect in the first year would be to:

A. increase net income and decrease CFO

B. increase net income and CFO

C. decrease net income and increase CFO

 128 - 1

LOS 32.h Determine
CFAI p. 506, Schweser p. 267

Non-current (Long-Term) Liabilities

Lessor Financial Reporting

Operating Lease

- Lessor reports leased asset on balance sheet
- Recognize lease payments as rental income
- Recognize depreciation expense on asset

Finance Lease

- Lessor reports lease receivable on balance sheet
- Recognize lease payments as part interest revenue and part return of capital
- **Treat as either sales-type lease or direct financing lease**

129

LOS 32.h Determine
CFAI p. 506, Schweser p. 267

Non-current (Long-Term) Liabilities

Sales-type Lease

- Lessor is typically a manufacturer or dealer of the leased equipment
- **PV of lease payments > Carrying value of leased asset (termed a sales-type lease under U.S. GAAP)**
- At lease inception, lessor recognizes gross profit
  - Sales = PV of lease payments
  - COGS = Carrying value of the asset
- Interest revenue recognized over lease term
- Difference between interest revenue (CFO) and payment reduces the lease receivable (CFI)

130

LOS 32.h Determine
CFAI p. 506, Schweser p. 267

Non-current (Long-Term) Liabilities

Direct Financing Lease

- Lessor is not the manufacturer or dealer of the leased equipment (e.g., finance company)
- **PV of lease payments = carrying value of leased asset**
- No gross profit is recognized at lease inception
- Lessor recognizes interest revenue over lease term
- Difference between interest revenue (CFO) and lease payment reduces the lease receivable (CFI)

131

LOS 32.h Determine
CFAI p. 506, Schweser p. 267

Non-current (Long-Term) Liabilities

Direct Financing Lease – Example

Rowlands, Inc. leases a machine to Hall Company. The lease qualifies as a finance lease. The terms of the lease are three years at $10,000 p.a. Rowlands estimates that the machine can be sold in three years for $5,000. The asset cost $24,000.

Rate Implicit in the Lease:

N	3	
PMT	$10,000	CPT I/Y = 19.897%
FV	$5,000	
PV	($24,000)	

132

LOS 32.h Determine
CFAI p. 506, Schweser p. 267

Non-current (Long-Term) Liabilities

Direct Financing Lease – Example

Year	Beginning lease receivable	Interest income	Annual end-of-year lease payment	Reduction in lease receivable	Year-end lease receivable
1	24,000	4,775	10,000	5,225	18,775
2	18,775	3,736	10,000	6,264	12,511
3	12,511	2,489	10,000	7,511	5,000
Total		11,000	30,000	19,000	

CFO — CFI

CFI permitted IFRS — CFO if leasing company

133

LOS 32.i Compare
CFAI p. 509, Schweser p. 275

Non-current (Long-Term) Liabilities

Lease Disclosure

Lessees and lessors are required to disclose:

- General description of leasing arrangements
- Nature, timing, and payments to be paid or received
  - In each of the next 5 years
  - Aggregated payments beyond 5 years
- Lease revenue and expense for each period presented in the income statement
- Amounts receivable and unearned revenues from leases
- Restrictions imposed by lease arrangements

134

Non-current (Long-Term) Liabilities

Lease – Problem

Under IFRS a lessor would be *most likely* to recognize depreciation expense related to a leased asset for a lease classified as a(n):

A. operating lease

B. financing lease.

C. sales-type lease.

135 - 2

LOS 32.j Describe
CFAI p. 509, Schweser p. 275

Non-current (Long-Term) Liabilities

Pensions

Defined Contribution Plan

- Employer contributes specified sum each period
- No guarantee of future benefits
- *Employee* bears investment risk

Defined Benefit Plan

- Employer promises specific payment stream beginning at retirement
- Contributions based on years of service, compensation at/near retirement
- *Employer* bears investment risk
- Separate legal entity manages plan assets

136

LOS 32.k Compare
CFAI p. 520, Schweser p. 276

Non-current (Long-Term) Liabilities

Defined Contribution Plan Reporting

Income Statement

- Pension expense = employer's contribution

Balance Sheet

- No future obligation to report as a liability
- Decrease in cash, or current liability if not paid by fiscal year-end

137

LOS 32.k Compare
CFAI p. 520, Schweser p. 276

Non-current (Long-Term) Liabilities

Defined Benefit Plan Reporting

Balance Sheet

- Plan assets < estimated obligation: Net pension liability
- Plan assets > estimated obligation: Net pension asset

Firm must estimate PV of pension obligations based on:

- Future compensation levels
- Employee turnover
- Average retirement age
- Mortality rates
- Appropriate discount rate

138

LOS 32.k Compare
CFAI p. 520, Schweser p. 276

Non-current (Long-Term) Liabilities

Defined Benefit Plan Reporting

Change in net pension asset or liability during year

- **Service costs**: PV of additional benefits earned
- **Past service costs**: Retroactive benefits awarded when plan is initiated or changed
- **Net interest expense/income**: Beginning value × assumed discount rate
- **Actuarial gains/losses**: Changes in assumptions
- **Return on plan assets**

Pension expense or other comprehensive income?
Different treatments under IFRS and U.S. GAAP

139

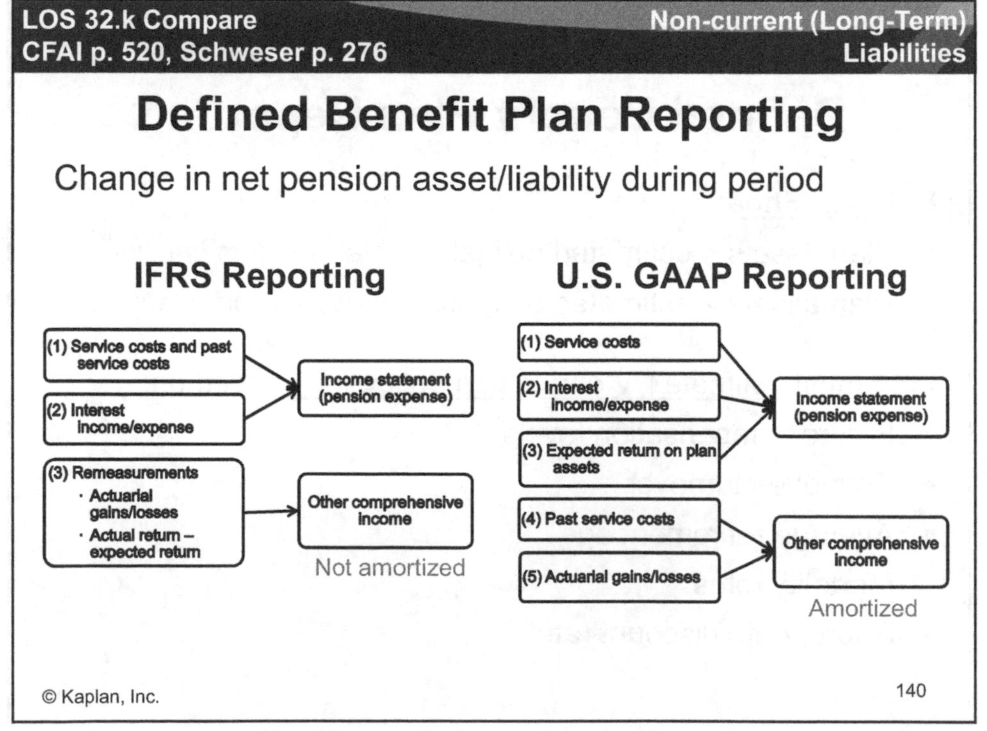

LOS 32.k Compare
CFAI p. 520, Schweser p. 276

Non-current (Long-Term) Liabilities

Defined Benefit Plan Reporting

Manufacturing companies allocate pension expense

- **Inventory** or **cost of goods sold** for employees who provide direct labor to production
- **Salary and administrative expense** for other employees

Pension expense details are disclosed in the financial statement notes

141

LOS 32.l Calculate/Interpret
CFAI p. 523, Schweser p. 278

Non-current (Long-Term) Liabilities

Solvency

- Solvency measures the firm's ability to satisfy its long-term obligations
- Leverage ratios
  - Balance sheet focus of measuring the amount of debt in the firm's capital structure
- Coverage ratios
  - Income statement focus of measuring the sufficiency of earnings to repay interest and other fixed charges

142

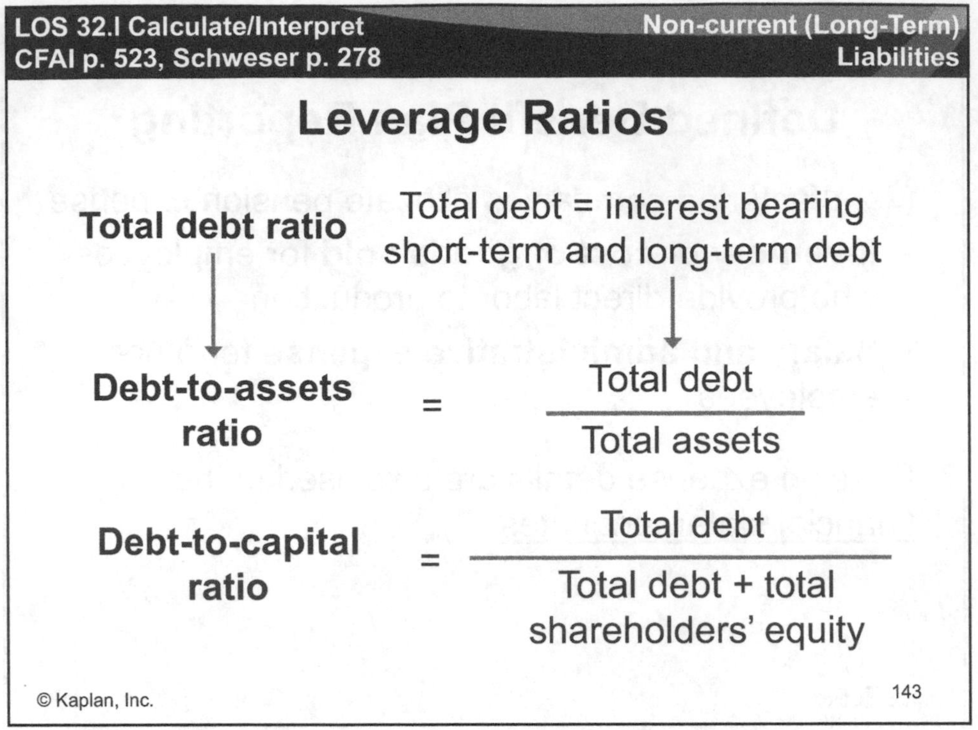

LOS 32.l Calculate/Interpret
CFAI p. 523, Schweser p. 278

Non-current (Long-Term) Liabilities

Leverage Ratios

$$\text{Debt-to-equity ratio} = \frac{\text{Total debt}}{\text{Total shareholders' equity}}$$

$$\text{Financial leverage ratio} = \frac{\text{Average total assets}}{\text{Average total equity}}$$

144

LOS 32.l Calculate/Interpret
CFAI p. 523, Schweser p. 278

Non-current (Long-Term) Liabilities

Coverage Ratios

$$\text{Interest coverage} = \frac{\text{EBIT}}{\text{Interest payments}}$$

$$\text{Fixed charge coverage} = \frac{\text{EBIT + lease payments}}{\text{Interest payments + lease payments}}$$

145

Inventories

Inventory Methods – Solution

For analytical purposes an analyst would prefer to use:

A. LIFO COGS and FIFO inventory.

Long-Lived Assets

Capitalizing Expenses – Solution

Firm Aggressive capitalizes certain expenses that Firm Conservative does not in year 20X0. In year 20X0, compared to Firm Aggressive, Firm Conservative will *most likely* have:

C. lower ROE.

Expensing firm will have lower net income and lower equity, but equity is typically greater than net income.

Long-Lived Assets

Depreciation Methods – Solution

Accelerated depreciation methods:

B. result in lower net income in early years, higher net income in later years.

Income Taxes

Deferred Taxes – Solution

A deferred tax asset would *most likely* be created by:

B. differing treatment of warranty expenses for taxes and for financial reporting.

Non-current (Long-Term) Liabilities

Bond Issuance – Solution

Acme issues an 8%, 10-year annual-pay bond when market yield is 7.5% for $1,034.32.

$$7.5\% \times 1{,}034.32 = \$77.57$$

Impact of the bond on net income in the first year is:

C. –$77.57, and NI is the same as with equal proceeds from par debt

Non-current (Long-Term) Liabilities

Leases – Solution

If Acme reports its lease of equipment as an operating lease rather than as a capital lease the effect in the first year would be to:

A. increase net income and decrease CFO

Non-current (Long-Term) Liabilities

Lease – Solution

Under IFRS a lessor would be *most likely* to recognize depreciation expense related to a leased asset for a lease classified as a(n):

A. operating lease

For a lessor, the leased asset remains on the balance sheet and is depreciated over the lease term.

Study Session 10

Financial Reporting and Analysis: Evaluating Financial Reporting Quality and Other Applications

Evaluating Financial Reporting Quality and Other Applications

33. Financial Reporting Quality: Red Flags and Accounting Warning Signs

Financial Reporting and Analysis

LOS 33.a Describe
CFAI p 538, Schweser p. 291

Financial Reporting Quality

Motivation: Over-report Earnings

- Meet analysts' expectations
- Meet debt covenants
- Improve incentive compensation

Motivation: Under-report Earnings

- Obtain trade relief
- Negotiate lower payments for contingent consideration
- Negotiate concessions from unions

 2

LOS 33.a Describe
CFAI p 538, Schweser p. 291 Financial Reporting Quality

Motivations: Manipulation of B/S

- Overstate assets/understate liabilities
  - Improve leverage ratios
  - Improve liquidity ratios
- Understate assets
  - Improve return on assets/asset turnover
  - Decrease solvency—negotiate concessions from creditors/employees
  - Report higher goodwill on acquisition

 3

LOS 33.b Describe
CFAI p. 539, Schweser p. 292 Financial Reporting Quality

Signs of Low Quality Earnings

1. Selecting alternatives within GAAP that bias or distort reported results
   - For example, inventory valuation, depreciation
2. Using loopholes or bright line criteria to report legal rather than economic substance
   - For example, operating vs. finance leases
3. Using unrealistic or inappropriate accounting estimates and assumptions
   - For example, economic lives and residual values of PP&E

 4

LOS 33.b Describe
CFAI p. 539, Schweser p. 292 Financial Reporting Quality

Signs of Low Quality Earnings

4. Stretching an accounting rule to achieve a desired result rather than economic substance
   - For example, past non-consolidation of SPEs
5. Fraudulent financial accounting (zero quality of earnings)
   - For example, capitalization of operating expenses

 5

LOS 33.c Describe
CFAI p. 539, Schweser p. 292 Financial Reporting Quality

The Fraud Triangle

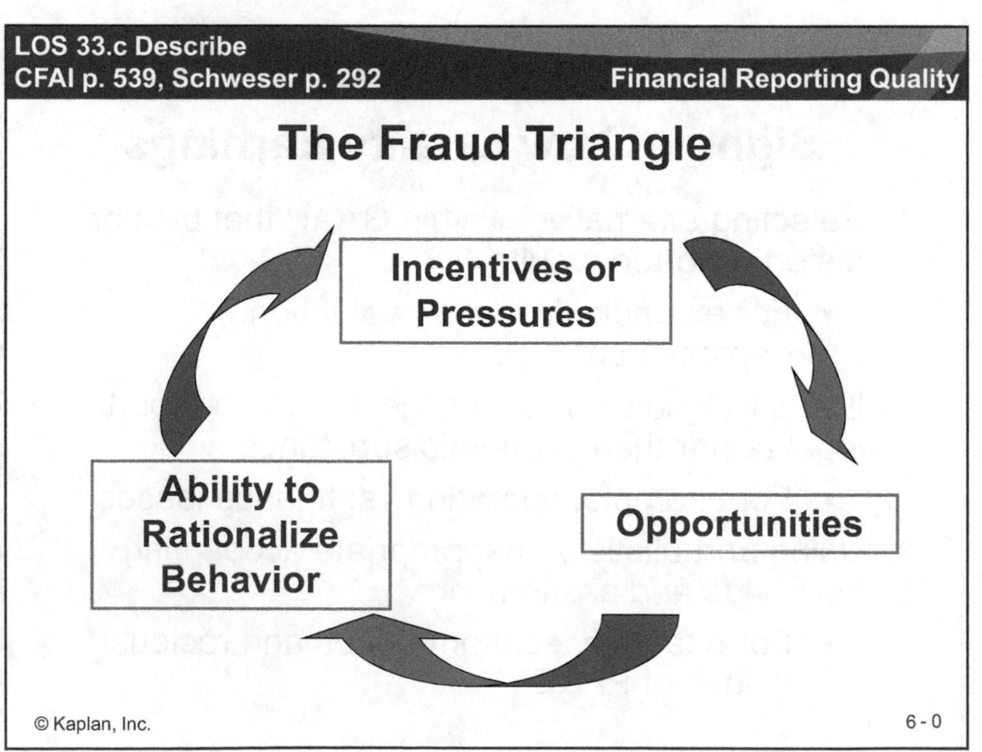

 6 - 0

LOS 33.c Describe
CFAI p. 539, Schweser p. 292 Financial Reporting Quality

Risk Factors: Incentives/Pressures

Economic, Industry, or Entity Operating Conditions

- Degree of competition/market saturation, declining margins
- Vulnerability to rapid change: technology, interest rates, product obsolescence
- Significant declines in consumer demand
- Operating losses—increasing bankruptcy, foreclosure or hostile takeover
- Recurring negative cash flows
- Rapid growth or unusual profitability
- New accounting/regulatory requirements

 7

LOS 33.c Describe
CFAI p. 539, Schweser p. 292 Financial Reporting Quality

Risk Factors: Incentives/Pressures

Pressure on Management from Third Parties

- Expectations of profitability/trends from analysts, institutional investors, significant creditors
- Need to obtain additional financing (debt & equity) to finance capex, R&D, etc.
- Exchange listing requirements
- Debt covenants
- Impact on pending transactions: business transactions, contract awards

 8

LOS 33.c Describe
CFAI p. 539, Schweser p. 292 Financial Reporting Quality

Risk Factors: Incentives/Pressures

Directors' personal financial position threatened

- Significant financial interests in entity
- Significant contingent compensation (bonuses, stock options)
- Personal guarantee of entity's debt

 9

LOS 33.c Describe
CFAI p. 539, Schweser p. 292 Financial Reporting Quality

Risk Factors: Opportunities

Nature of the industry or entity's operations

- Significant related-party transactions
- Strong financial position, power over customers/suppliers—non-arm's-length transactions
- Accounting transactions dependent on significant estimates, subjective judgements—difficult to corroborate
- Highly unusual transactions—substance over form
- International operations
- Operations in tax haven jurisdictions

 10

LOS 33.c Describe
CFAI p. 539, Schweser p. 292 Financial Reporting Quality

Risk Factors: Opportunities

Ineffective monitoring of management

- Domination of management by a single person, group, entity
- Ineffective audit committee
- Ineffective board of directors

 11

LOS 33.c Describe
CFAI p. 539, Schweser p. 292 Financial Reporting Quality

Risk Factors: Opportunities

Complex or unstable organizational structure

- Difficulty determining organizational structure
- Difficulty determining controlling interests
- Overly complex organizational structure/group structure
- High turnover of management, key staff, professional advisors, board members

 12

LOS 33.c Describe
CFAI p. 539, Schweser p. 292 Financial Reporting Quality

Risk Factors: Opportunities

Insufficient internal controls

- Inadequate monitoring of internal controls
- High turnover of accounting, internal audit, or IT staff
- Ineffective accounting and IT systems

 13

LOS 33.c Describe
CFAI p. 539, Schweser p. 292 Financial Reporting Quality

Risk Factors: Rationalizations

Attitudes/Justifications/Rationalizations

- Ineffective communication, support, and enforcement of ethical values
- Non-financial managers involved in selection of accounting principles/estimates
- History of violations
- Excessive focus on stock price, earnings trends
- Committing to analysts', investors', or creditors' unrealistic/aggressive forecasts
- Failure to correct known errors/breaches in a timely fashion

 14

LOS 33.c Describe
CFAI p. 539, Schweser p. 292 Financial Reporting Quality

Risk Factors: Rationalizations

Attitudes/Justifications/Rationalizations

- Focus on tax reduction
- Attempts to justify inappropriate accounting policy based on "materiality"
- Strained relationship with auditors
  - Turnover of auditors
  - Disputes, disagreements
  - Unreasonable demands—time pressure
  - Attempts to limit informational access
  - Attempt to influence auditors' scope

 15

LOS 33.d Describe
CFAI p. 539, Schweser p. 295 Financial Reporting Quality

SEC Improper Practice

Identified four categories based on enforcement actions:

1. Improper revenue recognition
2. Improper expense recognition
3. Improper accounting of business combinations
4. Other accounting and reporting issues

 16

LOS 33.d Describe
CFAI p. 539, Schweser p. 295 Financial Reporting Quality

Warning Signs

1. Aggressive revenue recognition
   - Bill-and-hold
   - Sales type leases (lessee operating)
   - Recording revenue before earnings activities are complete
     - Delivery of goods
     - Completion of all contract terms
   - Using swaps and barter agreements to generate sales

 17

LOS 33.d Describe
CFAI p. 539, Schweser p. 295 Financial Reporting Quality

Warning Signs

2. Divergence of CFO and earnings
   - Positive earnings, negative cash flows
   - CFO/NI less than 1 or declining trend

3. Growth of revenue out of line with peers
   - Quality of earnings
   - AR growing faster than revenues—indication of nonexistent sales

 18

LOS 33.d Describe
CFAI p. 539, Schweser p. 295 Financial Reporting Quality

Warning Signs

4. Growth in inventory out of line with peers/stock holding days increasing
   - Inventory management problems
   - Obsolete inventory
   - Overstatement of ending inventory

5. Classification of non-recurring or non-operating items as revenue
   - May mask sales decline

 19

LOS 33.d Describe
CFAI p. 539, Schweser p. 295 Financial Reporting Quality

Warning Signs

6. Deferral of expenses
   - Capitalization of operating expenses
7. Excessive use of operating leases
   - Off-balance-sheet finance
8. Classification of losses and expenses as extraordinary or non-recurring
   - Frequency of non-recurring items

 20

LOS 33.d Describe
CFAI p. 539, Schweser p. 295

Financial Reporting Quality

Warning Signs

9. LIFO liquidations
    - Firms using LIFO reducing stock levels
    - Review declines in LIFO reserve
10. Gross/operating margins out of line with peers
    - Indication of aggressive accounting policies
    - Overstatement of inventory
    - Capitalization of operating expenses

21

LOS 33.d Describe
CFAI p. 539, Schweser p. 295

Financial Reporting Quality

Warning Signs

11. Useful economic lives
    - Depreciation expense
    - Amortization expense
12. Aggressive pension assumptions
    - High discount rates
    - High expected returns
    - Low rates of compensation increase

22

LOS 33.d Describe
CFAI p. 539, Schweser p. 295

Financial Reporting Quality

Warning Signs

13. 4th quarter earnings surprises
    - Unusually high revenues
    - Unusually low expenses
    - Not linked to seasonality
14. Equity accounting/unconsolidated SPEs
    - Netting of assets and liabilities
    - Uncommon for industry
15. Off-balance-sheet financing

Evaluating Financial Reporting Quality and Other Applications

34. Accounting Shenanigans on the Cash Flow Statement

Financial Reporting and Analysis

LOS 34.a Analyze/Describe
CFAI p. 558, Schweser p. 302

Accounting Shenanigans on the Cash Flow Statement

Cash Flow Measurements

- Increased focus on cash flow statements post-accounting scandals
- Misconception: CFO cannot be manipulated
  - Difficult to manipulate change in total cash flow
  - Manipulation between classifications: CFO, CFI, CFF

 25

LOS 34.a Analyze/Describe
CFAI p. 558, Schweser p. 302

Accounting Shenanigans on the Cash Flow Statement

Motivations for Creative CF Reporting

- Higher share price from increasing expectations of higher CF
- Lower borrowing cost since operating CF and debt service ability are directly related; higher operating CF results in more borrowing capacity and lower interest rate
- Higher incentive compensation since managers often receive stock options or incentives based on CFs

 26

LOS 34.a Analyze/Describe
CFAI p. 558, Schweser p. 302

Accounting Shenanigans on the Cash Flow Statement

Stretching Out Payables

Delaying payment to suppliers—one-off boost to CFO

- Two views
  1. Sign that company is struggling with cash generation
  2. Company is utilizing a prudent cash management strategy
- Issues
  1. One-off boost (not sustainable)
  2. Suppliers may reduce future credit terms

 27

LOS 34.a Analyze/Describe
CFAI p. 558, Schweser p. 302

Accounting Shenanigans on the Cash Flow Statement

Stretching Out Payables

- Analysis

  Review days' sales payable (DSP)

$$\frac{\text{Average accounts payable}}{\text{Purchases}} \times 365$$

 28

LOS 34.a Analyze/Describe
CFAI p. 558, Schweser p. 302

Accounting Shenanigans on the Cash Flow Statement

Financing of Payables

- Use of borrowings to pay off accounts payable
- Manipulates timing of CFO
  1. Financial institution makes payment to the supplier
  2. Reclassify AP to notes payable ↓ CFO ↑ CFF
  3. Pay off notes payable ↓ CFF

 29

LOS 34.a Analyze/Describe
CFAI p. 558, Schweser p. 302

Accounting Shenanigans on the Cash Flow Statement

Securitization of Receivables

- Sell notes receivable / AR
  - Financing company
  - VIE
- Reduction in notes receivable / AR increases CFO
- Income statement impact

Cash received	X	Cash received	X
Notes receivable sold	(X)	Accounts rec.	(X)
Gain/(loss)	X	Gain/(loss)	(X)

 30

LOS 34.a Analyze/Describe
CFAI p. 558, Schweser p. 302

Accounting Shenanigans on the Cash Flow Statement

Tax Benefits From Stock Options

- Tax saving on exercise of employee options = # shares × (market price – exercise price) × tax rate
- Lower tax → ↑ CFO
- Issue: The boost to CFO is unsustainable

 31

LOS 34.a Analyze/Describe
CFAI p. 558, Schweser p. 302

Accounting Shenanigans on the Cash Flow Statement

Buybacks to Offset Dilution

	$
Share repurchase	24,000
Less: proceeds from exercise	(20,000)
Net cash outflow	4,000

- U.S. GAAP treats the $4,000 as CFF
- An analyst should reclassify it as CFO (part of employee compensation)

Evaluating Financial Reporting Quality and Other Applications

35. Financial Statement Analysis: Applications

Financial Reporting and Analysis

LOS 35.a Evaluate/Explain
CFAI p. 568, Schweser p. 308

Financial Statement Analysis: Applications

Evaluating Past Financial Performance

- How have key ratios changed and why?
- How do key ratios and trends compare with competitors/industry?
- What aspects of performance are critical for a competitive advantage?
- How did the company perform in these areas?
- What is the company's business model and strategy—are they reflected in key measures?

34

LOS 35.b Prepare
CFAI p. 576, Schweser p. 309

Financial Statement Analysis: Applications

Projecting Performance

1. Forecast expected GDP growth
2. Forecast expected industry sales based on historical relationship with GDP
3. Consider expected change of firm's market share
4. Forecast expected firm sales
5. Use historical margins for stable firms (gross, operating, net) or individual forecast for each expense item
   - Remove nonrecurring items
   - Historical margins are not relevant to new, volatile, or high fixed cost industries

 35

LOS 35.b Prepare
CFAI p. 576, Schweser p. 309

Financial Statement Analysis: Applications

Forecasting Net Income and Cash Flow

1. Spreadsheet can be developed based on the estimated growth rate of sales
2. Make assumptions about working capital, fixed assets, COGS, and SG&A as proportions of sales
3. Estimate interest rates for saving/borrowing, tax rate, and dividends
4. Project net income and cash flow based on assumptions

 36

LOS 35.b Prepare
CFAI p. 576, Schweser p. 309

Financial Statement Analysis: Applications

Financial Forecasting Example

- Sales expected to be $100 million in year 1 and increase 5% per year
- COGS = 20% of sales
- SG&A = 40% of sales
- Interest income = 5% of cash (beg. year)
- Tax rate = 30%
- No dividends
- Non-cash working capital = 70% of sales (beginning non-cash working capital = $67 mil)
- Fixed capital investment = 5% of sales

 37

LOS 35.b Prepare
CFAI p. 576, Schweser p. 309

Financial Statement Analysis: Applications

Financial Forecast

($ mil.)	Year 1	Year 2	Year 3
Sales	**100**	105	110
– COGS	20	21	22
– SG&A	40	42	44
+ Interest	0	1	2
Pretax income	40	43	46
– Taxes	12	13	14
Net income	28	30	32

 38 - 4

LOS 35.b Prepare
CFAI p. 576, Schweser p. 309

Financial Statement Analysis: Applications

Financial Forecast (continued)

($ mil.)	Beg.	Year 1	Year 2	Year 3
Working capital	67	70	73	77
Net income		28	30	32
– Inv. in working cap.		3	3	4
– Inv. in fixed capital		5	5	6
Change in cash		20	22	22
Beginning cash		0	20	42
Ending cash	0	20	42	64

39 - 6

LOS 35.c Describe
CFAI p. 585, Schweser p. 310

Financial Statement Analysis: Applications

Credit Risk

- Ability of issuer to meet interest and principal repayment on schedule (capacity)
- Cash flow forecast focus
- Variability of cash flows

- **Character**
- **Capacity**
- **Collateral**
- **Covenants**

4 Cs

Also in SS16

40

LOS 35.c Describe
CFAI p. 585, Schweser p. 310

Financial Statement Analysis: Applications

Credit Scoring

- Credit rating agencies employ formulas that are weighted averages of several specific accounting ratios and business characteristics

1. *Scale and diversification.* Size, product diversification, geographical diversification

2. *Operational efficiency*. Such items as operating ROA, operating margins, and EBITDA margins fall into this category, along with degree of vertical integration

 41

LOS 35.c Describe
CFAI p. 585, Schweser p. 310

Financial Statement Analysis: Applications

Credit Scoring

3. *Margin stability.* Stability of profitability margins indicates a higher probability of repayment (leads to a better debt rating and a lower cost of debt capital)

4. *Leverage.* Coverage ratios of operating earnings, EBITDA, or some measure of free cash flow to interest expense or total debt make up the most important part of the credit rating formula

 42

LOS 35.d Describe
CFAI p. 589, Schweser p. 311

Financial Statement Analysis: Applications

Equity Investment Screening

- Screening: Application of a set of criteria to reduce a set of investments to a smaller subset having desired characteristics
- Involves comparing ratios to min/max values

Growth investors:	Focus on earnings growth
Value investors:	Focus on low share price in relation to earnings or assets
Market oriented:	Neither value or growth focused

 43

LOS 35.e Determine/Justify
CFAI p. 592, Schweser p. 311

Financial Statement Analysis: Applications

Analyst Adjustments

- Adjust financial statements for **differences in accounting choices** (e.g., LIFO/FIFO, accelerated/straight line depreciation, revenue recognition criteria)
- Adjust financial statements for **differences in accounting standards** (e.g., IFRS vs. U.S. GAAP)

 44

LOS 35.e Determine/Justify
CFAI p. 592, Schweser p. 311

Financial Statement Analysis: Applications

Analyst Adjustments

- Required to ensure accounts are comparable before calculating ratios
- Investments
  - Held-to-maturity
  - Available-for-sale
  - Trading
  - IFRS: available-for-sale exchange rate gains taken to income statement

 45

LOS 35.e Determine/Justify
CFAI p. 592, Schweser p. 311

Financial Statement Analysis: Applications

Analyst Adjustments

- Inventory
  - FIFO/LIFO/AVCO
- Property, plant, and equipment
  - Depreciation methods
  - Estimated lives
  - Salvage values
  - IFRS allows revaluation
- Goodwill
  - Internally generated—not capitalized
  - Purchased—capitalized

 46

LOS 35.e Determine/Justify
CFAI p. 592, Schweser p. 311

Financial Statement Analysis: Applications

Analyst Adjustments

- Off-balance-sheet finance
  - Finance leases vs. operating leases
  - Equity accounted SPEs vs. non-qualifying SPEs
  - Sale of AR

Study Session 11

Corporate Finance

Corporate Finance

36. Capital Budgeting

Corporate Finance

LOS 36.a Describe/Distinguish
CFAI p. 6, Schweser p. 11

Capital Budgeting

Capital Budgeting Process

The **capital budgeting process** is used to determine and select (the most) profitable long-term (greater than one year) projects.

2

LOS 36.a Describe/Distinguish
CFAI p. 6, Schweser p. 11

Capital Budgeting

Steps in the Capital Budgeting Process

- Step 1: Idea generation
- Step 2: Analyze project proposals
- Step 3: Create the capital budgot for the firm
- Step 4: Monitor decisions and conduct a post-audit

3

LOS 36.a Describe/Distinguish
CFAI p. 6, Schweser p. 11

Capital Budgeting

Types of Capital Projects

- Replacement projects to maintain the business
- Replacement projects for cost reduction
- Expansion projects
- New products or markets
- Mandatory projects—safety and environment
- Other projects: pet projects, R&D

4

LOS 36.b Describe
CFAI p. 8, Schweser p. 12
Capital Budgeting

Principles of Capital Budgeting

- Decisions are made based on the changes in **after-tax cash flows**
- Do not consider **sunk costs** or any project-specific financing costs—financing costs are in discount rate used
- Consider cash **opportunity costs**
- Consider **externalities**—cannibalization
- **Timing** of cash flows is important

5

LOS 36.c Explain
CFAI p. 9, Schweser p. 14
Capital Budgeting

Project Interactions

- Independent projects vs. mutually exclusive projects
- Project sequencing—opportunity for profitable future projects
- Unlimited funds vs. capital rationing

6

LOS 36.d Calculate/Interpret
CFAI p. 10, Schweser p. 14
Capital Budgeting

Net Present Value (NPV)

- Uses discounted CFs and considers all CFs

$$NPV = CF_0 + \frac{CF_1}{(1+k)^1} + \frac{CF_2}{(1+k)^2} + \ldots + \frac{CF_n}{(1+k)^n}$$

Example (cost of capital of 9%):

End of Year	Project X	Discounted Cash Flow	
0	–$100	–$100.00	–100.00
1	25	22.94	+ 22.94
2	50	42.08	+ 42.08
3	75	57.91	+ 57.91

NPV = $22.93

 7

LOS 36.d Calculate/Interpret
CFAI p. 10, Schweser p. 14
Capital Budgeting

Net Present Value (NPV)

- NPV indicates the expected change in the value of the firm, in current (PV) dollars, if the project is accepted
- Accepting projects with NPV > 0 is expected to increase shareholder wealth
- Accepting a zero NPV project will not increase shareholder wealth, expected return just matches the cost of capital

Decision rule independent projects:
Accept all projects with NPV > 0

 8

LOS 36.d Calculate/Interpret
CFAI p. 10, Schweser p. 14 Capital Budgeting

Internal Rate of Return (IRR)

- IRR is the expected return on the project
- Technically, IRR is the discount rate that equates the PV of the project's CFs to the initial outlay (i.e., makes the NPV = 0)

$$NPV = 0 = CF_0 + \frac{CF_1}{(1+IRR)^1} + \frac{CF_2}{(1+IRR)^2} + \ldots + \frac{CF_n}{(1+IRR)^n}$$

 9

LOS 36.d Calculate/Interpret
CFAI p. 10, Schweser p. 14 Capital Budgeting

Internal Rate of Return (IRR)

Use the CF keys on your calculator

End of Year	Project X CFs	Discounted Cash Flow at 19.4%
0	–$100	–$100.00
1	25	20.94
2	50	35.07
3	75	44.06

Because NPV = 0
IRR = 19.4%

$\sum = 0.00 = NPV$

 10

LOS 36.d Calculate/Interpret
CFAI p. 10, Schweser p. 14

Capital Budgeting

Internal Rate of Return (IRR)

- **Decision rule** independent projects: Accept all projects with an IRR > cost of capital (hurdle rate)

This is equivalent to NPV > 0

If NPV > 0 or IRR > cost of capital,
then PV of cash flows > initial cash cost

11

LOS 36.d Calculate/Interpret
CFAI p. 10, Schweser p. 14

Capital Budgeting

Payback Period

- Primarily a measure of liquidity
- Projects with payback periods longer than an arbitrary number of years are rejected

Limitations

- Not a measure of value
- Ignores time value of money
- Ignores CFs beyond the payback period

12

LOS 36.d Calculate/Interpret
CFAI p. 10, Schweser p. 14
Capital Budgeting

Payback Period

Example:

End of Year	Project X	Cumulative Cash Flow
0	–$100	–$100
1	25	–75
2	50	–25
3	75	50

Payback period = 2 + 25 / 75 = 2.333 years

Firm recovers its initial investment in 2.333 years

13

LOS 36.d Calculate/Interpret
CFAI p. 10, Schweser p. 14
Capital Budgeting

Discounted Payback Period (DPP)

Cost of capital is 9%

End of Year	Project X	Discounted Cash Flow	Cumulative Discounted Cash Flow
0	–$100	–$100.00	–$100.00
1	25	22.94	–77.06
2	50	42.08	–34.98
3	75	57.91	22.93

DPP = 2 + 34.98 / 57.91 = 2.6 years

- Ignores CFs after payback
- Both payback methods focus on liquidity

14

LOS 36.d Calculate/Interpret
CFAI p. 10, Schweser p. 14 Capital Budgeting

Profitability Index (PI)

- Present value of future cash flows divided by initial cash outlay

$$PI = \frac{\text{PV Future CF}}{CF_0} = 1 + \frac{NPV}{CF_0}$$

- Independent projects: Accept all projects where PI > 1
- If NPV is > 0, then IRR > discount rate, and PI > 1

 15

LOS 36.e Explain/Compare/Describe
CFAI p. 16, Schweser p. 22 Capital Budgeting

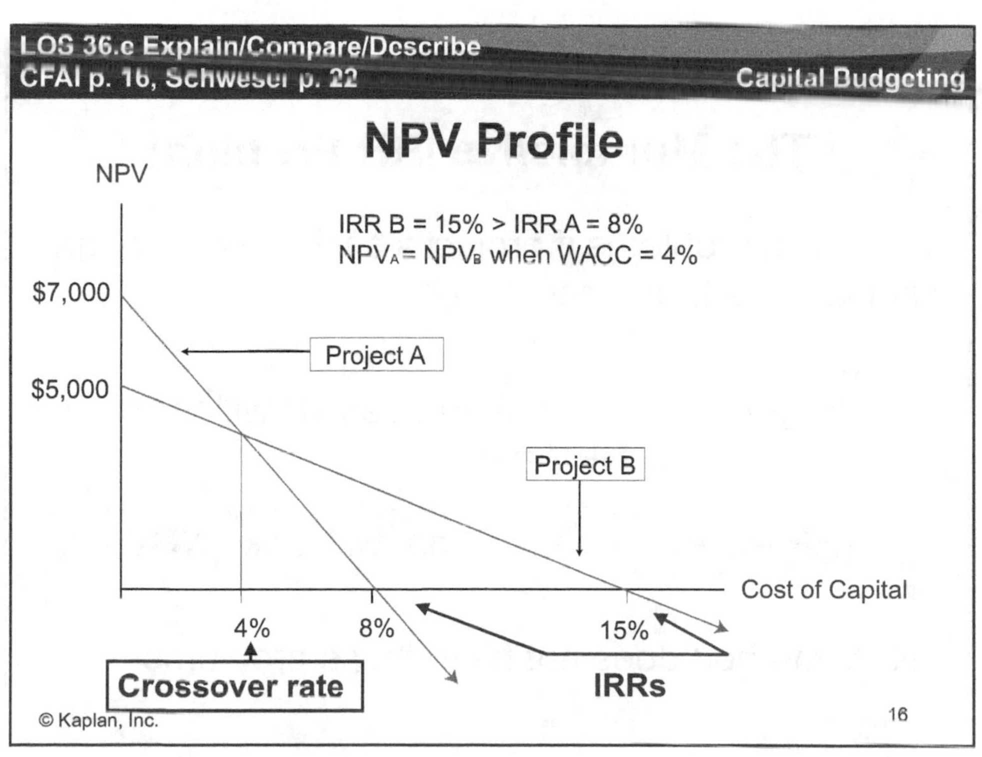

 16

LOS 36.e Explain/Compare/Describe
CFAI p. 16, Schweser p. 22 Capital Budgeting

IRR vs. NPV Project Rankings

- For **independent projects**, IRR and NPV give the **same** accept/reject decisions
- For **mutually exclusive projects**, IRR and NPV project rankings may differ, when:
  - Projects have different timing of CFs
  - The projects (CF_0) are different sizes
- Different **reinvestment rate assumptions**:
  IRR assumes CF reinvestment at project's IRR and NPV assumes CF reinvestment at the cost of capital (more conservative)

 17

LOS 36.e Explain/Compare/Describe
CFAI p. 16, Schweser p. 22 Capital Budgeting

The Multiple/No IRR Problem

Potential problems if project's cash flows change signs more than once:

Multiple IRRs – more than one IRR will make NPV = 0

No IRR – there is no IRR that will make NPV = 0

NPV method does not have these problems

 18

LOS 36.f Describe/Account/Explain
CFAI p. 25, Schweser p. 25

Capital Budgeting

Relative Popularity of Capital Budgeting Methods

- **By location:** European companies more likely to use payback period
- **By size of company:** Larger companies more likely to use NPV
- **Public vs. private companies:** Private companies more likely to use payback
- **By management education:** Educated managers more likely to use NPV

19

LOS 36.f,g Describe/Account/Explain
CFAI p. 25, Schweser p. 25

Capital Budgeting

Relationship Between NPV and Stock Price

- NPV is a direct measure of the expected change in shareholder wealth from a project
- Estimate increase in share value as NPV divided by number of shares

20

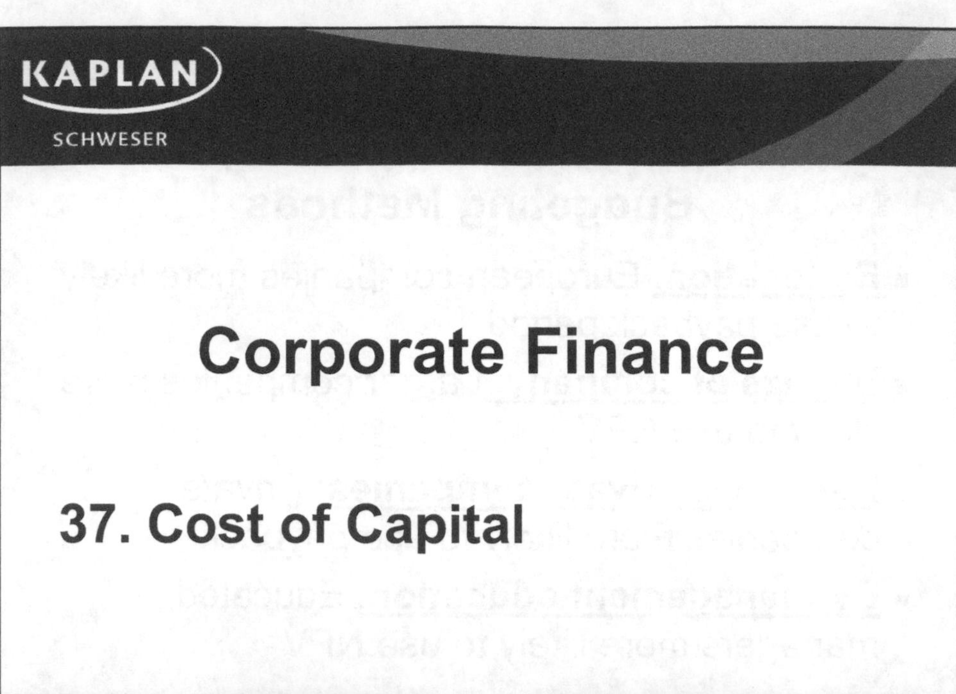

LOS 37.a Calculate/Interpret
CFAI p. 36, Schweser p. 35

Cost of Capital

Weighted-Average Cost of Capital

- The overall opportunity cost of the firm's capital is a weighted average of the opportunity costs of capital from **debt, preferred equity, and common equity**
- Project should be undertaken only if the return on invested capital is **greater than its opportunity cost**

22

LOS 37.a,b Calculate/Interpret/Describe
CFAI p. 36, Schweser p. 35 Cost of Capital

Weighted-Average Cost of Capital

- **k_d** Yield to maturity on existing/new debt; this is the before-tax cost of debt
- **$k_d(1 - t)$** After-tax cost of debt, where *t* is the marginal tax rate—only interest on debt is paid pre-tax
- **k_{ps}** Cost of preferred stock
- **k_{ce}** Cost of common equity

 23

LOS 37.a,b Calculate/Interpret/Describe
CFAI p. 36, Schweser p. 35 Cost of Capital

Weighted-Average Cost of Capital (WACC)

$$WACC = (w_d)[k_d(1 - t)] + (w_{ps})(k_{ps}) + (w_{ce})(k_{ce})$$

- **Example:** Firm X target capital structure is 10% preferred, 45% debt, and 45% common equity

$k_d = 7.5\%$, $t = 40\%$, $k_{ps} = 9.0\%$, and $k_{ce} = 11.5\%$

$$WACC = 0.45 \times 7.5\% (1 - 0.4) + 0.1 \times 9.0\% + 0.45 \times 11.5\% = 8.1\%$$

 24

LOS 37.c Explain
CFAI p. 38, Schweser p. 37

Cost of Capital

Target (Optimal) Capital Structure

Target capital structure: The proportions (based on market values) of debt, preferred stock, and equity that the firm expects to achieve over time

How do analysts determine target weights?

- Can use existing capital structure weights
- Can adjust existing weights for firm trends
- Can use industry average weights

25

LOS 37.d Explain
CFAI p. 40, Schweser p. 38

Cost of Capital

Marginal Cost of Capital (MCC)

- A firm's MCC is the cost of an additional dollar of capital
- MCC is the WACC of the next dollar of capital raised
- A firm's MCC increases as the firm increases the amount of capital it raises during a given period
- Thus, the **marginal cost of capital curve** slopes upward

26

LOS 37.d Explain
CFAI p. 40, Schweser p. 38

Cost of Capital

Optimal Capital Budget

- Given the expected returns (IRRs) on potential projects, we can order the **opportunities for investment** highest to lowest IRR
- This will allow us to construct a downward sloping **investment opportunity schedule**
- The intersection of the investment opportunity schedule with the marginal cost of capital curve identifies the **optimal capital budget**

27

LOS 37.d Explain
CFAI p. 40, Schweser p. 38

Cost of Capital

Optimal Capital Budget

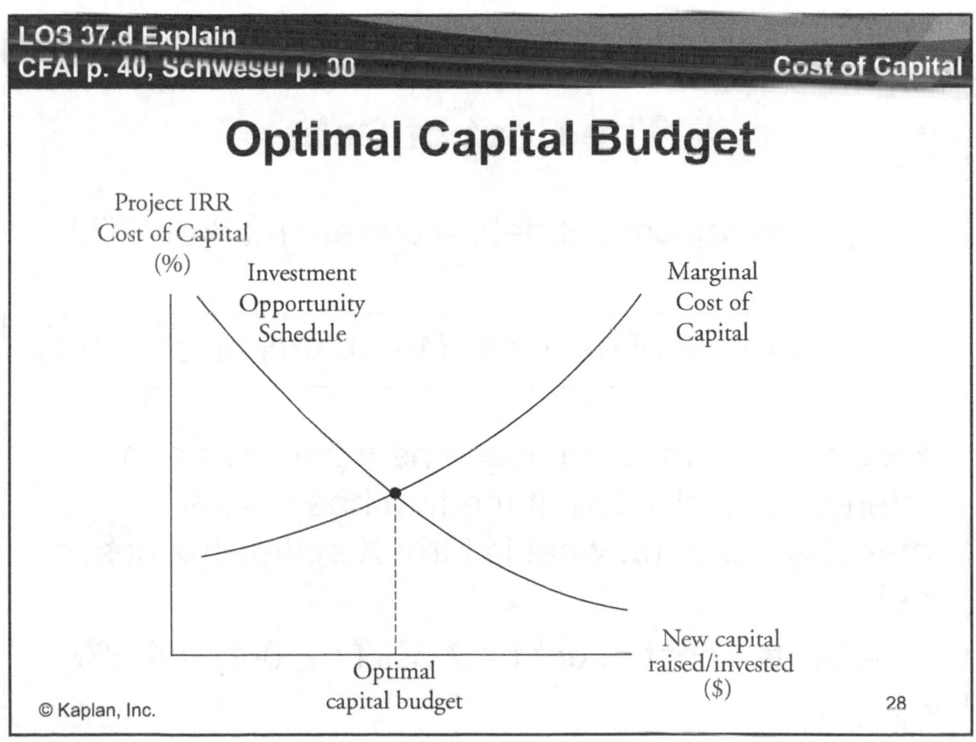

28

LOS 37.e Explain
CFAI p. 40, Schweser p. 39 Cost of Capital

Role of the WACC/MCC in Determining NPV of Projects

- The WACC is the appropriate discount rate (cost of capital) for projects that have the same level of risk as the firm's existing projects
- For a project with greater than average risk, use a discount rate greater than the firm's existing WACC
- For projects with below-average risk, use a discount rate less than the firm's WACC

 29

LOS 37.f Calculate/Interpret
CFAI p. 42, Schweser p. 39 Cost of Capital

The Cost of Debt

k_d = pretax cost of debt = current market YTM

After-tax cost of debt = k_d (1 – marginal tax rate)

Example: Firm X can issue new par debt at an interest rate of 7.5%. If the firm has a 40% marginal tax rate, what is Firm X's after-tax cost of debt?

After-tax cost of debt = 7.5% (1 – 0.4) = 4.5%

 30

LOS 37.f Calculate/Interpret
CFAI p. 42, Schweser p. 39

Cost of Capital

The Cost of Debt

- When available, use the **market rate of interest (YTM)** on firm's current debt for k_d
- If firm debt is not publicly traded, estimate the YTM using the **debt rating and maturity of existing debt**
- For firms that primarily use floating-rate debt, estimate the longer-term cost of the firm's debt using the **current yield curve** and firm's debt rating

31

LOS 37.g Calculate/Interpret
CFAI p. 44, Schweser p. 40

Cost of Capital

The Cost of Preferred Stock

$$k_{ps} = \frac{\text{preferred dividend}}{\text{market price of preferred}}$$

Example: New noncallable, nonconvertible preferred stock with a dividend of $8.50 has a value of $100/share. What is the firm's cost of preferred stock?

$$k_{ps} = \$8.50 / \$100.00 = 0.085 = 8.5\%$$

32

LOS 37.h Calculate/Interpret
CFAI p. 46, Schweser p. 41

Cost of Capital

The Cost of Common Equity

Method 1: CAPM

$$\text{CAPM: } k_{ce} = RFR + \beta[E(R_{mkt}) - RFR]$$

where: RFR = risk-free rate

β = beta (systematic risk) of firm's stock

$E(R_{mkt})$ = expected market return

Example: The T-bill rate is 5%, the expected return on the market is 11%, and Firm X's beta is 1.1

$$k_{ce} = 5\% + 1.1\ (11\% - 5\%) = 11.6\%$$

 33

LOS 37.h Calculate/Interpret
CFAI p. 46, Schweser p. 41

Cost of Capital

The Cost of Common Equity

Method 2: Dividend Discount Approach

$$k_{ce} = \frac{D_1}{P_0} + g$$

D_1 = **next year's** dividend

P_0 = current stock price

g = firm's expected constant growth rate
= (ROE)(retention rate)

 34

LOS 37.h Calculate/Interpret
CFAI p. 46, Schweser p. 41

Cost of Capital

The Cost of Common Equity

Method 3: Bond yield plus risk premium

$$k_{ce} = \text{bond market yield} + \text{risk premium}$$

(e.g., $k_{ce} = 7.5\% + 4\% = 11.5\%$)

- Assumes investors require a higher return on a firm's equity than on its debt
- Risk premium normally ranges from 3% to 5%
- Based on judgment: imprecise

35

Cost of Capital

Target Weights for Capital Sources – Problem

Which of the following methods for estimating the weights for calculating a firm's WACC is *least* acceptable?

A. Current proportions of debt and equity based on balance sheet values.

B. Industry average weights for debt and equity.

C. Firm's announced target capital structure weights.

36 - 1

LOS 37.i Calculate/Interpret
CFAI p. 51, Schweser p. 43

Cost of Capital

Cost of Capital for a Project

- Calculate cost of equity for the project using the pure play method
- Calculate the cost of debt for the company
- Calculate the cost of capital for the project using the debt/equity ratio of the subject company and the WACC formula

37

LOS 37.i Calculate/Interpret
CFAI p. 51, Schweser p. 43

Cost of Capital

Cost of Capital for a Project

Pure play method steps:

1. Calculate the beta of a comparable company (or companies) that is a pure play in the industry
2. Unlever it to adjust for differences in debt/equity ratio—this is the asset beta
3. Relever it to reflect the debt/equity ratio of the subject company—the project beta
4. Use the project beta to calculate the cost of equity for the project
5. Use that cost of equity to calculate WACC

38

LOS 37.i Calculate/Interpret
CFAI p. 51, Schweser p. 43
Cost of Capital

Asset Beta

Asset (unlevered) beta:

$$\beta_{ASSET} = \beta_{PURE\ PLAY}\left[\frac{1}{1+\left((1-t)\frac{D}{E}\right)}\right]$$

where: D/E is the *pure play company's* debt-to-equity ratio and *t* is its marginal tax rate

39

LOS 37.i Calculate/Interpret
CFAI p. 51, Schweser p. 43
Cost of Capital

Calculate the Company (Project) Beta

Company (project) beta:

$$\beta_{PROJECT} = \beta_{ASSET}\left[1+\left((1-t)\frac{D}{E}\right)\right]$$

use the *subject firm's* tax rate and debt-to-equity ratio for the company (project) to re-lever the asset beta

40

LOS 37.j Explain
CFAI p. 58, Schweser p. 45
Cost of Capital

Country Risk Premium

- **Problem**: CAPM problematic for estimating project cost of equity in developing markets
- **Solution:** Add country risk premium (CRP) to market risk premium when using CAPM

$$k_{ce} = R_F + \beta\left[E\left(R_{MKT}\right) - R_F + CRP\right]$$

41

LOS 37.j Explain
CFAI p. 58, Schweser p. 45
Cost of Capital

Country Risk Premium (cont.)

CRP =

sovereign yield spread

$$\times \left(\frac{\text{annualized } \sigma \text{ of equity index}}{\text{annualized } \sigma \text{ of sovereign bond market in terms of developed market currency}} \right)$$

Country must have sovereign bonds denominated in developed market currency

42

LOS 37.j Explain
CFAI p. 58, Schweser p. 45
Cost of Capital

Country Risk Premium Example

- Brazilian 10-year \$U.S. bond yield = 9.2%
- 10-year U.S. Treasury bond yield = 4.7%
- Annualized std. dev. Sao Paulo Equity Index = 34%
- Annualized std. dev. of Brazilian 10-year \$U.S. bond = 18%
- Beta of project = 1.32
- Expected market return = 10%
- Risk-free rate = 4.0%

MRP = 6%

43

LOS 37.j Explain
CFAI p. 58, Schweser p. 45
Cost of Capital

Country Risk Premium Example (cont.)

- **Country Risk Premium**

$$CRP = (0.092 - 0.047)\left(\frac{0.34}{0.18}\right) = 0.085$$

- **Cost of Equity**

$$k = 0.04 + 1.32[0.10 - 0.04 + 0.085]$$

$$k = 0.2314, \text{ or } 23.14\%$$

44

LOS 37.k Describe/Explain/Calculate/Interpret
CFAI p. 59, Schweser p. 46 Cost of Capital

Marginal Cost of Capital

- **MCC**: Opportunity cost of using an additional dollar of capital; WACC of raising an additional dollar
- Cost of each source of capital increases as the firm raises more new capital
- The result is an **upward sloping MCC schedule**

 45

LOS 37.k Describe/Explain/Calculate/Interpret
CFAI p. 59, Schweser p. 46 Cost of Capital

MCC and Investment Opportunity Schedules

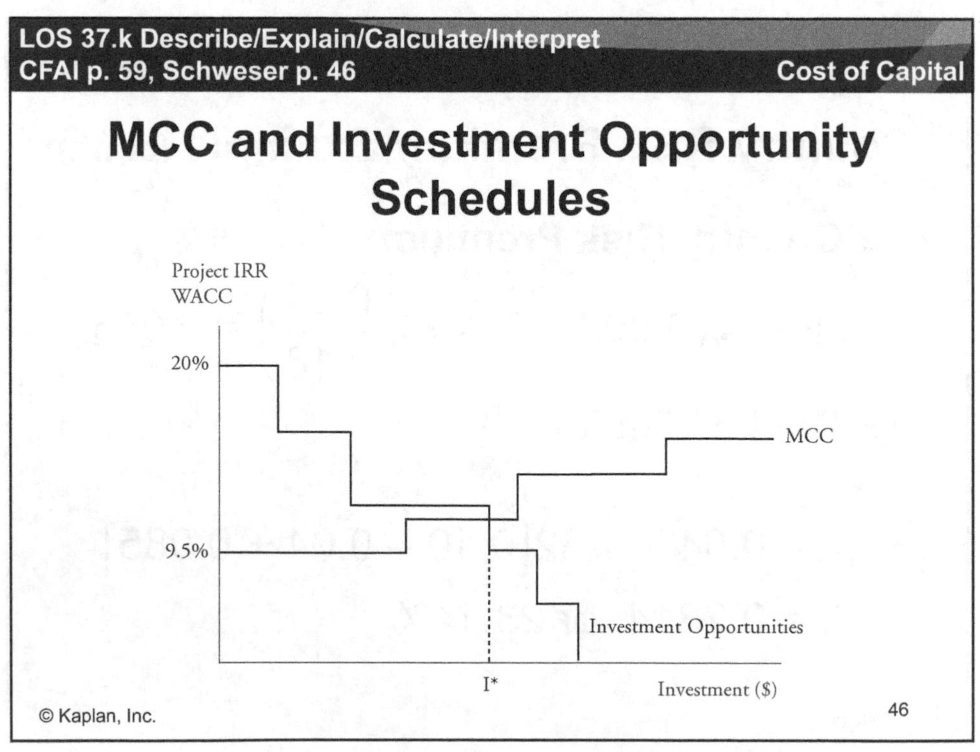

 46

LOS 37.k Describe/Explain/Calculate/Interpret
CFAI p. 59, Schweser p. 46 Cost of Capital

Calculating Breakpoints

The amount of new capital investment for which the WACC increases because the cost of one of the component costs of capital increases is termed a "breakpoint" and is:

$$\frac{\text{Amount of capital at which the component's cost of capital changes}}{\text{Weight of the component in the the capital structure}}$$

(e.g., cost of debt increases past $1.5 million raised, debt is 30% of the target capital structure: breakpoint = 1.5 / 0.3 = $5 million)

 47

LOS 37.l Explain/Demonstrate
CFAI p. 62, Schweser p. 48 Cost of Capital

Flotation Costs

Fees charged by investment bankers when a company raises external equity capital

- Range: 2% to 7%
- **Wrong way**: Adjust cost of equity
  - Cost is incorrectly carried through life of project
- **Right way:** Adjust initial cash outflow to include flotation costs when computing NPV
  - Correctly shows flotation cost as cash outflow at project inception

 48

Cost of Capital

Cost of Equity – Problem

At the beginning of last year, Acme Inc. had equity of $2 million and a share price of $15. For the year, net income was $200,000, dividends were $0.30/sh. on 200,000 outstanding shares. Acme's cost of equity capital is:

49 - 3

Corporate Finance

38. Measures of Leverage

Corporate Finance

LOS 38.a Define/Explain/Classify
CFAI p. 80, Schweser p. 00
Measures of Leverage

Definitions

- **Leverage:** Refers to the effect of fixed elements in cost structure

  Two types:
  - **Operating leverage:** Fixed operating expenses
  - **Financial leverage:** Fixed financing costs
- **Business risk:** Variability in EBIT
  - Affected by operating leverage
- **Financial risk:** Variability of EPS from fixed interest costs of debt financing

 51

LOS 38.b Calculate/Interpret
CFAI p. 83, Schweser p. 61

Measures of Leverage

Degree of Operating Leverage (DOL)

Definition/Interpretation: $$\text{DOL} = \frac{\%\text{ change in EBIT}}{\%\text{ change in sales}}$$

Calculation: $$\text{DOL} = \frac{\text{sales} - \text{TVC}}{\text{sales} - \text{TVC} - \text{fixed}}$$

When fixed costs are zero, DOL = 1, there is no operating leverage: %Δ EBIT = %Δ sales

52

LOS 38.b Calculate/Interpret
CFAI p. 83, Schweser p. 61

Measures of Leverage

Degree of Operating Leverage (DOL)

Example: A firm produced 5,000 units last year. Its fixed costs were \$70,000, its selling price was \$75, and its variable unit cost was \$50. What was the firm's DOL at 5,000 units?

$$\text{DOL} = \frac{\text{Sales} - \text{TVC}}{\text{Sales} - \text{TVC} - \text{Fixed}} = \frac{Q(P - V_{\text{Unit}})}{Q(P - V_{\text{Unit}}) - \text{Fixed}}$$

$$= \frac{5{,}000(75 - 50)}{5{,}000(75 - 50) - 70{,}000} = 2.27$$

53

LOS 38.b Calculate/Interpret
CFAI p. 83, Schweser p. 61
Measures of Leverage

Degree of Financial Leverage (DFL)

Definition/Interpretation: $DFL = \frac{\%\text{ change in EPS}}{\%\text{ change in EBIT}}$

Calculation: $DFL = \frac{EBIT}{EBIT - \text{interest}}$

When fixed financing costs are zero, DFL = 1, there is no financial leverage: %Δ EPS = %Δ EBIT

54

LOS 38.b Calculate/Interpret
CFAI p. 83, Schweser p. 61
Measures of Leverage

Degree of Financial Leverage (DFL)

Example: A firm has EBIT of $55,000 and interest expense of $20,000. **If EBIT increases by 3%,** what will be the effect on earnings per share?

$$DFL = \frac{55{,}000}{55{,}000 - 20{,}000} = 1.57$$

EPS will increase by 3% × 1.57 = **4.71%**

55

LOS 38.b Calculate/Interpret
CFAI p. 83, Schweser p. 61

Measures of Leverage

Degree of Total Leverage (DTL)

Definition/Interpretation: $DTL = \dfrac{\%\text{ change in EPS}}{\%\text{ change in sales}}$

$$DTL = DOL \times DFL$$

Two sources of leverage; multiplicative

$$DTL = \frac{Q(P - V)}{Q(P - V) - \text{fixed} - \text{interest}}$$

$$= \frac{\text{sales} - TVC}{\text{sales} - TVC - \text{fixed} - \text{interest}}$$

56

LOS 38.b Calculate/Interpret
CFAI p. 83, Schweser p. 61

Measures of Leverage

Degree of Total Leverage (DTL)

Example: What is the DTL of a firm that had sales last year of \$375,000, total variable costs of \$250,000, fixed costs of \$70,000, and interest expense of \$20,000?

$$DTL = \frac{\text{sales} - TVC}{\text{sales} - TVC - \text{fixed} - \text{interest}}$$

$$= \frac{375{,}000 - 250{,}000}{375{,}000 - 250{,}000 - 70{,}000 - 20{,}000} = 3.57$$

$DOL \times DFL = DTL; \quad 2.27 \times 1.57 = 3.57$

57

LOS 38.c Describe
CFAI p. 89, Schweser p. 64

Measures of Leverage

Firm Characteristics and Leverage

- Three rules of leverage:
  1. High fixed costs = high operating leverage
  2. High debt ratio = high financial leverage
  3. High fixed costs + high debt ratio = high total leverage

58

Measures of Leverage

Leverage – Problem

Polsen, Inc. has fixed operating costs of $1.5 million, fixed financing costs of $1.0 million, sells their output at $700 per unit, and has variable costs of $200 per unit. At an output of 5,000 units, a decrease in sales of 1% can be expected to decrease operating earnings by:

A. 1.0%.

B. 2.5%.

C. 3.5%.

59 - 2

LOS 38.d Calculate/Determine
CFAI p. 95, Schweser p. 66 Measures of Leverage

Breakeven Quantity of Sales

Breakeven quantity is the level of sales at which a firm's net income is zero

$$Q_{BE} = \frac{\text{Total Fixed Costs}}{\text{Price} - \text{Var. Cost per unit}}$$

Example: If P = \$85; V = \$60; FC = \$500,000; What is the firm's breakeven quantity of sales?

Q_{BE} = 500,000 / (85 – 60) = 20,000 units

 60

LOS 38.d Calculate/Determine
CFAI p. 95, Schweser p. 66 Measures of Leverage

Net Income at Various Sales Levels

Example: Assume the following for a firm:
P = \$85; VC = \$60; FC = \$500,000; Int = \$20,000;
Q = 25,000 units, no taxes

What is the firm's net income?

NI = Q(P – V) – fixed costs – interest
= 25,000(85 – 60) – 500,000 – 20,000

= \$105,000

 61

LOS 38.e Calculate/Interpret
CFAI p. 95, Schweser p. 66

Measures of Leverage

Operating Breakeven Quantity of Sales

Operating breakeven quantity is the level of sales that just covers a firm's fixed operating costs

$$Q_{OBE} = \frac{\text{Fixed Operating Costs}}{\text{Price} - \text{Var. Cost per unit}}$$

Example: If P = $85, V = $60, fixed operating costs = $300,000, what is the firm's operating breakeven quantity of sales?

Q_{OBE} = 300,000 / (85 – 60) = 12,000 units

Corporate Finance

39. Dividends and Share Repurchases: Basics

Corporate Finance

LOS 39.a Describe
CFAI p. 108, Schweser p. 75

Dividends and Share Repurchases: Basics

Types of Dividends

- **Cash dividends**: Payments made to shareholders in cash
- **Three** types:
    - Regular dividends
    - Special dividends
    - Liquidating dividends

64

LOS 39.a Describe
CFAI p. 108, Schweser p. 75

Dividends and Share Repurchases: Basics

Stock Dividends, Stock Splits

- **Stock dividend**: Payment to shareholders in shares of stock (e.g., 10% of existing shares)
- **Stock split**: Proportionate *increase* in shares outstanding (e.g., 2 for 1)
- **Reverse stock split**: Proportionate *decrease* in shares outstanding (e.g., 1 for 5)

Stock splits and stock dividends do not change value of stock outstanding

 65

LOS 39.a Describe
CFAI p. 108, Schweser p. 75

Dividends and Share Repurchases: Basics

Effects on Financial Ratios

- **Cash dividend:**
  Assets ↓ (cash)
  Equity ↓ (retained earnings)
  - Liquidity ratios decrease due to decrease in cash (current assets)
  - Leverage ratios increase due to decreases in assets, equity
- **Stock dividends, stock splits** do not affect liquidity ratios or leverage ratios

 66

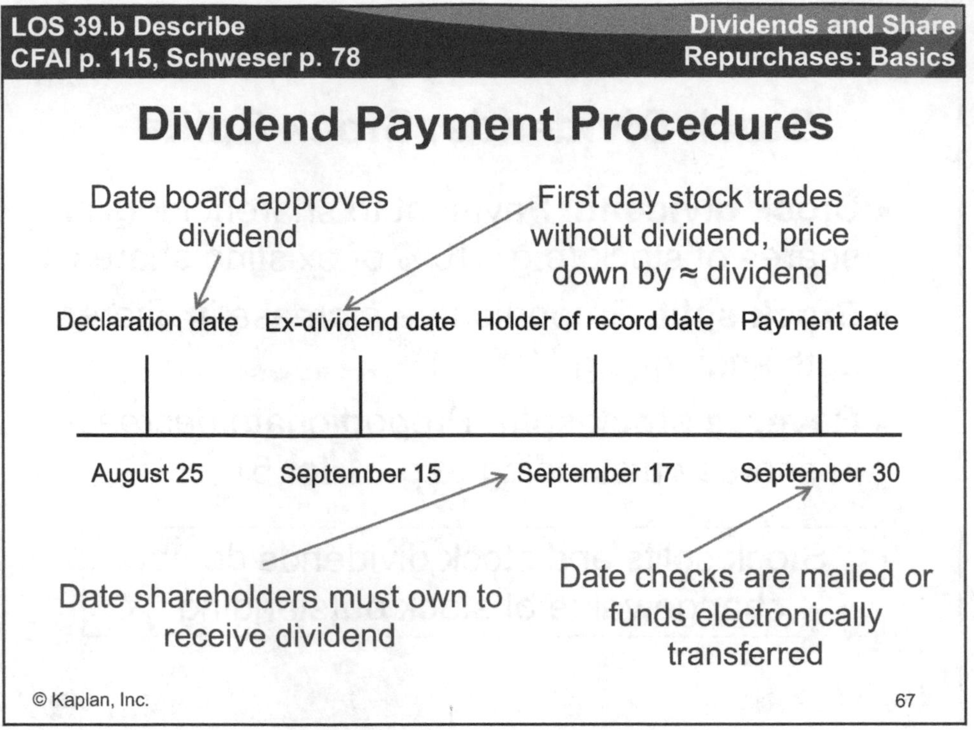

LOS 39.c Compare
CFAI p. 120, Schweser p. 79

Dividends and Share Repurchases: Basics

Share Repurchase Methods

- **Open market repurchase**
  - Buy at market price in the open market
  - Flexibility in timing
- **Tender offer**
  - Buy fixed number of shares at fixed price
  - Typically at a premium to market
  - May use Dutch auction to determine price
- **Direct negotiation**
  - Typically at a premium to market

68

LOS 39.c Compare
CFAI p. 120, Schweser p. 79

Dividends and Share Repurchases: Basics

Share Repurchase

Rationales for share repurchase instead of cash dividend:

1. Tax advantage to shareholders if tax rate on capital gains < tax rate on dividends
2. Signal to shareholders that management believes shares are undervalued

69

LOS 39.d Calculate/Compare
CFAI p. 122, Schweser p. 79

Dividends and Share Repurchases: Basics

Share Repurchase With Borrowed Funds

Price = \$50/share, 50,000 shares outstanding
EPS = \$4, after-tax cost of funds = 10%
Buy back 5,000 shares

Earnings yield = 4 / 50 = 8%

Interest cost = 5,000 × \$50 × 10% = \$25,000

$$\text{new EPS} = \frac{\$4(50{,}000) - \$25{,}000}{50{,}000 - 5{,}000} = \$3.89\,/\,\text{sh.}$$

When after-tax cost of funds is **greater** than earnings yield (EPS/Price), EPS **falls**

70

LOS 39.e Calculate
CFAI p. 124, Schwesser p. 82

Dividends and Share Repurchases: Basics

Share Repurchase Effect on BVPS

Price = \$50/share, 50,000 shares outstanding
BVPS = \$40, buy back 5,000 shares

Buyback amount = 5,000 × 50 = \$250,000
Original equity = 50,000 × 40 = \$2,000,000

$$\text{new BVPS} = \frac{\$2{,}000{,}000 - \$250{,}000}{50{,}000 - 5{,}000} = \$38.89\,/\,\text{sh.}$$

When share price is **greater** than book value, a repurchase **decreases** BV per share

71

LOS 39.f Explain
CFAI p. 125, Schweser p. 82

Dividends and Share Repurchases: Basics

Share Repurchase vs. Cash Dividend

If tax treatment and information effects are the same for either method, the effects of a cash dividend or a share repurchase in an equal amount are **the same**

Stock price = \$30 10,000 shares outstanding

Pay a cash dividend of \$3 per share = \$30,000

Cash dividend: Stock price = \$30 – \$3 = \$27

Market value of equity = 10,000 × 27 = **\$270,000**

Repurchase 1,000 shares for \$30,000

Repurchase: Shares outstanding decrease to 9,000

Market value of equity = 9,000 × 30 = **\$270,000**

72 - 2

WCM
1. Liquidity - access to cash
2. Short term horizon

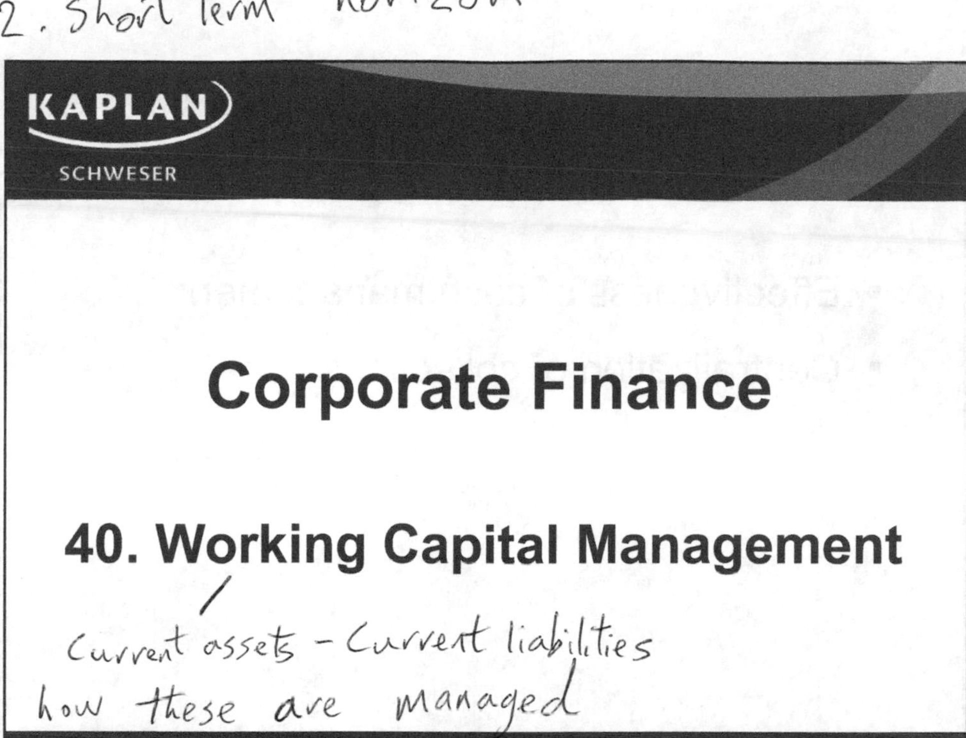

LOS 40.a Describe
CFAI p. 137, Schweser p. 89

Working Capital Management

Sources of Liquidity

- **Primary Sources** (from normal operations):
  - Cash, cash equivalents, collections, and investment income
  - Trade credit, bank lines of credit, and short-term investment portfolios
- **Secondary Sources** (may significantly change firm):
  - Renegotiation of debt, liquidation of assets, bankruptcy

74

LOS 40.a Describe
CFAI p. 137, Schweser p. 89

Working Capital Management

Factors Influencing Liquidity

- Effectiveness of cash management
- Centralization of collections
- Liquidity of short- and long-term assets

75

LOS 40.b Compare
CFAI p. 139, Schweser p. 90

Working Capital Management

Liquidity Ratios

$$\text{Current ratio} = \frac{\text{Current assets}}{\text{Current liabilities}}$$

$$\text{Quick ratio} = \frac{\text{Cash + ST securities + receivables}}{\text{Current liabilities}}$$

$$\text{Cash ratio} = \frac{\text{Cash + ST securities}}{\text{Current liabilities}}$$

76

LOS 40.b Compare
CFAI p. 139, Schweser p. 90

Working Capital Management

Liquidity Ratios

$$\text{Receivables turnover} = \frac{\text{Net annual sales}}{\text{Average receivables}}$$

$$\text{Inventory turnover} = \frac{\text{Cost of goods sold}}{\text{Average inventory}}$$

$$\text{Payables turnover} = \frac{\text{Purchases}}{\text{Average trade payables}}$$

77

LOS 40.b Compare
CFAI p. 139, Schweser p. 90

Working Capital Management

Liquidity Ratios

$$\text{\# days of receivables} = \frac{365}{\text{Receivables turnover}}$$

$$\text{\# days of inventory} = \frac{365}{\text{Inventory turnover}}$$

$$\text{\# days of payables} = \frac{365}{\text{Payables turnover}}$$

78

LOS 40.c Evaluate/Compare
CFAI p. 139, Schweser p. 92

Working Capital Management

Operating and Cash Conversion Cycles

Operating cycle = days of inventory + days of receivables

Cash conversion cycle = days of inventory + days of receivables – days of payables

- Cash conversion cycle is also called ***net*** *operating cycle*

79

LOS 40.c Evaluate/Compare
CFAI p. 139, Schweser p. 92

Working Capital Management

Operating and Cash Conversion Cycles

Buy raw materials

Sell goods on credit

Collect cash

Inventory days

Receivables days

OPERATING CYCLE

Payables days

CASH CONVERSION CYCLE

80

LOS 40.d Explain
CFAI p. 143, Schweser p. 92

Working Capital Management

Managing Net Daily Cash

- **Goal:** Keep enough cash for routine needs, but not so much cash that the firm foregoes interest income
- Forecast cash inflows and outflows by type (e.g., sales, collections, purchases, wages, taxes, interest, dividends, transfers to/from subsidiaries)
  - Short-term horizon: Next few weeks
  - Medium-term horizon: Next 12 months
  - Long-term horizon: Multi-year

81

LOS 40.e Calculate/Interpret/Compare/Evaluate
CFAI p. 149, Schweser p. 93

Working Capital Management

Short-term Investments

Invest excess cash in **short-term securities**:

- U.S. Treasury bills
- Short-term federal agency securities
- Bank certificates of deposit
- Banker's acceptances
- Time deposits
- Repurchase agreements
- Commercial paper
- Money market mutual funds
- Adjustable-rate preferred stock

82

LOS 40.e Calculate/Interpret/Compare/Evaluate
CFAI p. 149, Schweser p. 93

Working Capital Management

Comparing Short-term Yields

$$\% \text{ discount} = \frac{\text{Face value} - \text{price}}{\text{Face value}}$$

$$\text{Discount basis (bank discount) yield} = \% \text{ discount} \times \frac{360}{\text{Days}}$$

$$\text{Money market yield} = \left(\frac{\text{Face value} - \text{price}}{\text{Price}}\right)\left(\frac{360}{\text{Days}}\right) = \text{HPY} \times \frac{360}{\text{days}}$$

$$\textbf{Bond equivalent yield} = \left(\frac{\text{Face value} - \text{price}}{\text{Price}}\right)\left(\frac{365}{\text{Days}}\right) = \text{HPY} \times \frac{365}{\text{Days}}$$

83

LOS 40.e Calculate/Interpret/Compare/Evaluate
CFAI p. 149, Schweser p. 93

Working Capital Management

Cash Management IPS

- Purpose and objective of investment portfolio
- Strategy guidelines
- Types of securities
- Individuals responsible for the portfolio
- Corrective steps
- Limitations

84

LOS 40.f Evaluate
CFAI p. 153, Schweser p. 95

Working Capital Management

Accounts Receivable Aging Schedule $ 000's

Days Outstanding	Mar	Apr	May
< 31 days	200	212	195
31–60 days	150	165	140
61–90 days	100	90	92
> 90 days	50	70	66

Can also be presented as percentage of total receivables

85

LOS 40.f Evaluate
CFAI p. 153, Schweser p. 95

Working Capital Management

Weighted-Average Collection Period

Days Outstanding	Average Collection Days	% Weight	Days × Weight
< 31 days	22	40%	8.8
31–60 days	44	30%	13.2
61–90 days	74	20%	14.8
> 90 days	135	10%	13.5
Weighted-average collection period			**50.3**

86

LOS 40.f Evaluate
CFAI p. 153, Schweser p. 95

Working Capital Management

Evaluating Performance

- **Receivables:** Trade-off between credit terms and sales
- **Inventories:** Too low can lead to stock-outs, too high increases carrying costs
- **Payables:** Early payment can take advantage of discounts but gives up potential interest on cash; late payment increases interest costs, can damage supplier relationships

87

LOS 40.g Evaluate/Recommend
CFAI p. 167, Schweser p. 98

Working Capital Management

Sources of Short-term Funding

- Lines of credit
  - Committed: Requires fee
  - Revolving: Fee, larger, strongest (U.S.)
  - Uncommitted: Less reliable, no fee (U.S.)
- Bankers' acceptances: Import/export
- Factoring: Smaller users, higher fees
- Commercial paper: Large, strong credit
- Nonbank finance companies: Weak credit

88

Working Capital Management

Cash Management – Problem

Firm A's operating cycle is 38 days. Firm B's operating cycle is longer at 42 days but its cash conversion cycle is shorter than that of Firm A. We can conclude that:

A. Firm A has better inventory management.

B. Firm B has better receivables management.

C. Firm B has lower payables turnover.

Corporate Finance

41. The Corporate Governance of Listed Companies: A Manual for Investors

Corporate Finance

LOS 41.a Define
CFAI p. 182, Schweser p. 105

Corporate Governance of Listed Companies

What is Corporate Governance?

- Corporate governance refers to the firm's **internal controls** and the procedures by which the firm is managed
- Defines **rights and responsibilities** of management, the board, and shareholders
- Good corporate governance ensures that **shareholder interests are protected**

91

LOS 41.a Define
CFAI p. 182, Schweser p. 105

Corporate Governance of Listed Companies

Factors Affecting Corporate Governance

- **Board of directors**—independent directors, qualifications of directors, terms, committee structure
- **Management**—code of ethics, board oversight, compensation, alignment of interests

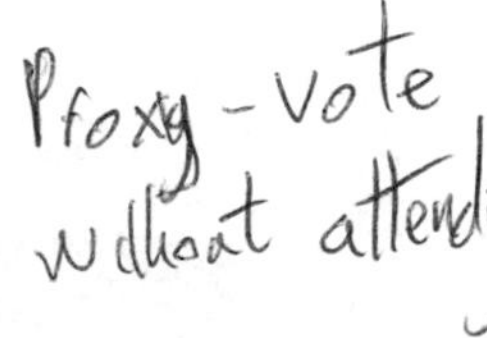

- **Shareholder rights**—voting rights (e.g., cumulative), proxy voting, actions requiring shareholder approval

92

LOS 41.b Describe/Determine
CFAI p. 183, Schweser p. 100

Corporate Governance of Listed Companies

What Makes a Good Board?

- Acts in the **best interest of shareholders**
  - Independent majority
  - Sometimes meets without managers present
- Ability to **hire outside consultants** with specialized knowledge (e.g., risk management, technology, legal)
- **Annual terms** give shareholders more control than longer, possibly staggered, terms
- **Negative factors**: CEO (or past CEO) is chair, members are closely related to customers or suppliers

93

LOS 41.c Describe/Explain
CFAI p. 188, Schweser p. 107

Corporate Governance of Listed Companies

Independent Board Members

- Board members who do not have material relationships with management or significant shareholders
- No compensation from firm for other than board service (e.g., no consulting or finder's fees)
- Works to protect shareholders' long-term interest

94

LOS 41.d Identify
CFAI p. 189, Schweser p. 107

Corporate Governance of Listed Companies

What Makes a Good Board Member?

- Qualifications and experience
  - Can they make informed decisions?
  - Do they understand the business?
  - Are they ethical?
  - Have they had legal or regulatory problems?
  - Have they had other board experience?
  - Do they attend meetings?

95

LOS 41.e Describe/Identify
CFAI p. 194, Schweser p. 108

Corporate Governance of Listed Companies

Board Committees

- **Audit**: Ensures quality of financial reporting
  - Proper procedures (e.g., GAAP)
  - Controls auditors
- **Compensation**: Sets executive compensation
  - Links compensation to LT performance
  - Need independence from management
- **Nominations**: Nominates/recruits new members

 96

LOS 41.f Explain
CFAI p. 201, Schweser p. 110

Corporate Governance of Listed Companies

Code of Ethics

- Strong code of ethics needed
- Policies should prevent personal use of corporate assets
  - Board members should not serve as consultants
  - Board members should not receive finder's fees for M&A or sales opportunities

 97

LOS 41.f Explain
CFAI p. 201, Schweser p. 110

Corporate Governance of Listed Companies

Provisions of a Code of Ethics

- Congruent with local laws
- Prohibit advantages to firm insiders
- Conditions for waivers (and frequency of use)
- Require timely information to board
- Periodic audits/reviews of code

Weak code allows related-party transactions and personal use of company assets

 98

LOS 41.g Evaluate
CFAI p. 208, Schweser p. 111

Corporate Governance of Listed Companies

Shareholders and Proxy Voting Rules

Easy proxy voting = better shareholder rights

Negatives:

- Limits on proxy voting
- Meetings timed inconveniently
- Require attendance
- Allows "share blocking"
- Cumulative voting with large minority shareholder group (e.g., founding family)

 99

LOS 41.g Evaluate
CFAI p. 208, Schweser p. 111

Corporate Governance of Listed Companies

Shareholder Sponsored Action

Greater ability to influence board = greater shareholder protection

- Board nominations
- Resolutions/proposals
- Issues:
  - When can they be made?
  - Can board member be removed?
  - Simple majority vs. supermajority

100

LOS 41.g Evaluate
CFAI p. 200, Schweser p. 111

Corporate Governance of Listed Companies

Different Classes of Stock

- Classes separate voting rights and economic value
- Potential acquirers may only deal with one class of stockholders
- Generally, separation of voting rights works to the impairment of at least one set of shareholders
- Different classes lead to trouble raising equity capital

101

LOS 41.g Evaluate
CFAI p. 208, Schweser p. 111

Corporate Governance of Listed Companies

Takeover Defense and Share Value

Takeover defenses reduce shareholder value

- Golden parachutes
- Poison pills
- Greenmail

Is shareholder approval required to implement?

Past acquisition interest?

Government intervention in acquisition likely?

102

Corporate Governance of Listed Companies

Corporate Governance – Problem

Which of the following characteristics of a board is *least* supportive of shareowner protection?

A. Firm suppliers, customers, and consultants are not represented on the board. +

B. The board chairman is the ex-CEO of the firm. –

C. The board often meets without firm management present. +

103 - 1

Cost of Capital

Target Weights for Capital Sources – Solution

Which of the following methods for estimating the weights for calculating a firm's WACC is *least* acceptable?

A. Current proportions of debt and equity based on balance sheet values.

Cost of Capital

Cost of Equity – Solution

At the beginning of last year, Acme Inc. had equity of $2 million and a share price of $15. For the year, net income was $200,000, dividends were $0.30/sh. on 200,000 outstanding shares. Acme's cost of equity capital is:

g = ROE x RR =

$$\frac{200{,}000}{2{,}000{,}000} \times \left[1 - \frac{0.3\,(200{,}000)}{200{,}000}\right] = 10\%(1 - 0.3) = 7\%$$

K_{ce} = div. yld. + growth = 0.30/15 + 7% = 9%

Measures of Leverage

Leverage – Solution

Polsen, Inc. has fixed operating costs of $1.5 million, fixed financing costs of $1.0 million, sells their output at $700 per unit, and has variable costs of $200 per unit. At an output of 5,000 units, a decrease in sales of 1% can be expected to decrease operating earnings by:

B. 2.5%.

$$\text{Op. Leverage} = \frac{5{,}000(700-200)}{5{,}000(700-200)-1{,}500{,}000} = 2.5$$

Expected change in op. earnings = 2.5 (–1%) = –2.5%

Working Capital Management

Cash Management – Solution

Firm A's operating cycle is 38 days. Firm B's operating cycle is longer at 42 days but its cash conversion cycle is shorter than that of Firm A. We can conclude that:

C. Firm B has lower payables turnover.

Corporate Governance – Solution

Which of the following characteristics of a board is *least* supportive of shareowner protection?

B. The board chairman is the ex-CEO of the firm.

Study Session 12

Portfolio Management

Portfolio Management

42. Portfolio Management: An Overview

Portfolio Management

LOS 42.a Describe
CFAI p. 225, Schweser p. 125

Portfolio Management: An Overview

The Portfolio Perspective

- Evaluate investments based on their contribution to risk and return of an investor's overall portfolio (not in isolation)
- Adding a risky asset can actually reduce portfolio risk
- **Diversification ratio** =

$$\frac{\text{standard deviation of portfolio returns}}{\text{average std. dev. of returns on portfolio assets}}$$

2

LOS 42.b Describe
CFAI p. 233, Schweser p. 126

Portfolio Management: An Overview

Pension Plans

Defined Contribution Plans

- No guarantee of future payment
- Individual bears risk, makes decisions

Defined Benefit Plans

- Obligation for future payment
- Time horizon: Long
- Risk tolerance: High
- Income needs: Depend on age of beneficiaries
- Liquidity needs: Low

 3

LOS 42.b Describe
CFAI p. 233, Schweser p. 126

Portfolio Management: An Overview

Endowments

- Provide ongoing financial support
- Time horizon: Long
- Risk tolerance: High
- Income needs: Low
- Liquidity needs: Low

 4

LOS 42.b Describe
CFAI p. 233, Schweser p. 126

Portfolio Management: An Overview

Insurance Companies

Property Casualty (P&C) and Life

- Time horizon: Long for Life
  Short for P&C
- Risk tolerance: Low
- Income needs: Low
- Liquidity needs: High

5

LOS 42.b Describe
CFAI p. 233, Schweser p. 126

Portfolio Management: An Overview

Banks

Loans are assets, excess reserves invested primarily in fixed-income and money market securities

- Time horizon: Short
- Risk tolerance: Low
- Income needs: Must pay interest on deposits
- Liquidity needs: High

6

LOS 42.b Describe
CFAI p. 233, Schweser p. 126

Portfolio Management:
An Overview

Other Types of Investors

Mutual funds

- Liquidity needs: High
- Time horizon, risk tolerance, and income needs all depend on the type of fund and fund objective

Sovereign wealth funds

- Various investment goals
- Invest for future generations
- Manage foreign exchange reserves
- Manage government assets (e.g., state pensions)

7

LOS 42.c Describe
CFAI p. 239, Schweser p. 127

Portfolio Management:
An Overview

Portfolio Management Process

1. Planning

- Understand client needs and constraints
- Write an Investment Policy Statement (IPS)
- Develop an investment strategy consistent with the IPS
- Specify performance benchmark

8

LOS 42.c Describe
CFAI p. 239, Schweser p. 127

Portfolio Management: An Overview

Portfolio Management Process

2. Execution

- Analyze risk and return characteristics of asset classes
- Analyze market conditions to identify attractive asset classes
- Identify attractive securities within asset classes
- Portfolio construction: Target/strategic asset allocations, individual securities weightings, risk management

9

LOS 42.c Describe
CFAI p. 239, Schweser p. 127

Portfolio Management: An Overview

Portfolio Management Process

3. Feedback

- Monitor and update investor's needs
- Monitor and update market conditions
- Rebalance portfolio as needed
- Measure and report performance

10

LOS 42.d Describe/Compare
CFAI p. 243, Schweser p. 128

Portfolio Management: An Overview

Pooled Investments

1. **Open-end mutual funds**
   - Purchase or redeem shares at NAV
   - Number of shares changes with purchases and redemptions
   - Fee (%) for ongoing management
   - Load funds: Up-front charges, redemption charges, or both
   - No-load funds: Neither type of charges

 11

LOS 42.d Describe/Compare
CFAI p. 243, Schweser p. 128

Portfolio Management: An Overview

Pooled Investments

2. **Closed-end mutual funds**
   - Fixed number of shares
   - Issued as an IPO
   - Trade like shares of stock, commission and spread, and margin and shorting
   - Fee (%) for ongoing management
   - Market prices can (do) differ from NAV
   - Do not need to hold cash or sell shares to meet redemptions as open-end funds do

 12

LOS 42.d Describe/Compare
CFAI p. 243, Schweser p. 128

Portfolio Management: An Overview

Pooled Investments

Types of mutual funds by investment objective

- Money market funds
- Bond funds: High yield, global, domestic, government, corporate, long-term, short-term, tax-exempt, etc.
- Stock funds
  - Actively managed funds
  - Index funds
- Balanced funds

13

LOS 42.d Describe/Compare
CFAI p. 243, Schweser p. 128

Portfolio Management: An Overview

Pooled Investments

3. **Exchange-Traded Funds (ETFs)**
   - Typically index funds
   - Trade like shares of closed-end funds
   - Can be shorted or margined
   - Dividends typically paid out
   - In-kind purchase and redemptions keep market price close to NAV
   - May have tax advantage over open-end index funds

14

LOS 42.d Describe/Compare
CFAI p. 243, Schweser p. 128

Portfolio Management: An Overview

Pooled Investments

4. **Separately managed accounts**
   - Owned by a single investor
   - Also called "wrap accounts"
   - Minimum investment $100–500K
5. **Buyout funds**
   - Buy all public shares and take company private
   - Heavy use of debt, high leverage
   - Hope to restructure, improve cash flow, and resell as an IPO at a profit

 15

LOS 42.d Describe/Compare
CFAI p. 243, Schweser p. 128

Portfolio Management: An Overview

Pooled Investments

6. **Venture capital funds**
   - Provide start-up/early-stage financing
   - Expect failures but with some big successes
   - Active in management of portfolio firms
7. **Hedge funds**
   - Not registered or offered to the public
   - Small number of "accredited" investors
   - High minimum investment, high leverage, derivatives
   - Many strategies are used (e.g., long/short, global macro, event driven)

 16

Portfolio Management

43. Portfolio Risk and Return: Part I

Portfolio Management

LOS 43.a Calculate/Interpret/Describe
CFAI p. 260, Schweser p. 136

Portfolio Risk and Return: Part I

Return Measures

Holding Period (Total) Return

$$\frac{\text{End-of-period value}}{\text{Beginning-of-period value}} - 1$$

Average Return

$$\frac{R_1 + R_2 + R_3 + \ldots\ldots\ldots\ldots + R_n}{n}$$

18

LOS 43.a Calculate/Interpret/Describe
CFAI p. 260, Schweser p. 136

Portfolio Risk and Return: Part I

Return Measures

Geometric Mean Return

$$\sqrt[n]{(1+R_1)(1+R_2)(1+R_3)........(1+R_n)}-1$$

19

LOS 43.a Calculate/Interpret/Describe
CFAI p. 260, Schweser p. 136

Portfolio Risk and Return: Part I

Return Measures

Money-weighted returns are an IRR measure

$$CF_0 + \frac{CF_1}{1+MWR} + ... + \frac{CF_N}{(1+MWR)^N} = 0$$

Periods must be equal length, use shortest period with no significant cash flows

Remember, use time-weighted for performance

20

Portfolio Risk and Return: Part I

Money-Weighted Return – Problem

Invest $1,000 in an account at t = 0

Value at end of Year 1 is $1,200, investor **adds $800**.

Value at end of Year 2 is $2,200.

Calculate the annual MWR.

MWR =

21 - 3

LOS 43.a Calculate/Interpret/Describe
CFAI p. 260, Schweser p. 136

Portfolio Risk and Return: Part I

Return Measures

Gross Return: Return before management fees

Net Return: Return after management fees

After-tax Return: After deducting tax liability

Real Return: After adjusting for inflation

Leveraged Return: Return on cash investment

22

Portfolio Risk and Return: Part I

Return Measures – Problem

An investor buys 500 shares at $35 with 50% margin. After one year, the shares are sold for $50. The investor is subject to a 15% tax on gains, and inflation over the year was 4%. Ignoring interest and commissions, the investor's real after-tax leveraged return is:

23 - 3

LOS 43.b Calculate/Interpret
CFAI p. 261, Schweser p. 139

Portfolio Risk and Return: Part I

Mean, Variance, Covariance

Year	Asset A	Asset B
1	+0.05	+0.07
2	–0.02	–0.04
3	+0.12	+0.18

Mean return, Asset A = (5 – 2 + 12) / 3 = 5%

Mean return, Asset B = (7 – 4 + 18) / 3 = 7%

24

LOS 43.b Calculate/Interpret
CFAI p. 261, Schweser p. 139

Portfolio Risk and Return: Part I

Mean, Variance, Covariance, Correlation

Year	Asset A	Asset B
1	+0.05	+0.07
2	–0.02	–0.04
3	+0.12	+0.18
Mean	0.05	0.07

$$Var_A = \frac{(5-5)^2 + (-2-5)^2 + (12-5)^2}{3-1} = 49\,(0.0049) \quad \text{Std. Dev.} = 7\%$$

$$Var_B = \frac{(7-7)^2 + (-4-7)^2 + (18-7)^2}{3-1} = 121(0.0121) \quad \text{Std. Dev.} = 11\%$$

 25

LOS 43.b Calculate/Interpret
CFAI p. 261, Schweser p. 139

Portfolio Risk and Return: Part I

Mean, Variance, Covariance, Correlation

Year	Asset A	Asset B
1	+0.05	+0.07
2	–0.02	–0.04
3	+0.12	+0.18
Mean	0.05	0.07

Covariance of returns for Assets A and B:

$$\frac{(5-5)(7-7) + (-2-5)(-4-7) + (12-5)(18-7)}{3-1} = 77 = 0.0077$$

 26

LOS 43.b Calculate/Interpret
CFAI p. 261, Schweser p. 139

Portfolio Risk and Return: Part I

Mean, Variance, Covariance, Correlation

$Cov_{AB} = 0.0077; \sigma_A = 0.07; \sigma_B = 0.11$

$$\rho_{A,B} = \frac{Cov_{A,B}}{\sigma_A \sigma_B}$$

$$\rho_{A,B} = \frac{0.0077}{(0.07)(0.11)} = 1$$

The returns on Assets A and B are perfectly positively correlated in this example

27

LOS 43.c Describe
CFAI p. 275, Schweser p. 142

Portfolio Risk and Return: Part I

Major Asset Classes

Asset Class	Annual Returns	Standard Deviation
Small-cap	11.7%	33.0%
Large-cap	9.6%	20.9%
LT Corporate Bonds	5.9%	8.4%
LT Treasury Bonds	5.7%	9.4%
Treasury Bills	3.7%	3.1%
Inflation	3.0%	4.2%

Source: 2009 Ibbotson SBBI Classic Yearbook

28

LOS 43.d Explain
CFAI p. 282, Schwesser p. 143

Portfolio Risk and Return: Part I

Risk Aversion

Risk aversion means investors prefer less risk to more risk

- When two investments have the same expected return, investors **prefer the lower risk investment**
- When two investments have the same risk, investors prefer the investment with the **higher expected return**

Investors do not *minimize* risk. It's a trade-off!

29

Portfolio Risk and Return: Part I

Risk Aversion – Problem

Abner is risk averse. Which of the following statements is *most likely* correct?

A. He will choose relatively safe investments.

B. He may hold some very risky investments.

C. His risk tolerance is relatively low.

30 - 1

LOS 43.e Calculate/Interpret
CFAI p. 290, Schweser p. 144

Portfolio Risk and Return: Part I

Portfolio Standard Deviation

$$Var(R_p) = \sigma_A^2 w_A^2 + \sigma_B^2 w_B^2 + 2w_A w_B Cov_{AB}$$

$$\text{Note}: Cov_{AB} = \rho_{AB}\sigma_A\sigma_B$$

$$Var(R_p) = \sigma_A^2 w_A^2 + \sigma_B^2 w_B^2 + 2w_A w_B \rho_{AB}\sigma_A\sigma_B$$

31

LOS 43.e Calculate/Interpret
CFAI p. 290, Schweser p. 144

Portfolio Risk and Return: Part I

Portfolio Standard Deviation Example

A portfolio is 30% invested in stocks, σ = 20%, with the remainder in bonds, σ = 12%. The correlation of bond returns with stock returns is 0.60. What is the standard deviation of portfolio returns?

$$\sqrt{0.2^2 0.3^2 + 0.12^2 0.7^2 + 2(0.3)(0.7)(0.6)(0.2)(0.12)}$$

$$= 12.9\% = \text{portfolio standard deviation}$$

If correlation were equal to 1.0, portfolio standard deviation would be 0.3(20%) + 0.7(12%) = 14.4%

32 - 1

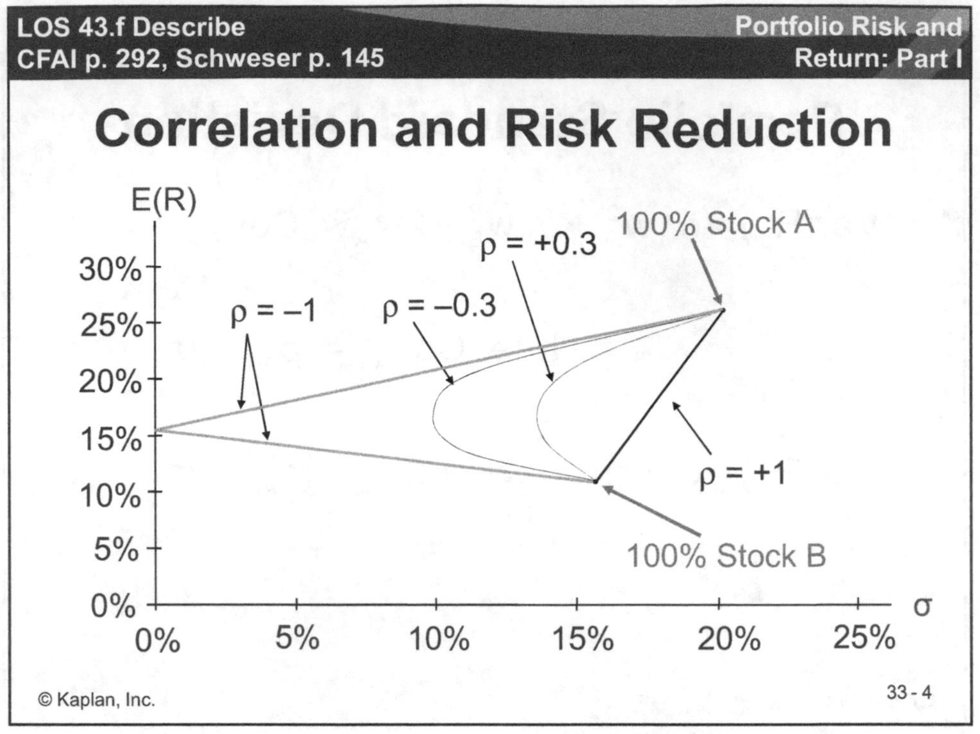

Portfolio Risk and
Return: Part I

Portfolio Risk – Problem

An asset has correlation with a portfolio's return that is less than 1 but has the same standard deviation of returns as the portfolio. What effect will adding some of this asset to the portfolio have on the portfolio risk? Portfolio risk:

A. will decrease.

B. will increase.

C. may increase or decrease depending on the individual securities mix in the portfolio.

34 - 1

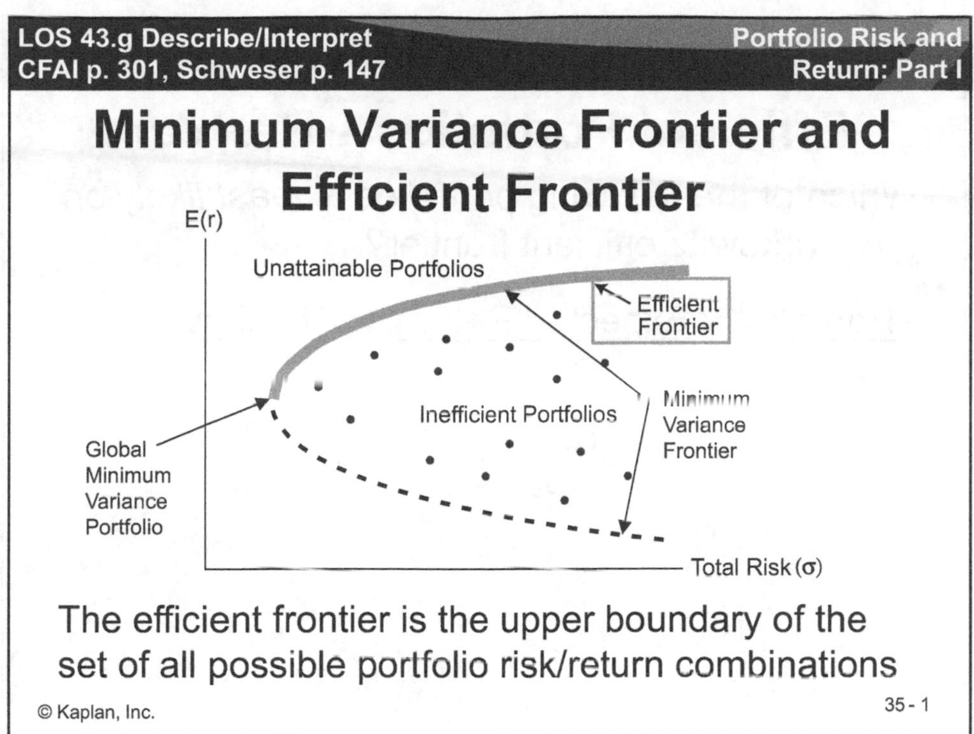

LOS 43.g Describe/Interpret
CFAI p. 301, Schweser p. 147

Portfolio Risk and Return: Part I

Efficient Frontier

Efficient frontier is the set of portfolios among all the possible portfolios of combinations of individual risky assets that offers the highest expected return for each level of risk (standard deviation)

36

Efficient Portfolios – Problem

Which of the following portfolios is *least likely* on the Markowitz efficient frontier?

Portfolio	Expected Return	Std. Dev.
A.	10%	12%
B.	12%	16%
C.	14%	15%

Capital Allocation Line

When a risk-free asset is combined with a risky asset or portfolio, the risk/return of each possible combination is referred to as the CAL

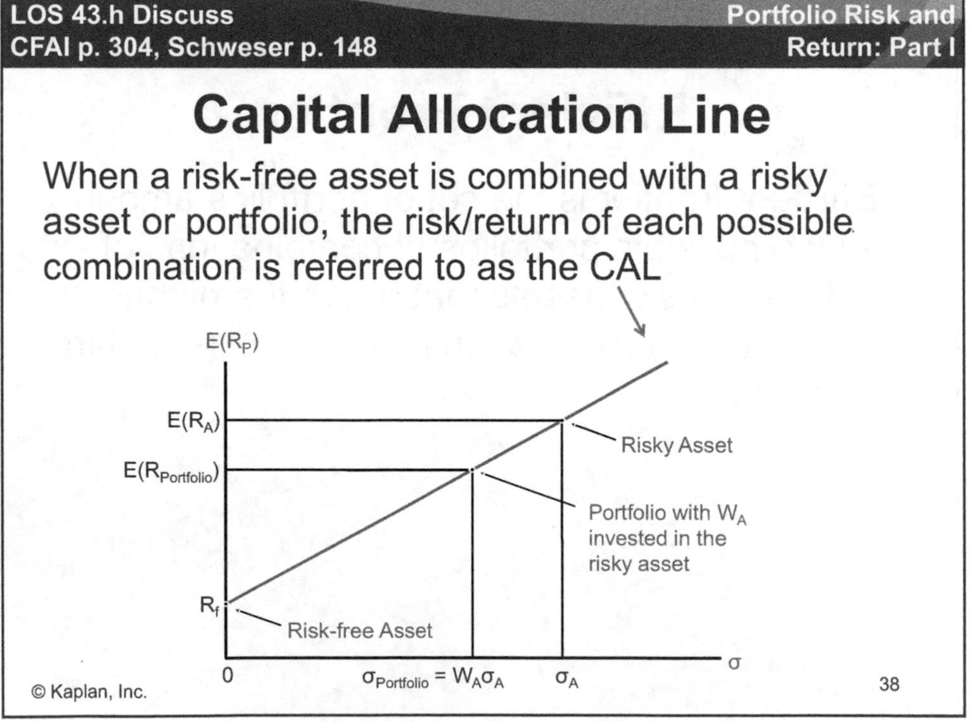

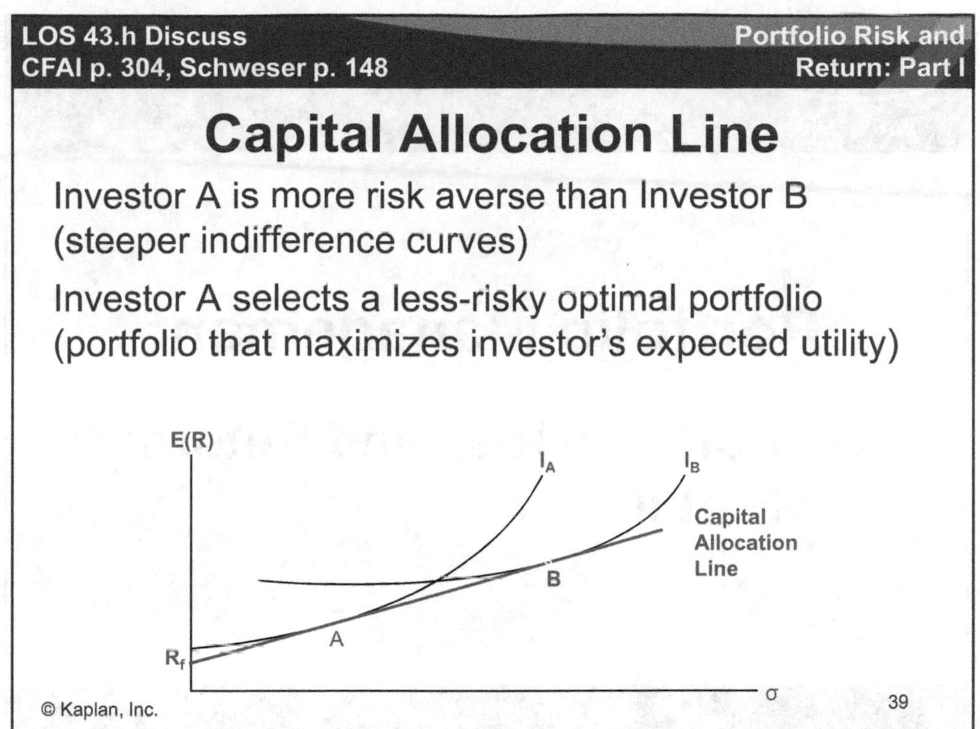
LOS 43.h Discuss
CFAI p. 304, Schweser p. 148
Portfolio Risk and
Return: Part I
Capital Allocation Line
Investor A is more risk averse than Investor B
(steeper indifference curves)
Investor A selects a less-risky optimal portfolio
(portfolio that maximizes investor's expected utility)
E(R)
I_A
I_B
Capital
Allocation
Line
B
A
R_f
σ
© Kaplan, Inc.
39

Portfolio Management

44. Portfolio Risk and Return: Part II

Portfolio Management

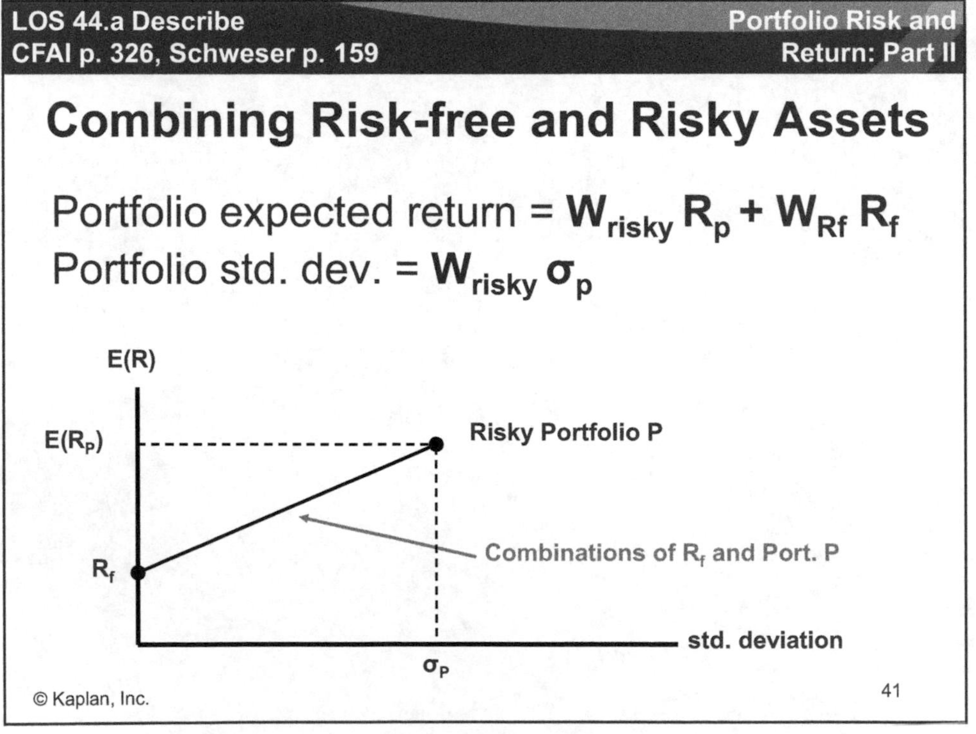

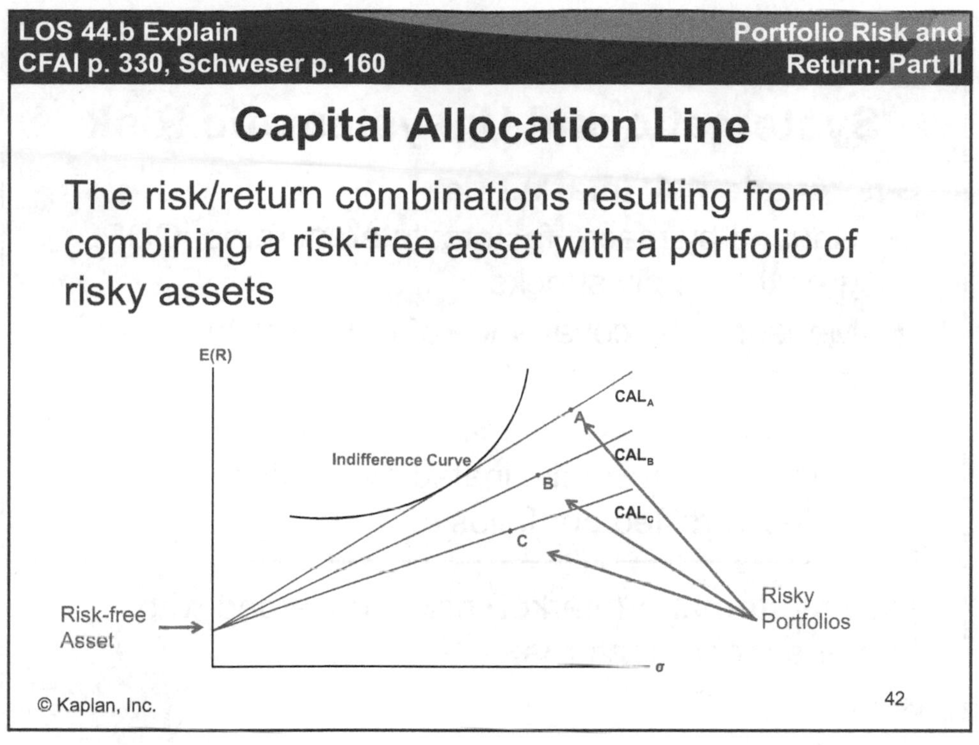
LOS 44.b Explain
CFAI p. 330, Schweser p. 160
Portfolio Risk and Return: Part II
Capital Allocation Line
The risk/return combinations resulting from combining a risk-free asset with a portfolio of risky assets
E(R)
CAL_A
A
Indifference Curve
CAL_B
B
CAL_C
C
Risky Portfolios
Risk-free Asset
σ
© Kaplan, Inc.
42

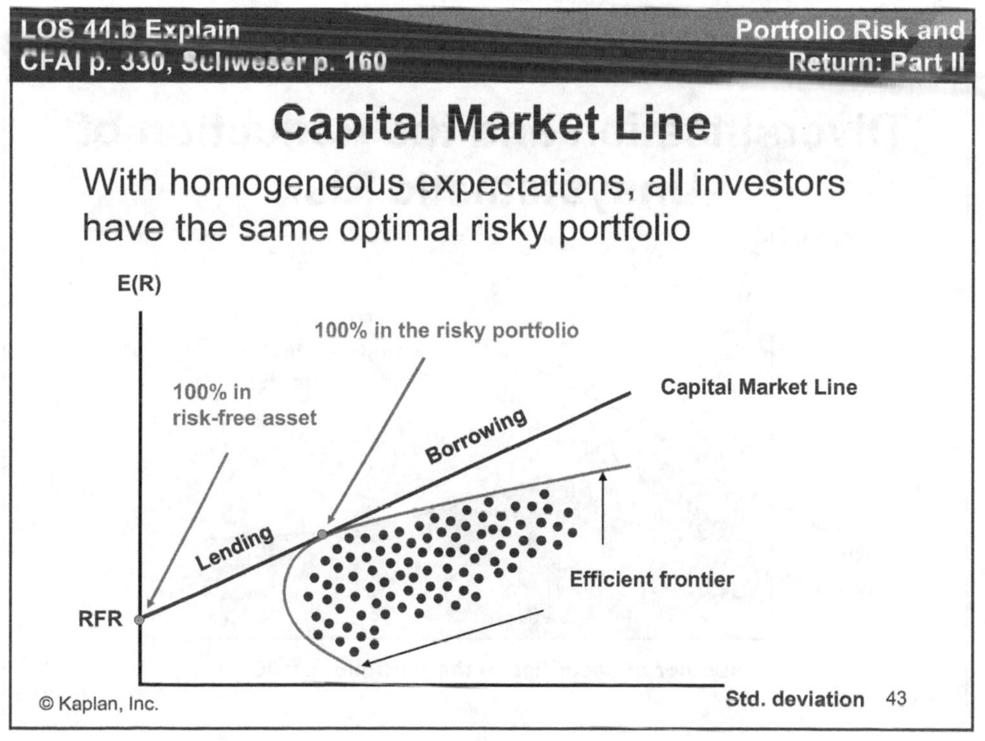
LOS 44.b Explain
CFAI p. 330, Schweser p. 160
Portfolio Risk and Return: Part II
Capital Market Line
With homogeneous expectations, all investors have the same optimal risky portfolio
E(R)
100% in the risky portfolio
100% in risk-free asset
Capital Market Line
Borrowing
Lending
Efficient frontier
RFR
© Kaplan, Inc.
Std. deviation
43

LOS 44.c Explain
CFAI p. 338, Schweser p. 164

Portfolio Risk and Return: Part II

Systematic and Unsystematic Risk

Systematic risk (market risk)

- Caused by macro factors: Interest rates, GDP growth, supply shocks
- Measured by covariance of returns with returns on the market portfolio

Unsystematic risk (firm-specific risk)

- Can be reduced/eliminated by holding well-diversified portfolios

Only **systematic** (market) risk is rewarded with higher expected returns

LOS 44.c Explain
CFAI p. 338, Schweser p. 164

Portfolio Risk and Return: Part II

Diversification and the Reduction of Unsystematic Risk

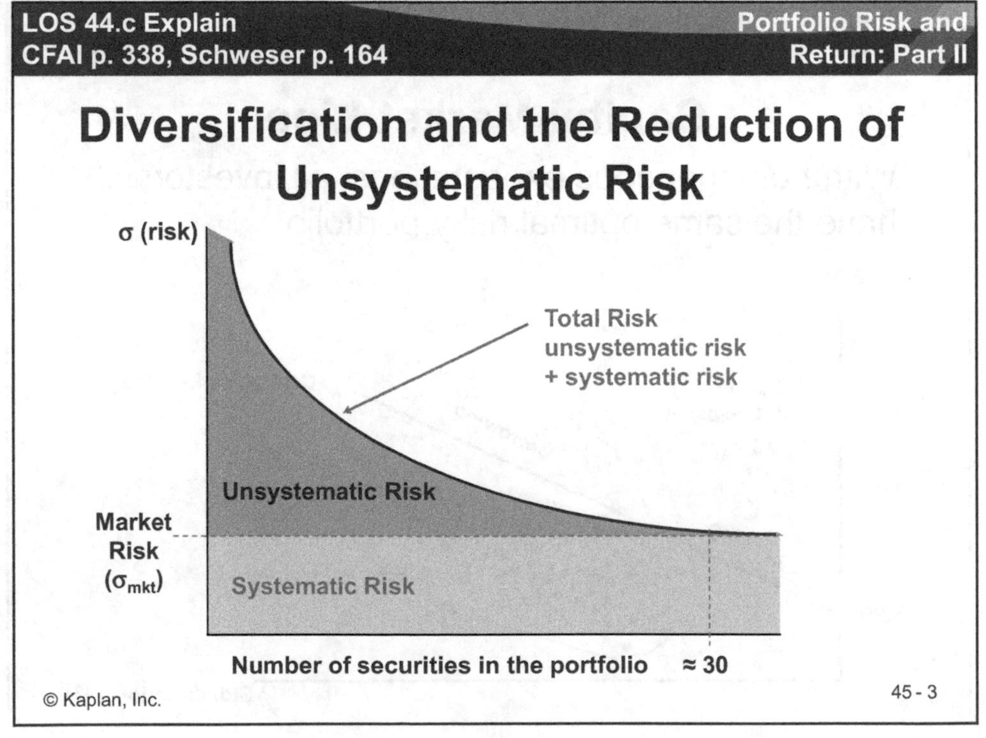

LOS 44.d Explain
CFAI p. 340, Schweser p. 166

Portfolio Risk and Return: Part II

Returns Generating Models

The Market Model

$$R_i = \alpha_i + \beta_i R_m + e_i$$

- The market model has a single risk factor, the return on the market
- The asset's beta (β_i) is the sensitivity of its returns to this risk factor
- Asset returns are a linear function of market returns

46

LOS 44.d Explain
CFAI p. 340, Schweser p. 166

Portfolio Risk and Return: Part II

Returns Generating Models

Multi-factor Models

$$E[R_i] - R_f = \beta_{i,1} E[F_1] + \beta_{i,2} E[F_2] + \ldots + \beta_{i,K} E[F_K]$$

The factors (F's) are the expected values of each risk factor

The betas ($\beta_{i,k}$) are the asset's <u>factor sensitivities</u> or <u>factor loadings</u> for each risk factor

47

LOS 44.d Explain
CFAI p. 340, Schweser p. 166

Portfolio Risk and Return: Part II

Returns Generating Models

Multi-factor Models

$$E[R_i] - R_f = \beta_{i,1} E[F_1] + \beta_{i,2} E[F_2] + \ldots\ldots + \beta_{i,K} E[F_K]$$

Risk factors (F) of three types:

1. Macroeconomic factors (e.g., GDP growth, inflation, consumer confidence)
2. Fundamental factors (e.g., earnings, earnings growth, firm size, research expenditures)
3. Statistical factors, no basis in finance theory

 48

LOS 44.d Explain
CFAI p. 340, Schweser p. 166

Portfolio Risk and Return: Part II

Returns Generating Models

Fama and French 3-factor Model

Risk factors are:

1. Firm size
2. Book-to-market ratio
3. Excess return on the market portfolio

Carhart added a fourth factor, momentum

These models explain U.S. equity returns better than the market (single-index) model

 49

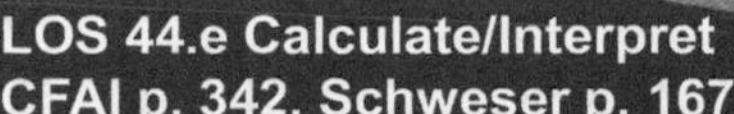

LOS 44.e Calculate/Interpret
CFAI p. 342, Schweser p. 167

Portfolio Risk and Return: Part II

Calculating Beta

In the market model, beta is often estimated as the slope of a regression of asset returns on market returns: **Characteristic Line**

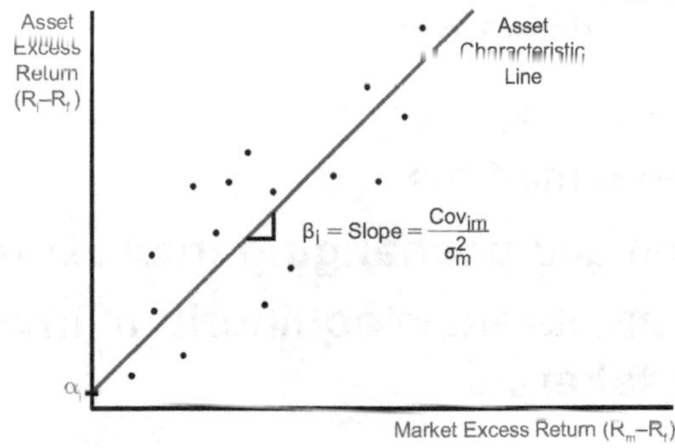

50

LOS 44.e Calculate/Interpret
CFAI p. 342, Schweser p. 167

Portfolio Risk and Return: Part II

Calculating Beta

$$Beta_i = \frac{Cov_{i,mkt}}{\sigma^2_{mkt}} \qquad Beta_{Portfolio} = \sum_{i=1}^{n} w_i Beta_i$$

$$Beta_i = \rho_{i,mkt}\left(\frac{\sigma_i}{\sigma_{mkt}}\right) = \frac{Cov_{i,mkt}}{\sigma_i \sigma_{mkt}}\left(\frac{\sigma_i}{\sigma_{mkt}}\right) = \frac{Cov_{i,mkt}}{\sigma^2_{mkt}}$$

$$Beta_{mkt} = \rho_{mkt,mkt}\left(\frac{\sigma_{mkt}}{\sigma_{mkt}}\right) = 1$$

51

LOS 44.f Explain
CFAI p. 346, Schwesser p. 169

Portfolio Risk and Return: Part II

Assumptions of Capital Market Theory

- Investors use **mean-variance** framework
- Unlimited **lending and borrowing** at R_f
- Homogeneous **expectations**
- **One-period** time horizon
- **Divisible** assets
- **Frictionless** markets
- No inflation and **unchanging interest rates**
- Capital markets are in **equilibrium, investors are price takers**

52

LOS 44.f Explain
CFAI p. 346, Schweser p. 169

Portfolio Risk and Return: Part II

The Capital Asset Pricing Model

SML equation:

$$E(R_i) = RFR + \beta_i\,[E(R_{mkt}) - RFR]$$

- Beta is a measure of systematic risk
- Beta is the standardized covariance of an asset's returns with returns on the market portfolio

$$\beta_i = \frac{Cov_{i,mkt}}{\sigma^2_{mkt}}$$

53

LOS 44.f Explain
CFAI p. 346, Schweser p. 169

Portfolio Risk and Return: Part II

Capital Asset Pricing Model (CAPM)

- CAPM: The expected return on an asset based only on the asset's systematic risk or beta
- CAPM is also used to determine the required return on an asset based on the asset's systematic risk (beta)
- Required return and expected return are the same in equilibrium

54

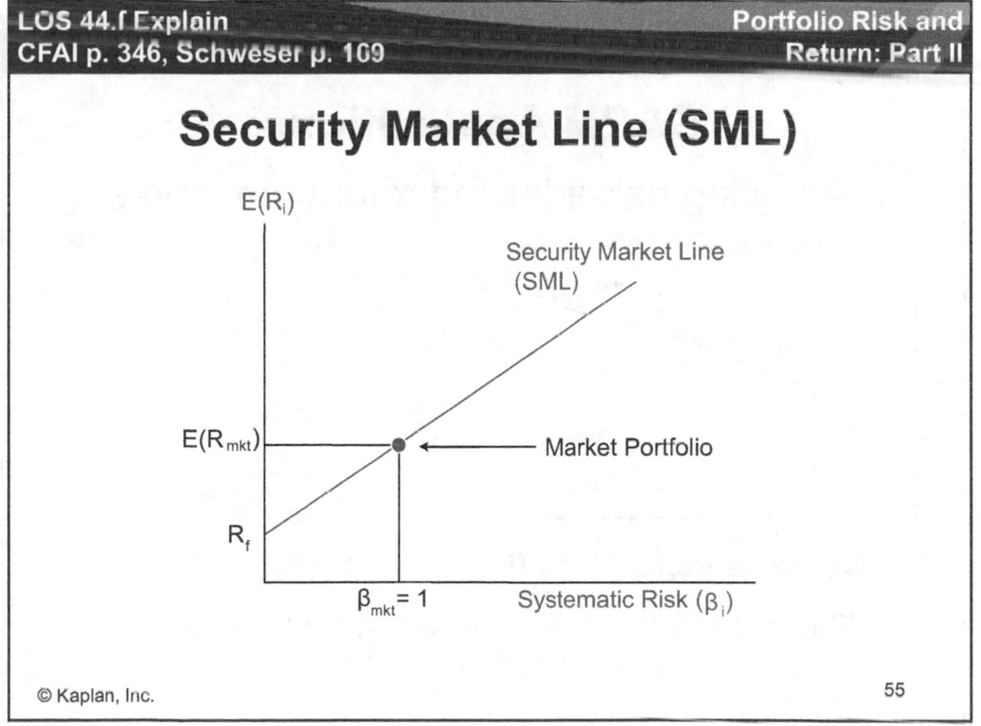

LOS 44.g Calculate/Interpret
CFAI p. 349, Schweser p. 173

Portfolio Risk and Return: Part II

CAPM Expected Returns Example

A stock has a beta of 1.2, the expected return on the market is 8%, and the risk-free rate is 2%. What is the stock's expected return?

Expected return = 2% + 1.2 (8% – 2%) = 9.2%

(Risk-free Rate → 2%; Market Risk Premium → (8% – 2%); Beta → 1.2)

In equilibrium the expected return and the required return in the market are equal

56

LOS 44.h Describe/Demonstrate
CFAI p. 351, Schweser p. 174

Portfolio Risk and Return: Part II

CAPM Applications

Calculating risk-adjusted return measures

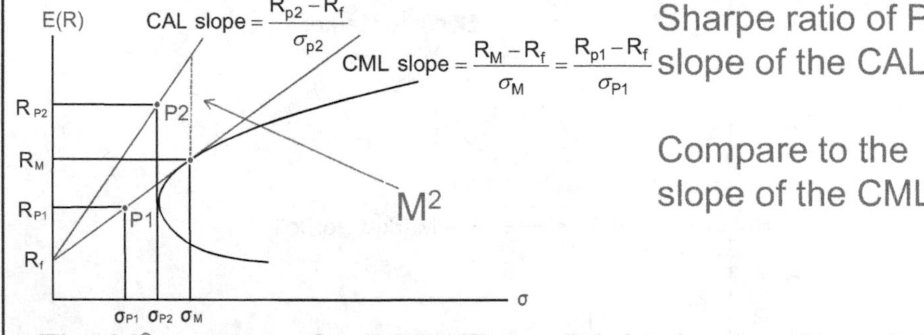

Sharpe ratio of P2 is slope of the CAL

Compare to the slope of the CML

The M^2 measure for P2 is $(R_{P2} - R_f)(\sigma_M/\sigma_{P2}) - (R_M - R_f)$

M^2 is the extra % return for a (leveraged) portfolio with same risk as the market portfolio

57 - 4

LOS 44.h Describe/Demonstrate
CFAI p. 351, Schweser p. 174

Portfolio Risk and Return: Part II

CAPM Applications

Calculating risk-adjusted return measures

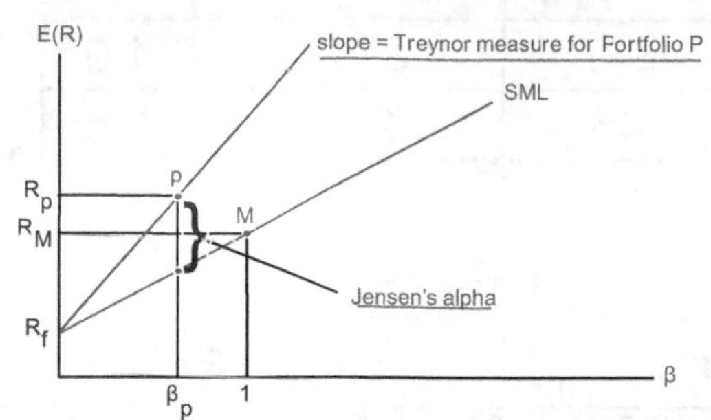

Treynor measure = $(R_P - R_f)/\beta_P$

Compare to the slope of the SML

Jensen's alpha = $R_P - [R_f + \beta_P (R_M - R_f)]$

Jensen's alpha is the % return above the equilibrium return for a portfolio with beta = β_P

58 - 3

LOS 44.h Describe/Demonstrate
CFAI p. 351, Schweser p. 174

Portfolio Risk and Return: Part II

Forecast Returns and the CAPM Example

An analyst has forecast the following for three stocks. R_f = 7% $E(R_{mkt})$ = 15%

Stock	Price Today	E (price) in 1 year	E (dividend) in 1 year	Beta
A	$25	$27	$1.00	1.0
B	40	45	2.00	0.8
C	15	17	0.50	1.2

Are these stocks overpriced, underpriced, or at their equilibrium prices? Show where they plot on the SML graph.

59

LOS 44.h Describe/Demonstrate
CFAI p. 351, Schweser p. 174

Portfolio Risk and Return: Part II

Forecast Returns and the CAPM Example

Stock	Price Today	E (price) in 1 year	E (dividend) in 1 year	Beta
A	$25	$27	$1.00	1.0
B	40	45	2.00	0.8
C	15	17	0.50	1.2

$R_f = 7\%$ $E[R_{mkt}] = 15\%$

Stock	Forecast Return	Required Return
A	(27 – 25 + 1) / 25 = 12.0%	0.07 + 1.0(0.15 – 0.07) = 15.0%
B	(45 – 40 + 2) / 40 = 17.5%	0.07 + 0.8(0.15 – 0.07) = 13.4%
C	(17 – 15 + 0.50) / 15 = 16.6%	0.07 + 1.2(0.15 – 0.07) = 16.6%

R_f

MRP

60 - 4

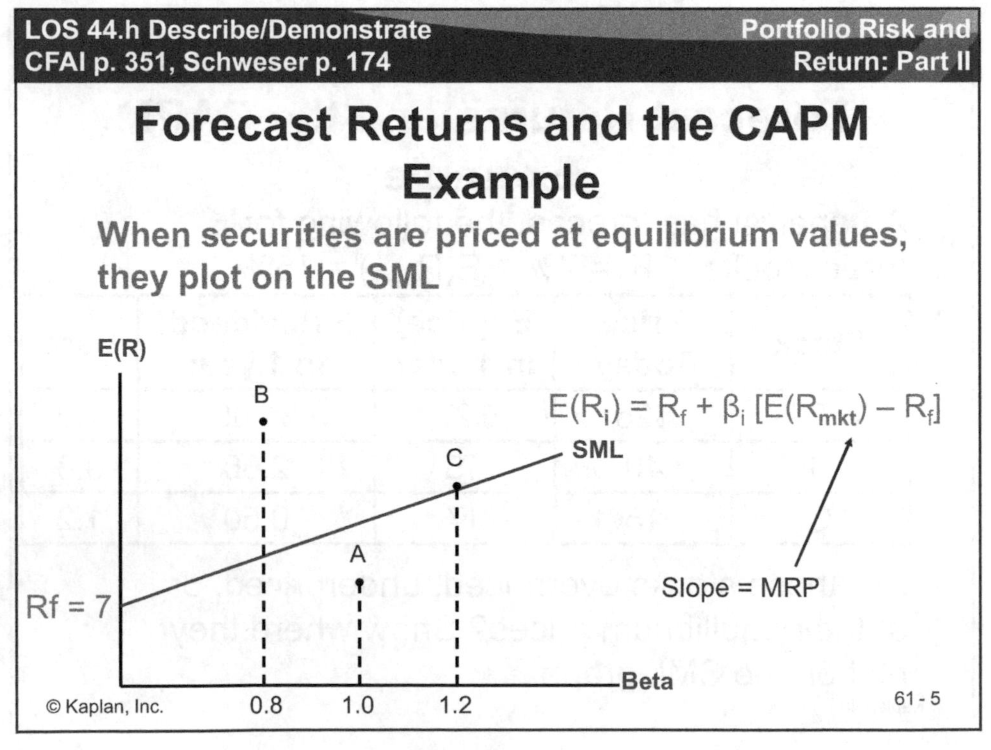

LOS 44.h Describe/Demonstrate
CFAI p. 351, Schweser p. 174

Portfolio Risk and Return: Part II

Forecast Returns and the CAPM

Stock	Forecast Return	Required Return
A	12.0%	15.0%
B	17.5%	13.4%
C	16.6%	16.6%

Stock A is overvalued (sell it or sell it short)
Stock B is undervalued (buy it)
Stock C is properly valued (indifferent)

 62

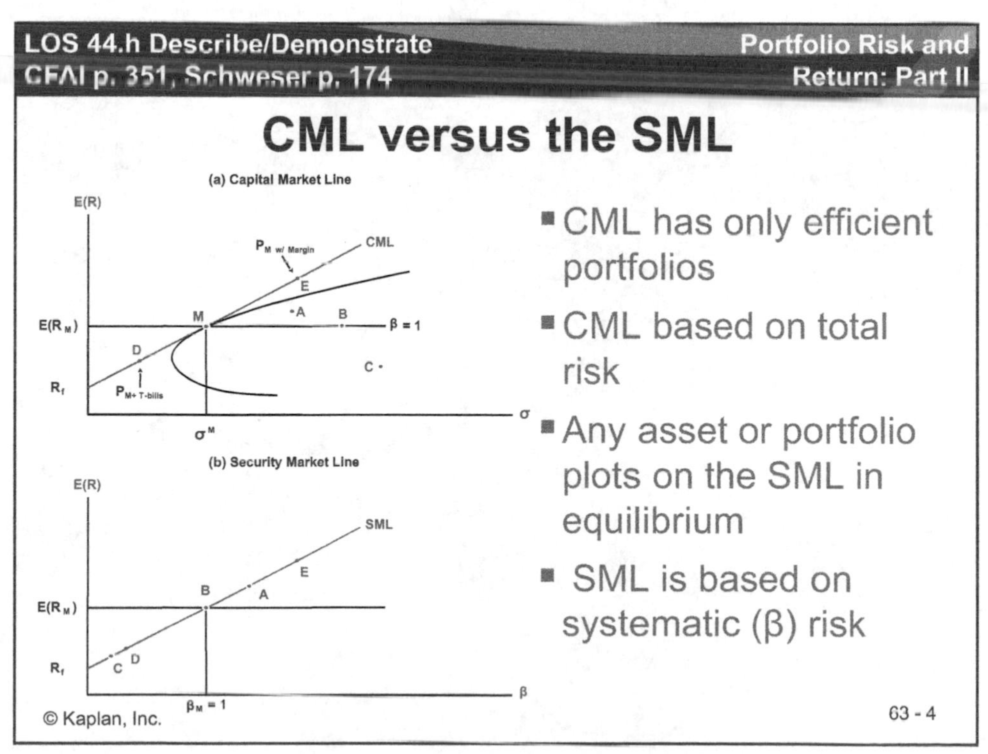

Portfolio Risk and Return: Part II

SML Pricing – Problem

$E[R_{mkt}]$ = 15% RFR = 8% Stock X's beta = 1.25
Forecast $R_{Stock\ X}$ = 17%

Using these data and the CAPM, which of the following statements about Stock X is true based on the analyst forecast? Stock X is:

A. overvalued by 1.75 percentage points.
B. properly valued.
C. undervalued by 0.25 percentage points.

64 - 2

Portfolio Management

45. Basics of Portfolio Planning and Construction

Portfolio Management

LOS 45.a Describe
CFAI p. 376, Schweser p. 104

Basics of Portfolio Planning and Construction

Investment Policy Statement

- Identifies client objectives and constraints
- Clear statement of client risk tolerance
- Imposes investment discipline on both client and manager
- Identifies risks
- Identifies a benchmark portfolio consistent with client preferences

66

LOS 45.b Describe
CFAI p. 377, Schweser p. 184

Basics of Portfolio Planning and Construction

Major Components of an IPS

- Description of client circumstances
- Purpose of the IPS
- Duties and responsibilities of all parties
- Procedures to update IPS, resolve problems
- Investment objectives and constraints
- Investment guidelines
- Evaluation of performance, benchmark
- Appendices: Strategic asset allocation, permitted deviations, rebalancing procedures

 67

LOS 45.c Describe
CFAI p. 377, Schweser p. 185

Basics of Portfolio Planning and Construction

Investment Objectives

Investment objectives should include both risk and return objectives because of the trade-off between risk and expected return

Factors affecting investor risk tolerance:

- Psychological factors
- Personal factors: Age, family situation, existing wealth, insurance coverage, cash reserves, income

 68

LOS 45.d Distinguish
CFAI p. 379, Schweser p. 186

Basics of Portfolio Planning and Construction

Risk Tolerance

Ability to bear risk depends on investment horizon, insurance, income, wealth, financial responsibilities

Willingness to bear risk depends on attitudes and beliefs about investment risk

Willingness > ability: Advisor should go with ability

Ability > willingness: Educate the investor about investment risk, do not attempt to change personality/psychological characteristics

LOS 45.e Describe
CFAI p. 384, Schweser p. 186

Basics of Portfolio Planning and Construction

Investment Constraints

- **Liquidity:** The potential need for cash
- **Legal and regulatory:** Applies more to institutional investors, but this constraint also affects individual investors (e.g., IRA accounts)
- **Time horizon:** The time until the proceeds of the investment will be required
- **Tax concerns:** Is the account taxable, tax-deferred, or tax-exempt?
- **Unique needs and preferences:** Anything that does not fit into the above categories

LOS 45.f Explain
CFAI p. 391, Schweser p. 188

Basics of Portfolio Planning and Construction

Strategic Asset Allocation

- Based on risk, returns, and correlations of asset classes
- Correlations of returns of assets within an asset class should be relatively high
- Correlations of returns between asset classes should be low

71

LOS 45.f Explain
CFAI p. 391, Schweser p. 188

Basics of Portfolio Planning and Construction

Strategic Asset Allocation Example

Cash	2%
Large-cap U.S. Equity	13%
Mid- Small-cap U.S. Equity	8%
International Developed Equity	12%
Emerging Markets Equity	9%
High-yield Bonds	7%
U.S. Bonds	18%
International Bonds	14%
Real Estate	11%
Hedge Funds	6%

72

LOS 45.g Discuss
CFAI p. 391, Schweser p. 189

Basics of Portfolio Planning and Construction

Portfolio Construction

- Use risk, return, and correlations of asset classes to construct an <u>efficient frontier</u>
- Use objectives and constraints from IPS to select an <u>optimal portfolio</u> (strategic asset allocation)
- <u>Tactical asset allocation</u> (deviations from strategic) and security selection as permitted and appropriate
- <u>Risk budgeting</u> allocates permitted risk to strategic allocation, tactical allocation, and security selection

73

Portfolio Risk and Return: Part I

Money-Weighted Return – Solution

Invest $1,000 in an account at t = 0

Value at end of Year 1 is $1,200, investor **adds $800**.

Value at end of Year 2 is $2,200.

Calculate the annual MWR.

MWR = 13.623%

$$-1000 + \frac{-800}{1.13623} + \frac{2{,}200}{1.13623^2} = 0$$

$CF_0 = -1{,}000$; $CF_1 = -800$; $CF_2 = 2{,}200$; IRR = 13.623%

MWR places more weight on second period returns

Portfolio Risk and Return: Part I

Return Measures – Solution

An investor buys 500 shares at $35 with 50% margin. After one year, the shares are sold for $50. The investor is subject to a 15% tax on gains, and inflation over the year was 4%. Ignoring interest and commissions, the investor's real after-tax leveraged return is:

Leveraged return = (50 – 35) / 17.50 = 85.7%

After-tax return = 85.7% × (1 – 15%) = 72.8%

Real after-tax return = 1.728 / 1.04 – 1 = 66.2%

Portfolio Risk and Return: Part I

Risk Aversion – Solution

Abner is risk averse. Which of the following statements is *most likely* correct?

B. He may hold some very risky investments.

Portfolio Risk – Solution

An asset has correlation with a portfolio's return that is less than 1 but has the same standard deviation of returns as the portfolio. What effect will adding some of this asset to the portfolio have on the portfolio risk? Portfolio risk:

A. will decrease.

Efficient Portfolios – Solution

Which of the following portfolios is *least likely* on the Markowitz efficient frontier?

Portfolio	Expected Return	Std. Dev.
B.	**12%**	**16%**

B has <u>lower return</u> and <u>higher standard deviation</u> compared to C, therefore B can't be efficient

Portfolio Risk and Return: Part II

SML Pricing – Solution

$E[R_{mkt}]$ = 15% RFR = 8% Stock X's beta = 1.25
Forecast $R_{Stock\ X}$ = 17%

Using these data and the CAPM, which of the following statements about Stock X is true based on the analyst forecast? Stock X is:

C. undervalued by 0.25 percentage points.

8 + 1.25(15 – 8) = 16.75   17 – 16.75 = 0.25

Study Session 13

Equity: Market Organization, Market Indices, and Market Efficiency

Market Organization, Market Indices, and Market Efficiency

46. Market Organization and Structure

Equity Investments

LOS 46.a Explain
CFAI p. 6, Schweser p. 198

Market Organization and Structure

Financial System Functions

- Allow entities to borrow, save, issue equity, manage risk, exchange assets, utilize info
- Determine the returns that equate savings and borrowing across the economy
- Allocate capital efficiently (to its highest valued uses)

2

LOS 46.a Explain
CFAI p. 6, Schweser p. 198

Market Organization and Structure

Financial System Functions

- An **investor** expects to earn equilibrium (fair) returns over time
- An **information trader** expects to earn positive risk-adjusted returns (i.e., active management strategies)
- A **hedger** takes on a position to offset an existing risk

 3

LOS 46.b Describe
CFAI p. 14, Schweser p. 200

Market Organization and Structure

Classifications of Assets

- Financial vs. real assets
- Debt vs. equity securities
- Public vs. private securities
- Physical derivatives vs. financial derivatives

 4

LOS 46.b Describe
CFAI p. 14, Schweser p. 200

Market Organization and Structure

Classifications of Markets

- Spot markets (immediate delivery) vs. futures markets
- Primary markets vs. secondary markets
- Call vs. continuous markets
- Money markets vs. capital markets
- Traditional markets vs. alternative investment markets

5

LOS 46.c Describe
CFAI p. 16, Schweser p. 201

Market Organization and Structure

Types of Assets

Securities

- Equity
- Fixed income
- Pooled investments
  - Mutual funds (including REITs)
  - ETFs
  - Asset-backed securities
  - Hedge funds

6

LOS 46.c Describe
CFAI p. 16, Schweser p. 201

Market Organization and Structure

Types of Assets (continued)

- **Currencies**
- **Contracts:** forwards; futures; swaps; options; insurance
- **Commodities**
- **Real assets**

7

LOS 46.d Describe
CFAI p. 28, Schweser p. 204

Market Organization and Structure

Financial Intermediary Roles

- **Brokers, exchanges**: Connect buyers, sellers of same security at same location and time
- **Dealers**: Match buyers, sellers of same security at different points in time
- **Arbitrageurs:** Transact with buyers, sellers of same security at same time but in different markets

8

LOS 46.d Describe
CFAI p. 28, Schweser p. 204

Market Organization and Structure

Financial Intermediary Roles

- **Securitizers, depository institutions**: Sell interests in a diversified pool of assets
- **Insurance companies**: Manage a diversified pool of risks
- **Clearinghouses**: Reduce counterparty risk and promote market integrity

 9

LOS 46.e Compare
CFAI p. 38, Schweser p. 207

Market Organization and Structure

Investor Positions

- **Long position**: Gains when asset values increase (purchase stock or calls, sell puts, take long futures or forward positions)
- **Short position**: Gain when asset values decrease (sell short, sell/write calls, purchase puts, take short positions in futures and forwards)
- **Financial leverage**: Borrow part of purchase price or post less than asset value with futures

 10

LOS 46.e Compare
CFAI p. 38, Schweser p. 207

Market Organization and Structure

Selling Short

1. Investor **borrows stock** and sells it
2. Later, **repurchases the stock** and returns it to the lender (covers the short position)
3. Short seller's **profit (loss)** is the original selling price minus the repurchase price (interest, commissions)

Rules of short selling:

- Short sellers **pay all dividends** to the lender
- Short seller **deposits margin/collateral**

Sell high and buy low

 11

LOS 46.f Calculate/Interpret
CFAI p. 41, Schweser p. 209

Market Organization and Structure

Buying Stock on Margin

- **Margin:** Borrow part of the money needed to buy stock
- Brokers hold the stock as collateral
- **Margin requirement:** Required equity percentage is set by the Federal Reserve Board in the United States (currently 50%)
- **Maintenance margin**: Minimum equity in position

Equity percentage =

(stock value – loan) / stock value

 12

LOS 46.f Calculate/Interpret
CFAI p. 41, Schweser p. 209

Market Organization and Structure

Return on Margin Position Example

- An investor buys 1,000 shares of a stock on margin at a price of $60 per share
- Initial margin requirement is 50% and margin loan rate is 2%
- Stock pays annual dividend of $0.40 per share
- Commission is $0.01 per share on purchase, sale
- One year later, investor sells stock at $66 per share
- **Calculate** the leverage ratio and the investor's return on the margin position

 13

LOS 46.f Calculate/Interpret
CFAI p. 41, Schweser p. 209

Market Organization and Structure

Return on Margin Position Example

Leverage ratio
= 1 / minimum margin requirement
= 1 / 0.50 = **2.0**

Ignoring transactions costs and commissions, a return of +10% on the stock would result in a return of +20% on equity investment

 14

LOS 46.f Calculate/Interpret
CFAI p. 41, Schweser p. 209

Market Organization and Structure

Return on Margin Position Example

- Investor equity = 0.50 × \$60 × 1,000 = \$30,000
- Commission on purchase = \$0.01 × 1,000 – \$10
- Total investment = \$30,010

15

LOS 46.f Calculate/Interpret
CFAI p. 41, Schweser p. 209

Market Organization and Structure

Return on Margin Position Example

- Dividends = 1,000 × \$0.40 = \$400
- Interest on loan = \$30,000 × 2% = \$600
- Sale proceeds = \$66 × 1,000 = \$66,000
- Commission on sale = \$0.01 × 1,000 = \$10
- Remaining equity = \$66,000 + \$400 – \$30,000 – \$600 – \$10 = \$35,790
- **Return** on margin position = (\$35,790 / \$30,010) – 1 = **19.26%**

16 - 6

LOS 46.f Calculate/Interpret
CFAI p. 41, Schweser p. 209

Market Organization and Structure

Margin Call

If equity < **maintenance margin**, investor must add cash or marginable securities, or must close the position

$$\textbf{Trigger price} = P_0\left(\frac{1-\text{initial margin}}{1-\text{maintenance margin}}\right)$$

LOS 46.f Calculate/Interpret
CFAI p. 41, Schweser p. 209

Market Organization and Structure

Margin Call Example

An investor buys a stock on margin at a price of \$70. The initial margin requirement is 40% and the maintenance margin is 25%. At what stock price will the investor receive a margin call?

$$\$70 \times \frac{1-0.40}{1-0.25} = \mathbf{\$56}$$

LOS 46.g Compare
CFAI p. 44, Schweser p. 210

Market Organization and Structure

Trading Instructions

Execution: How to trade

- Market orders: Best price available
- Limit orders: Specified price or better

Validity: When to trade

- Good-till-cancelled, immediate-or-cancel, day orders
- Stop orders: Execute if price reaches specified level

Clearing: How to settle trade

19

LOS 46.g Compare
CFAI p. 44, Schweser p. 210

Market Organization and Structure

Order Execution

- Dealer buys at **bid** price, sells at **ask** price
- **Bid-ask spread** → dealer profit
- **Best bid**: Highest bid price
- **Best offer**: Lowest ask (offer) price
- The best bid and best offer **"make" the market**
- A trade accepting a current bid or offer is said to **"take" the market**

20

LOS 46.h Compare
CFAI p. 44, Schweser p. 210

Market Organization and Structure

Types of Orders

Market order: Immediate execution at best available price

- Useful when trading based on information
- Can execute at unfavorable price

Limit order

- **Buy** at limit price or lower
- **Sell** at limit price or higher
- Avoids execution price uncertainty
- Order might not be filled

21

LOS 46.h Compare
CFAI p. 44, Schweser p. 210

Market Organization and Structure

Types of Orders

Stop (loss) orders: A trade at the stop (trigger) price activates a market order

- Trader who owns a stock trading at 35 might enter a stop sell order at 31.50
- Trader who is short a stock trading at 35 might enter a stop buy order at 39
- Technician who believes that a trade above 60 indicates a strong upward move will follow, might enter a stop buy at 60

22

Market Organization and Structure

Types of Orders – Problem

A trader who owns a stock that is trading at 48 and would like to buy more shares if it increases in value to 52 should enter a:

A. limit buy order at 52.

B. market buy order at 52.

C. stop buy order at 52.

23 - 2

LOS 46.i Define/Explain
CFAI p. 50, Schweser p. 213

Market Organization and Structure

Primary vs. Secondary Capital Markets

- **Primary capital markets**: Sales of new issues of stocks and bonds (IPOs and seasoned offerings); proceeds less underwriting fees to issuer
- **Secondary capital markets**: Where securities trade after their initial offerings (e.g., NYSE, Nasdaq, other OTC)
- Secondary markets are important because they **provide liquidity** and **information about value** to investors

24

LOS 46.i Define/Explain
CFAI p. 50, Schweser p. 213

Market Organization and Structure

Primary Markets

- **Underwritten offer**: Investment bank guarantees security sale
- **Best efforts**: Investment bank acts as broker
- **Private placement**: Sell directly to qualified investors
- **Shelf registration**: Issue securities over time
- **Dividend reinvestment plan**: Issue new shares to shareholders who reinvest dividends
- **Rights offering**: Sell new shares to current shareholders

25

LOS 46.j Describe
CFAI p. 54, Schweser p. 215

Market Organization and Structure

Market Structures

Quote-driven: Investors trade with dealers

Order-driven: Rules used to match buyers and sellers

Brokered markets: Brokers find counterparty for a trade

26

LOS 46.j Describe
CFAI p. 54, Schweser p. 215

Market Organization and Structure

Call vs. Continuous Markets

Call markets: Securities trade at specific times

- All bids and asks are accumulated, then price is set that clears the market
- Used in smaller markets and to open major markets

Continuous markets:

- Trades occur any time the market is open
- Price is set by auction or by dealer bid-ask quotes

27

LOS 46.k Describe
CFAI p. 58, Schweser p. 217

Market Organization and Structure

Well-Functioning Financial System

- **Complete**: Assets and contracts are available
- **Operationally efficient**: Low transactions costs
- **Informationally efficient**: Prices reflect fundamental (intrinsic) value
- Financial intermediaries facilitate transactions

28

LOS 46.l Describe
CFAI p. 60, Schweser p. 218

Market Organization and Structure

Objectives of Market Regulation

- Protect unsophisticated investors
- Require minimum standards of competency
- Prevent trading on inside information
- Require common financial reporting standards
- Require minimum levels of capital

29

Market Organization and Structure

Margin – Problem

An investor who purchases 400 shares of stock at 42 and posts initial margin of 40% when the maintenance margin requirement is 30% will get a margin call if the stock price falls below:

A. 34.20.

B. 36.00.

C. 38.20

30- 2

Market Organization, Market Indices, and Market Efficiency

47. Security Market Indices

Equity Investments

LOS 47.a Describe
CFAI p. 78, Schweser p. 226 Security Market Indices

Security Market Index

- Represents value/performance of an asset class, security market, or market segment over time
- Index value is calculated from market prices of index's constituent securities
- There are various weighting schemes for constituent securities' values/performance

 32

LOS 47.b Calculate/Interpret
CFAI p. 79, Schweser p. 226

Security Market Indices

Price Return and Total Return

- **Price return** = (ending price / beginning price) – 1
- **Total return** includes cash flows from the securities in the index (dividends, interest)

$$\text{total return} = \frac{\text{ending value + cash flows}}{\text{beginning value}} - 1$$

 33

LOS 47.c Describe
CFAI p. 82, Schweser p. 227

Security Market Indices

Index Construction Decisions

- What market does the index represent?
- Which securities will be included?
- Which weighting method will be used?
- When will the index be rebalanced?
- When will the index's securities be re-examined?

 34

LOS 47.d Compare
CFAI p. 83, Schweser p. 227 Security Market Indices

Price-Weighted Index (PWI)

$$PWI = \frac{\text{sum of stock prices}}{\text{\# stocks in index, adjusted for splits}}$$

- Match by buying an **equal number of shares** of each stock in the index
- Given percentage price change in high-priced stock affects the index more than it does for a low-priced stock
- DJIA and Nikkei Dow Jones Stock averages are price-weighted indexes

 35

LOS 47.d Compare
CFAI p. 83, Schweser p. 227 Security Market Indices

Market-Cap Weighted Index

$$MCWI = \frac{\Sigma\ (\text{price}_{\text{today}})(\text{\# shares})}{\Sigma\ (\text{price}_{\text{base year}})(\text{\# shares})} \times \text{beg. index value}$$

- Match portfolio weights to each stock's % of total market value of index stocks
- Firms with larger market capitalizations influence the index more than firms with smaller market capitalizations
- S&P 500, NYSE Index, and Wilshire 5000 are market-capitalization weighted indexes
- **Momentum tilt:** Overpriced are over-represented

 36

LOS 47.d Compare
CFAI p. 83, Schweser p. 227 Security Market Indices

Float-adjusted Index Weights

- Market float-weighted index with number of shares equal to investable shares (excludes shares of controlling investors and often those held by government or corporations)
- **Free float** when shares not available to foreign investors are excluded

 37

LOS 47.d Compare
CFAI p. 83, Schweser p. 227 Security Market Indices

Fundamental Index Weights

- Proportions of index (weights) are based on proportion to total value of a fundamental factor (e.g., revenue, earnings, book value, cash flow)
- Leads to a **value tilt**: High book-to-market have higher weights
- GDP weights are used in multi-market indexes

 38

LOS 47.d Compare
CFAI p. 83, Schweser p. 227 Security Market Indices

Equal-Weighted Index Returns

- An equal-weighted index gives the **same weight to the performance each index stock**
- Match with portfolio of equal dollar investment in each index stock
- Index return is the average HPR on index stocks
- Rebalancing—often quarterly

 39

LOS 47.d Compare
CFAI p. 83, Schweser p. 227 Security Market Indices

Comparing Weighting Schemes

Compared to market-cap weighted index:

- **Price-weighted index** places more weight on high-price stocks and less on low price stocks; stock splits change all weights (and divisor)
- **Equal-weighted index** places more weight on small-cap stocks and less on large-cap stocks; must be rebalanced
- **Float-adjusted index** more closely matches investable shares proportions
- **Fundamental-weighted index** has a value tilt

 40

LOS 47.e Calculate/Analyze
CFAI p. 83, Schweser p. 229

Security Market Indices

Calculating a Price-Weighted Index

	Nov. 30			Dec. 31		
Stock	Share Price	# of Shares	Market Value	Share Price	# of Shares	Market Value
A	\$20	300	\$6,000	\$22	300	\$6,600
B	\$30	200	\$6,000	\$27	200	\$5,400
C	\$40	100	\$4,000	\$44	100	\$4,400
Total	\$90		\$16,000	\$93		\$16,400

Price-weighted index:

\$90 / 3 = 30.0 \$93 / 3 = 31.0

93 / 90 – 1 = +3.33%

 41

LOS 47.e Calculate/Analyze
CFAI p. 83, Schweser p. 229

Security Market Indices

Calculating a Cap-Weighted Index

	Nov. 30			Dec. 31		
Stock	Share Price	# of Shares	Market Cap	Share Price	# of Shares	Market Cap
A	\$20	300	\$6,000	\$22	300	\$6,600
B	\$30	200	\$6,000	\$27	200	\$5,400
C	\$40	100	\$4,000	\$44	100	\$4,400
Total	\$90		\$16,000	\$93		\$16,400

Beginning index value Nov. 30 = 100

New value Dec. 31 = (16,400 / 16,000) × 100 = 102.5

The total market value of all index stocks is up 2.5%

 42

LOS 47.e Calculate/Analyze
CFAI p. 83, Schweser p. 229

Security Market Indices

Calculating an Equal-Weighted Index

Stock	Initial Cost	Current Price	HPR
X	$30.00	$27.00	–10%
Y	$10.00	$15.00	+50%
Z	$20.00	$22.00	+10%

$$\text{Arithmetic mean} = \frac{-10\% + 50\% + 10\%}{3} = +16.67\%$$

Initial index value = 100

Current index value = 116.67

LOS 47.f Describe
CFAI p. 91, Schweser p. 233

Security Market Indices

Rebalancing and Reconstitution

- **Rebalancing**: Updating the index weights on a periodic basis
- **Reconstitution**: Periodically adding and deleting securities

Security Market Indices

Index Weighting – Problem

Compared to a market-cap weighted index, a fundamental weighted index based on dividends will place more weight on firms with higher:

A. dividend yields.

B. dividends per share.

C. total dividend payments.

45 - 2

LOS 47.g Describe
CFAI p. 93, Schweser p. 234

Security Market Indices

Uses of Indexes

- Reflection of market sentiment
- Performance benchmark
- Measure of market return
- Calculate beta
- Calculate expected and risk-adjusted returns
- Model portfolio for index funds

46

LOS 47.h Describe
CFAI p. 94, Schweser p. 234 Security Market Indices

Types of Equity Indexes

- Broad market – Various weighting schemes
- Multi-market market-cap weighted
- Multi-market with fundamental (GDP) weighting
- Sector – Health care, technology, finance consumer goods, etc.
- Style – Large-cap, mid-cap, small-cap; Value vs. growth

 47

LOS 47.i Describe
CFAI p. 97, Schweser p. 235 Security Market Indices

Fixed Income Indexes

- By maturity, type of issuer, country, region, sector, collateral
- Construction issues
  - Broad universe, high turnover
  - Lack of price data
  - Illiquidity

 48

LOS 47.j Describe
CFAI p. 100, Schweser p. 236

Security Market Indices

Alternative Asset Indexes

- **Commodity indexes**
  - Indexes of futures contracts; performance may differ from commodity
  - Wide variety of commodity weights
- **Real estate indexes**
  - Appraisals, repeat sales, REITs
- **Hedge fund indexes**
  - Upward bias from self-selection and survivorship bias

49

Security Market Indices

Index Weighting – Problem

The type of index weighting that is *most likely* to be similar to a momentum strategy is:

A. market-cap weighting.

B. fundamental weighting.

C. equal weighting.

50 - 2

LOS 47.k Compare
CFAI p. 102, Schweser p. 237
Security Market Indices

Types of Security Market Indexes

Index	*Reflects*	*Constituent Securities*	*Weighting Method*	*Notes*
Dow Jones Industrial Average	Large U.S. stocks	30	Price	Stocks chosen by WSJ editors.
Nikkei Stock Average	Large Japanese stocks	225	Modified Price	Contains some illiquid stocks. Adjusted for high-priced shares.
TOPIX	All stocks on the Tokyo Stock Exchange First Section	Variable	Market-capitalization, adjusted for float	Contains 93% of Japanese market cap. Many small, illiquid stocks.

LOS 47.k Compare
CFAI p. 102, Schweser p. 237
Security Market Indices

Types of Security Market Indexes

Index	*Reflects*	*Constituent Securities*	*Weighting Method*	*Notes*
MSCI All Country World Index	Stocks in 23 developed and 22 emerging markets	Variable	Market-capitalization, adjusted for float	Available in both U.S. dollars, local currency
S&P Developed Ex-U.S. BMI Energy Sector Index	Global energy stocks outside United States	Variable	Market-capitalization, adjusted for float	Model portfolio for an ETF
Barclays Capital Global Aggregate Bond Index	Global investment-grade bonds	Variable	Market-capitalization	Formerly compiled by Lehman Brothers

LOS 47.k Compare
CFAI p. 102, Schweser p. 237
Security Market Indices

Types of Security Market Indexes

Index	*Reflects*	*Constituent Securities*	*Weighting Method*	*Notes*
Markit iBoxx Euro High-Yield Bond Indices	Below investment-grade bonds	Variable	Market-capitalization	Represents liquid portion of market
FTSE EPRA/ NAREIT Global Real Estate Index	Global real estate	335	Market-capitalization, adjusted for float	Represents publicly traded REITs
HFRX Global Hedge Fund Index	Global hedge funds	Variable	Asset-weighted	Contains variety of hedge fund strategies

 53

LOS 47.k Compare
CFAI p. 102, Schweser p. 237
Security Market Indices

Types of Security Market Indexes

Index	*Reflects*	*Constituent Securities*	*Weighting Method*	*Notes*
HFRX Equal Weighted Strategies EUR Index	Global hedge funds	Variable	Equal-weighted	Contains same strategy funds as HFRX Global Hedge Fund Index and is equal-weighted
Morningstar Style Indices	U.S. stocks grouped by value/growth and market cap	Variable	Market-capitalization, adjusted for float	9 categories classified by combinations of 3 cap, 3 value/growth categories

 54

Market Organization, Market Indices, and Market Efficiency

48. Market Efficiency

Equity Investments

LOS 48.a Describe
CFAI p. 116, Schweser p. 245

Market Efficiency

What are Efficient Capital Markets?

- **Efficient** in this context means **informational efficiency**: security prices quickly and fully reflect available information in a statistical sense
- Prices are efficient with respect to a particular information set if investors **cannot** use that information **earn positive abnormal (risk-adjusted) returns** <u>**on average**</u>

LOS 48.b Distinguish
CFAI p. 118, Schweser p. 246
Market Efficiency

Market Value and Intrinsic Value

- **Market value**: Price at which asset can be bought or sold
- **Intrinsic value**: Value rational investors would place on an asset with full knowledge of its characteristics
- If markets are not efficient, market values differ from intrinsic values in predictable ways

57

LOS 48.c Explain
CFAI p. 120, Schweser p. 246
Market Efficiency

Factors Affecting Market Efficiency

- Number of market participants
- Availability of information
- Impediments to trading
- Transactions and information costs

58

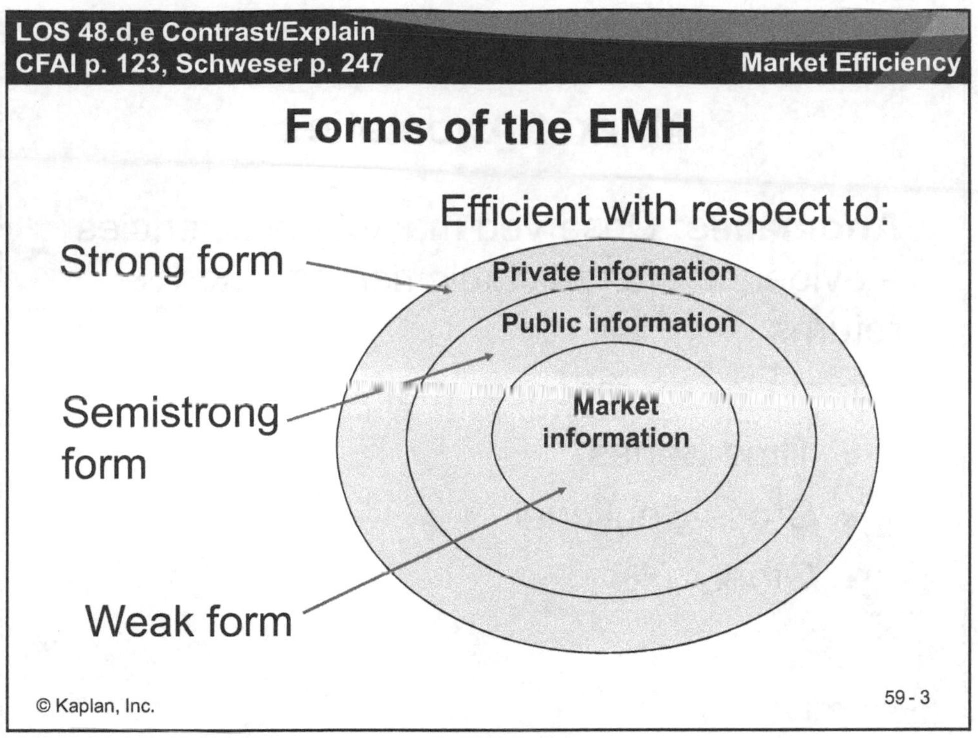

LOS 48.e Explain
CFAI p. 128, Schweser p. 248
Market Efficiency

Roles for Portfolio Managers in Efficient Markets

- Establish portfolio risk/return objectives
- Portfolio diversification
- Implement asset allocation based on risk/return objectives
- Tax minimization

60

LOS 48.f Describe
CFAI p. 129, Schweser p. 249

Market Efficiency

Market Anomalies

Anomalies: Observed market inefficiencies – evidence of predictable risk-adjusted returns

Anomalies by research method:

- Time Series
- Cross-Sectional
- Other

61

LOS 48.f Describe
CFAI p. 129, Schweser p. 249

Market Efficiency

Time Series Anomalies

- **Calendar effects:** January, turn-of-month, day-of-week, weekend, holiday
- **Overreaction:** Prices inflated after good news, depressed after bad news
- **Momentum:** High short-term returns continue in following periods

62

LOS 48.f Describe
CFAI p. 129, Schweser p. 249
Market Efficiency

Cross-Sectional Anomalies

- **Size effect:** Small-cap stocks outperform large-cap stocks
- **Value effect:** Low P/E, low market-to-book, high dividend yield stocks outperform

63

LOS 48.f Describe
CFAI p. 129, Schweser p. 249
Market Efficiency

Other Anomalies

- **Closed-end funds** sell at a discount
- Slow adjustment to **earnings surprises**
- **IPOs**: Initial overreaction, long-term underperformance
- Stocks react to **economic fundamentals** (but perhaps they should)

64

LOS 48.f Describe
CFAI p. 129, Schweser p. 249 Market Efficiency

Data Mining

Repeated tests on the same historical data

1. Analysts' tests of many different strategies will result in some that show positive abnormal returns just by chance
2. Some researchers may "snoop" the data for strategies that would have worked in the past, without regard to economic rationale

No reason to believe these strategies will work in the future

 65

LOS 48.f Describe
CFAI p. 129, Schweser p. 249 Market Efficiency

Anomaly Evidence

- Most evidence appears to result from methodology (expected returns) used
- Many anomalies are not profitable when transactions costs are considered
- Some strategies have ceased to work after being identified
- Some strategies only work in some time periods
- Portfolio management should not be based on anomalies with no economic basis

 66

LOS 48.g Contrast
CFAI p. 136, Schweser p. 252 Market Efficiency

Behavioral Finance

- Investors behave in ways that are not rational
- Investors have cognitive biases

Loss aversion: Risk aversion is asymmetrical, investors dislike losses more than they like gains.

Overconfidence: Investors overestimate their ability to value securities.

Gambler's fallacy: Recent results affect estimates of future probabilities.

 67

LOS 48.g Contrast
CFAI p. 136, Schweser p. 252 Market Efficiency

Behavioral Finance

- **Mental accounting:** Considering different investments' performance separately instead of viewing them as a portfolio
- **Disposition effect:** Willing to realize gains but not losses
- **Information cascades**: Uninformed investors mimic actions of informed investors

Markets can still be efficient even if investors exhibit irrational behavior

 68

Market Organization and Structure

Types of Orders – Solution

A trader who owns a stock that is trading at 48 and would like to buy more shares if it increases in value to 52 should enter a:

C. stop buy order at 52.

A limit buy order at 52 and a market buy order would both execute immediately.

Market Organization and Structure

Margin – Solution

An investor who purchases 400 shares of stock at 42 and posts initial margin of 40% when the maintenance margin requirement is 30% will get a margin call if the stock price falls below:

B. 36.00.

$$42(1 - 0.4) / (1 - 0.3) = 36$$

Security Market Indices

Index Weighting – Solution

Compared to a market-cap weighted index, a fundamental weighted index based on dividends will place more weight on firms with higher:

A. dividend yields.

Firms with higher dividend yields as a percentage of firm value have higher dividend proportions than market-cap proportions

Security Market Indices

Index Weighting – Solution

The type of index weighting that is *most likely* to be similar to a momentum strategy is:

A. market-cap weighting.

Firms with price increases (decreases) have higher (lower) weights in the index.

Study Session 14

Equity Analysis and Valuation

Equity Analysis and Valuation

49. Overview of Equity Securities

Equity Investments

LOS 49.a,b Describe
CFAI p. 156, Schweser p. 258

Overview of Equity Securities

Equity Security Characteristics

- Dividends are variable; no obligation to pay dividends
- Common shareholders have a residual claim to firm assets
- Common shareholders vote for board members
- Different classes of common shares can have different voting rights

2

LOS 49.a,b Describe
CFAI p. 156, Schweser p. 258 Overview of Equity Securities

Cumulative Voting

Allows minority shareholders greater representation

Example: 3 board positions are up for vote, shareholder owns 100 shares:

- **Statutory (non-cumulative) voting**: Shareholder can give maximum of 100 votes to each of 3 candidates
- **Cumulative voting**: Shareholder can give maximum of 300 votes to one candidate

 3

LOS 49.a,b Describe
CFAI p. 156, Schweser p. 258 Overview of Equity Securities

Preferred Stock (Preference Shares)

Similarities to common stock:

- Dividends not an obligation
- No maturity date

Similarities to debt:

- Fixed payment (scheduled dividends)
- Usually no voting rights
- Does not participate when firm does well

 4

LOS 49.a,b Describe
CFAI p. 156, Schweser p. 258 Overview of Equity Securities

Types of Preferred Stock

- **Cumulative preferred** must receive any unpaid dividends before common shares may be paid dividends—less risk than non-cumulative preferred shares
- **Participating preferred** receives extra payment if firm does well, claim can exceed par value if firm is liquidated

 5

LOS 49.a,b Describe
CFAI p. 156, Schweser p. 258 Overview of Equity Securities

Convertible Preferred Stock

- Preferred shares can be converted to common shares at a conversion ratio
- Advantages:
  - Preferred dividend > common dividend
  - Shareholders can benefit from firm growth by converting to common
  - Less risky than common stock

 6

LOS 49.a,b Describe
CFAI p. 156, Schweser p. 258 Overview of Equity Securities

Callable and Putable Shares

Both common and preferred equity can have a **call feature** or **put feature**

- **Callable shares** give the firm the right to repurchase the shares at the call price—more risk than regular shares
- **Putable shares** give shareholders the right to sell the shares back to the firm at the put price—less risk than regular shares

 7

LOS 49.c Distinguish
CFAI p. 163, Schweser p. 260 Overview of Equity Securities

Private Equity

Advantages compared to public equity:

- Reporting requirements less
- More able to focus on long term
- Potentially greater return for investors once firm goes public

Disadvantages compared to public equity:

- Less liquid
- Less ability to raise capital
- Less disclosure, may weaken governance

 8

LOS 49.c Distinguish
CFAI p. 163, Schweser p. 260 Overview of Equity Securities

Private Equity Investments

- **Venture capital:** Provides financing for early stages of firm development
- **Leveraged buyout** (LBO): Uses debt to buy all outstanding stock
- **Management buyout** (MBO): Management-led LBO
- **Private Investment in Public Entity** (PIPE): Public firm raises equity capital in private placement

 9

LOS 49.d Describe
CFAI p. 165, Schweser p. 261 Overview of Equity Securities

Investing in Foreign Equities

Disadvantages of **direct investing** on a foreign exchange:

- Investment and return may be denominated in foreign currency
- Often less liquidity
- Often less transparency
- Exchange regulations and procedures may be quite different

 10

LOS 49.d Describe
CFAI p. 165, Schweser p. 261 Overview of Equity Securities

Depository Receipts

- Shares are deposited in a bank
- Claims to deposited shares (receipts) trade like a local stock in local currency
- Accounting standards and market procedures are those of the local market

 11

LOS 49.d Describe
CFAI p. 165, Schweser p. 261 Overview of Equity Securities

Depository Receipts

Sponsored depository receipts:

- Firm is involved with issue
- Investor has same voting and dividend rights as foreign shareholders
- Greater firm reporting requirements (must be registered with SEC in U.S.)

Unsponsored depository receipts:

- Depository buys shares in foreign market
- Bank retains voting rights

 12

LOS 49.d Describe
CFAI p. 165, Schweser p. 261 Overview of Equity Securities

Investing in Foreign Securities

- **Global Depository Receipts**: Issued outside U.S. and outside firm's home country; most denominated in USD, some in pounds and euros
- **American Depository Receipts**: Denominated in U.S. dollars and traded on U.S. exchanges; oldest and most common type
- **Global Registered Shares**: Identical common shares that trade in local currencies on stock exchanges worldwide (1998)
- **Baskets of Listed Depository Receipts**: ETFs; portfolio of depository receipts

 13

LOS 49.e Compare
CFAI p. 170, Schweser p. 262 Overview of Equity Securities

Return Characteristics of Equity

Components of equity return:

- Dividends
- Capital gain or loss
- Share repurchases
- Possible foreign exchange gain or loss

Compounding of reinvested dividends has historically been an important part (2/3 +) of investors' compound returns on equity securities

 14

LOS 49.e Compare
CFAI p. 170, Schweser p. 262
Overview of Equity Securities

Risk Characteristics of Equity

Preferred stock is **less risky** than common stock

- Fixed dividend
- Receives distributions before common stock
- Claim to par value if firm is liquidated; after claims of debt holders but before claims of common stockholders

LOS 49.f Explain
CFAI p. 173, Schweser p. 263
Overview of Equity Securities

Equity Issuance

- Provides funds to buy productive assets to increase shareholder wealth
- Can be used to buy other companies or for employee incentive compensation
- Decreases firm's reliance on debt financing

LOS 49.g Distinguish
CFAI p. 173, Schweser p. 263 Overview of Equity Securities

Book and Market Value of Equity

- **Book value** of equity: Value of the firm's balance sheet assets minus liabilities
- **Market value** of equity: Reflects investor expectations regarding firm risk, amount and timing of future cash flows

 17

LOS 49.h Compare
CFAI p. 178, Schweser p. 264 Overview of Equity Securities

ROE and Cost of Equity

- **ROE** (net income / average equity) measures the return management is generating on equity capital
- **Cost of equity** is investors' minimum **required rate of return** on the firm's equity securities—difficult to estimate compared to required return on debt

 18

Equity Analysis and Valuation

50. Introduction to Industry and Company Analysis

Equity Investments

LOS 50.a Explain
CFAI p. 188, Schweser p. 271

Introduction to Industry and Company Analysis

Uses of Industry Analysis

- Understanding a firm's business environment—growth, competition, risks
- Active management—industry analysis can be used to weight a portfolio and rotate among industries
- Performance attribution—industry selection as a source of portfolio return

20

LOS 50.b Compare/Classify
CFAI p. 189, Schweser p. 271

Introduction to Industry and Company Analysis

Approaches to Industry Groupings

- **Products and services**: Group by sector or primary business activity
- **Business cycle sensitivity**: Cyclical or non-cyclical
  - **High sensitivity:** Consumer discretionary, energy, financials, industrials, technology, materials
  - **Low sensitivity:** Consumer staples, health care, telecommunications, utilities

21

LOS 50.b Compare/Classify
CFAI p. 189, Schweser p. 271

Introduction to Industry and Company Analysis

Approaches to Industry Groupings

Statistical groupings: Groups of firms with highly correlated historical returns, low correlations between groups

- Limitations:
  - Historical correlations may not persist
  - Firm groups can be non-intuitive
  - Firm groups may change for different time periods and countries

22

LOS 50.b Compare/Classify
CFAI p. 189, Schweser p. 271

Introduction to Industry and Company Analysis

Commercial Classification Systems

3 or 4 tiers: Sectors, Industry Groups, Industries, Sub-industries

Sectors:

Basic Materials	Consumer Discretionary
Consumer Staples	Energy
Financial Services	Health Care
Industrial Durables	Technology
Telecommunications	Utilities

23

LOS 50.b Compare/Classify
CFAI p. 189, Schweser p. 271

Introduction to Industry and Company Analysis

Government Classification Systems

Facilitate comparison over time and across countries

North American Industry Classification:

2 digits: sector
3 digits: subsector
4 digits: industry group
5 digits: industry
6 digits: country

Do not distinguish between public and private, large and small, for profit and non-profit

Updated less frequently than commercial systems

24 - 1

LOS 50.c Explain
CFAI p. 190, Schweser p. 274

Introduction to Industry and Company Analysis

Business Cycle Sensitivity

- **Cyclical**: Earnings highly dependent on the business cycle
- **Non-cyclical**: Earnings largely independent of the business cycle
  - **Defensive**: Basic goods and services with relatively stable demand
  - **Growth**: Demand is so strong the firm is largely unaffected by business cycle

25

LOS 50.d Explain
CFAI p. 197, Schweser p. 275

Introduction to Industry and Company Analysis

Peer Groups

- Start with narrowest commercial classification
  - Find specific competitors—annual report
  - Find comparable companies—industry reports, management comments
  - Determine similar business model/activity
- Peer group companies should have similar business activities, demand drivers, cost structure drivers, availability of capital

26

LOS 50.e Describe
CFAI p. 202, Schweser p. 276

Introduction to Industry and Company Analysis

Elements of Industry Analysis

- Evaluate relationships between macroeconomic variables and industry
- Estimate industry projections using different approaches and scenarios
- Cross-check analysis against that from other analysts
- Compare industry valuations across time to determine risk and rotation strategies
- Analyze industry prospects using strategic groups (similar business or product delivery)

27

LOS 50.e Describe
CFAI p. 202, Schweser p. 276

Introduction to Industry and Company Analysis

Elements of Industry Analysis

- Classify industries within **life-cycle stage** (embryonic, growth, shakeout, mature, or declining)
- Position industry on **experience curve** (cost per unit relative to output)
- Consider demographic, macroeconomic, governmental, social, and technological influences
- Examine **forces that determine industry competition**

28

LOS 50.f Describe
CFAI p. 204, Schweser p. 276

Introduction to Industry and Company Analysis

Porter's Five Forces

Intensity of industry competition depends on:

1. Rivalry among existing competitors
2. Threat of new entrants
3. Threat of substitute products
4. Bargaining power of buyers
5. Bargaining power of suppliers

29

LOS 50.g Explain
CFAI p. 206, Schweser p. 278

Introduction to Industry and Company Analysis

Barriers to Entry

- High barriers to entry limit new competitors
- To determine ease of entry, examine industry composition over time (if same firms over time, entry is difficult)
- Barriers to entry may not imply pricing power if competition among existing firms is strong
  - Undifferentiated products
  - High barriers to exit (→ overcapacity)
- Barriers to entry and competitive environment may change over time

30

LOS 50.g Explain
CFAI p. 206, Schweser p. 278

Introduction to Industry and Company Analysis

Industry Concentration

- High industry concentration does not necessarily imply pricing power
- Absolute market share may not matter as much as relative market share (having larger share than next-largest competitor)
- Low industry concentration (market fragmentation) usually results in strong competition, little pricing power

31

LOS 50.g Explain
CFAI p. 206, Schweser p. 278

Introduction to Industry and Company Analysis

Industry Capacity

- Undercapacity (demand exceeds supply) often implies pricing power
- Overcapacity can lead to strong price competition, especially when barriers to exit are high
- Capacity is fixed in the short run and variable in the long run
- Producers may overshoot future required capacity, especially in cyclical markets

32

LOS 50.g Explain
CFAI p. 206, Schweser p. 278

Introduction to Industry and Company Analysis

Industry Capacity

- Non-physical capacity (e.g., capital, skills) can be reallocated more quickly to new industries than physical capacity
- Physical capacity comes into production more slowly than non-physical capacity
- If capacity is physical and specialized, there may be overcapacity if producers overshoot

33

LOS 50.g Explain
CFAI p. 206, Schweser p. 278

Introduction to Industry and Company Analysis

Market Share Stability

- Highly variable market shares suggest competitive industry, firms with little pricing power
- Stable market shares suggest less intense competition
- High **switching costs** contribute to market share stability

34

LOS 50.h Describe/Classify
CFAI p. 213, Schweser p. 280

Introduction to Industry and Company Analysis

Industry Life Cycle

- **Embryonic stage**: Slow growth, high prices, large investment required, high risk of failure
- **Growth stage**: Rapid demand growth, low competition, falling prices, increasing profitability
- **Shakeout stage**: Slower growth, intense competition, increasing overcapacity, declining profitability, cost cutting, increased failures

35

LOS 50.h Describe/Classify
CFAI p. 213, Schweser p. 280

Introduction to Industry and Company Analysis

Industry Life Cycle

Mature stage: Slow growth, industry consolidation, high barriers to entry including brand loyalty and efficient cost structure

- Superior products lead to market share increases
- With stable demand, firms avoid price competition
- During economic downturns, overcapacity can lead to intense price competition

36

LOS 50.h Describe/Classify
CFAI p. 213, Schweser p. 280

Introduction to Industry and Company Analysis

Industry Life Cycle

Decline stage: Negative growth, excess capacity leads to price competition, higher production costs as demand falls, weak companies merge or exit

Reasons for decline:

- Technology: Decline of newspapers
- Global competition: Decline of U.S. textile industry
- Social change and changing tastes: Declining beer sales per capita in Germany

37

LOS 50.h Describe/Classify
CFAI p. 213, Schweser p. 280

Introduction to Industry and Company Analysis

Limitations of Life-Cycle Analysis

- Most useful during stable periods
- Stages may not be as long as anticipated or might be skipped altogether
- Some firms will experience dissimilar growth and profits due to competitive position

38

LOS 50.i Compare
CFAI p. 219, Schweser p. 282

Introduction to Industry and Company Analysis

Elements of Strategic Industry Analysis

- Major firms
- Barriers to entry/success
- Industry concentration
- Influence of industry capacity on pricing
- Industry stability
- Life cycle
- Competition

39

LOS 50.i Compare
CFAI p. 219, Schweser p. 282

Introduction to Industry and Company Analysis

Elements of Strategic Industry Analysis

- Demographic influences
- Government influence
- Social influences
- Technological influences
- Whether the industry is growth, defensive, or cyclical

40

LOS 50.j Describe
CFAI p. 221, Schweser p. 282

Introduction to Industry and Company Analysis

External Industry Influences on Growth, Profitability, and Risk

- **Macroeconomic factors**: Economic output, interest rates, credit availability, inflation
- **Technology**: New or improved products
- **Demographics**: Age distribution, population
- **Social influences**: How people conduct their lives and choose to spend their incomes
- **Government**: Tax rates, business regulation, purchases

41

LOS 50.k Describe
CFAI p. 227, Schweser p. 283

Introduction to Industry and Company Analysis

Elements of Company Analysis

- Firm overview
- Industry characteristics
- Product demand
- Product costs
- Pricing environment
- Financial ratios
- Projected financial statements and firm valuation

42

LOS 50.k Describe
CFAI p. 227, Schweser p. 283

Introduction to Industry and Company Analysis

Elements of Company Analysis

Company analysis should examine the firm's **competitive strategy**

- **Cost leadership (low cost)**: Lowest costs of production, lowest prices; sell enough volume to earn superior return
- **Product or service differentiation**: Distinctive in terms of type, features, quality, or delivery; achieve price premium

43

Equity Analysis and Valuation

51. Equity Valuation: Concepts and Basic Tools

Equity Investments

LOS 51.a Evaluate
CFAI p. 244, Schweser p. 291

Equity Valuation: Concepts and Basic Tools

Security Valuation

- Market price < estimated value: Asset is **undervalued**
- Market price > estimated value: Asset is **overvalued**

44

LOS 51.a Evaluate
CFAI p. 244, Schweser p. 291

Equity Valuation: Concepts and Basic Tools

Security Valuation

- For security valuation to be profitable, the security must be misvalued now and must converge towards intrinsic value in the future
- Market price is more likely to be correct when a security is followed by many analysts

45

LOS 51.b Describe
CFAI p. 246, Schweser p. 292

Equity Valuation: Concepts and Basic Tools

Types of Equity Valuation Models

1. **Discounted Cash Flow Models**
   Estimated value is the PV of:
   - Future cash distributed to shareholders (**dividend discount** models), or
   - Future cash available to shareholders (**free cash flow to equity** models)

46

LOS 51.b Describe
CFAI p. 246, Schweser p. 292

Equity Valuation: Concepts and Basic Tools

Types of Equity Valuation Models

2. **Multiplier Models**
   - Price multiplier: Ratio of stock price to earnings, sales, book value, or cash flow
   - Enterprise value multiplier: Ratio of enterprise value to sales or EBITDA
3. **Asset-Based**
   Equity value = total asset value minus liabilities and preferred stock values

47

LOS 51.c Explain/Describe
CFAI p. 248, Schweser p. 292

Equity Valuation: Concepts and Basic Tools

Valuing Common Stock: Multiple-Year Holding Period

For an *n*-year holding period:

$$\text{Value} = \frac{D_1}{(1+k_e)^1} + \ldots\ldots + \frac{D_n}{(1+k_e)^n} + \frac{P_n}{(1+k_e)^n}$$

P_n is the assumed sale price immediately after D_n is paid

48

LOS 51.c Explain/Describe
CFAI p. 248, Schweser p. 292

Equity Valuation: Concepts and Basic Tools

Valuing Common Stock Example

A stock paid a $1.50 dividend last year that will grow at 8% every year. You require a 12% return and you expect the stock price to be $51.00 at the end of Year 3. What is the stock's value today?

$$\frac{1.50(1.08)}{1.12}+\frac{1.50(1.08)^2}{1.12^2}+\frac{1.50(1.08)^3}{1.12^3}+\frac{51.00}{1.12^3}=\$40.50$$

LOS 51.c Explain/Describe
CFAI p. 248, Schweser p. 292

Equity Valuation: Concepts and Basic Tools

Dividend Discount Model

$$V_0=\sum_{t=1}^{\infty}\frac{D_t}{(1+k_e)^t}$$

- Corporation has an indefinite life
- Investor must receive future cash dividends to be willing to invest today

LOS 51.c Explain/Describe
CFAI p. 248, Schweser p. 292

Equity Valuation: Concepts and Basic Tools

Free Cash Flow to Equity Model

$$V_0 = \sum_{t=1}^{\infty} \frac{FCFE_t}{(1+k_e)^t}$$

FCFE: Cash available after a firm meets its debt obligations and necessary capital expenditures

FCFE = CFO – FCInv + Net borrowing

51

LOS 51.c Explain/Describe
CFAI p. 248, Schweser p. 292

Equity Valuation: Concepts and Basic Tools

FCFE Model Rationale

- FCFE reflects the firm's capacity to pay dividends
- Useful for firms that currently do not pay a dividend
- Analyst does not have to project the amount and timing of future dividend payments

52

LOS 51.d Calculate
CFAI p. 251, Schweser p. 296

Equity Valuation: Concepts and Basic Tools

Preferred Stock Valuation

- **Preferred stock** (usually) pays a fixed dividend and has no maturity date

$$V_0 = \frac{\text{Preferred dividend}}{k_P}$$

LOS 51.e Calculate/Interpret
CFAI p. 254, Schweser p. 297

Equity Valuation: Concepts and Basic Tools

Gordon (constant) Growth Model

Assumptions:

- Dividends grow at a constant rate forever
- k_e must be greater than g_c

$$P_0 = \frac{D_1}{(k_e - g_c)}$$

Expected dividend next period

where g_c = constant dividend growth rate

LOS 51.e Calculate/Interpret
CFAI p. 254, Schweser p. 297

Equity Valuation: Concepts and Basic Tools

Gordon Growth Model Example

A stock paid a dividend of $1.50 per share last year, which is expected to grow at a rate of 8.0% forever. If an investor requires a 12% return, what is the value of the stock today?

This is D_0

$$P_0 = \frac{D_1}{(k_e - g_c)}$$

$$= \frac{1.50\ (1+0.08)}{(0.12-0.08)} = \$40.50$$

55 - 1

LOS 51.e Calculate/Interpret
CFAI p. 254, Schweser p. 297

Equity Valuation: Concepts and Basic Tools

Estimating the Value of *g*

***g* represents the earnings and dividend growth rate in the constant growth model**

g = (RR)(ROE)

where:

RR = earnings retention rate

ROE = return on equity

RR = (1 – dividend payout ratio)

56

Equity Valuation: Concepts and Basic Tools

Stock Valuation – Problem

Acme has an ROE of 18%, EPS of $2.00 for last year, and paid a dividend of $1.20. If the ROE and payout ratio remain the same and the required rate of return is 13%, the value of the stock according to the Gordon Growth Model is *closest* to:

A. $22.18.

B. $40.24.

C. $60.44.

 57 - 2

LOS 51.e Calculate/Interpret
CFAI p. 254, Schweser p. 297

Equity Valuation: Concepts and Basic Tools

Multistage DDM

- For companies experiencing temporary rapid growth
- Assumes that dividend growth will be constant at some future date
- Estimate dividends during the rapid growth period
- Use Gordon growth model to find the terminal value of the firm when growth is constant

 58

LOS 51.e Calculate/Interpret
CFAI p. 254, Schweser p. 297

Equity Valuation: Concepts and Basic Tools

Multistage DDM Example

- Calculate the value of a stock if:
  - Last year's dividend = $1.00
  - Dividend will grow at 15% for two years
  - Dividend will grow at 5% after two years
  - Required return is 11%

59

LOS 51.e Calculate/Interpret
CFAI p. 254, Schweser p. 297

Equity Valuation: Concepts and Basic Tools

Multistage DDM Example

Step 1: Forecast the dividend for each year of rapid growth and for the first year of constant growth

$$D_1 = \$1.00(1.15)^1 = \$1.15$$

$$D_2 = \$1.00(1.15)^2 = \$1.32$$

$$D_3 = \$1.00(1.15)^2\ (1.05) = \$1.39$$

Identify the first dividend that will grow at a constant growth rate

60

LOS 51.e Calculate/Interpret
CFAI p. 254, Schweser p. 297

Equity Valuation: Concepts and Basic Tools

Multistage DDM Example

Step 2: Use the constant growth model to find the value of the stock one period before the dividend that will grow at a constant rate (D_2)

Using: $P_1 = D_2 / (k - g)$

We have: $1.32 / (0.11 – 0.05) = $22.00

(annotations: D_2 under $1.32; P_1 above $22.00)

61

LOS 51.e Calculate/Interpret
CFAI p. 254, Schweser p. 297

Equity Valuation: Concepts and Basic Tools

Multistage DDM Example

Step 3: Find the PV of expected dividends and of the expected future stock price

$$P_0 = \frac{D_1}{1+k} + \frac{P_1}{1+k}, \text{ where } P_1 = \frac{D_2}{k-g}$$

$$P_0 = \frac{1.15}{1.11} + \frac{22.00}{1.11} = \$20.86 \qquad 22.00 = \frac{1.32}{0.11-0.05}$$

(annotations: D_1 → 1.15; P_1 → 22.00; D_2 → 1.32)

62

LOS 51.e Calculate/Interpret
CFAI p. 254, Schweser p. 297

Equity Valuation: Concepts and Basic Tools

Multistage DDM Example

We could apply the constant growth model to D_3 and get a mathematically equivalent value (difference due to rounding).

$$P_0 = \frac{D_1}{1+k} + \frac{D_2}{(1+k)^2} + \frac{P_2}{(1+k)^2}, \text{ where } P_2 = \frac{D_3}{k-g}$$

$$P_0 = \frac{1.15}{1.11} + \frac{1.32}{1.11^2} + \frac{23.17}{1.11^2} = \$20.91 \qquad 23.17 = \frac{1.39}{0.11-0.05}$$

P_2 D_3

63

Equity Valuation: Concepts and Basic Tools

Stock Valuation – Problem

A stock is not expected to pay dividends until three years from now. The dividend is then expected to be \$2.00 per share, the dividend payout ratio is expected to be 40%, and the return on equity is expected to be 15%. If the required rate of return is 12%, the value of the stock today is *closest* to:

A. \$33.

B. \$53.

C. \$67.

64 - 2

LOS 51.f Identify
CFAI p. 258, Schweser p. 302

Equity Valuation: Concepts and Basic Tools

Dividend Discount Model Use

Gordon growth model is most appropriate for firms that pay a dividend that will grow at a constant rate, such as:

- Stable and mature firms
- Noncyclical firms

65

LOS 51.f Identify
CFAI p. 258, Schweser p. 302

Equity Valuation: Concepts and Basic Tools

Dividend Discount Model Use

- **2-stage DDM** appropriate for:
  - Firms with high current growth that will fall to a stable rate in the future
  - Older firms that were in the constant growth phase, but are now in a high growth phase or are losing market share
- **3-stage DDM** appropriate for:
  - Young firms still in the high growth phase

66

LOS 51.g Explain/Distinguish
CFAI p. 262, Schweser p. 303

Equity Valuation: Concepts and Basic Tools

P/E Based on Fundamentals

Begin with the constant growth value:

$$P_0 = \frac{D_1}{k - g}$$

Divide both sides of the equation by next year's projected earnings (E_1) to get P/E:

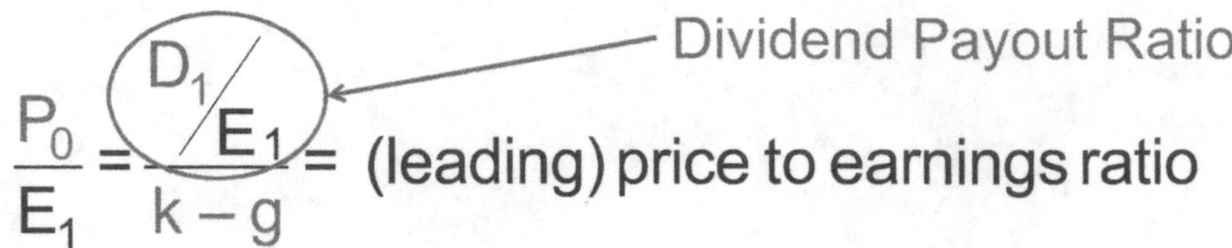

67

LOS 51.g Explain/Distinguish
CFAI p. 262, Schweser p. 303

Equity Valuation: Concepts and Basic Tools

P/E Based on Fundamentals

$$\frac{P_0}{E_1} = \frac{D_1 / E_1}{k - g}$$

- The primary determinants of a P/E ratio are the required rate of return (k) and the growth rate (g)
- The same factors that affect a stock's price affect the stock's P/E ratio

68

LOS 51.g Explain/Distinguish
CFAI p. 262, Schweser p. 303

Equity Valuation: Concepts and Basic Tools

P/E Based on Fundamentals

$$\frac{P_0}{E_1} = \frac{D_1 / E_1}{k - g}$$

Other things equal, fundamental P/E ratio (price) is higher if firm has:

- Higher dividend payout ratio
- Higher growth rate
- Lower required return

Note that increasing the payout ratio will decrease the growth rate: g = ROE × (1 – payout ratio)

 69

LOS 51.g Explain/Distinguish
CFAI p. 262, Schweser p. 303

Equity Valuation: Concepts and Basic Tools

P/E Based on Fundamentals Example

You expect a firm to pay out 30% of its earnings as dividends. Earnings and dividends are expected to grow at a constant rate of 6%. If you require a 13% return on the stock, what is the stock's expected P/E ratio?

$$\frac{P_0}{E_1} = \frac{D_1 / E_1}{k - g} = \frac{0.30}{0.13 - 0.06} = 4.3 \times$$

 70 - 3

LOS 51.h Calculate/Interpret
CFAI p. 262, Schweser p. 303

Equity Valuation: Concepts and Basic Tools

Price Multiples

- **P/E** = stock price / earnings per share
- **P/S** = stock price / sales per share
- **P/B** = stock price / book value per share
- **P/CF** = stock price / cash flow per share, where cash flow = operating cash flow or free cash flow

71

LOS 51.h Calculate/Interpret
CFAI p. 262, Schweser p. 303

Equity Valuation: Concepts and Basic Tools

Using Price Multiple Comparables

- Based on the **law of one price:** Two comparable assets should sell for the same multiple
- P/E, P/S, P/B, or P/CF ratio lower than industry average or comparable stock suggests stock is undervalued

72

LOS 51.i Explain/Demonstrate
CFAI p. 271, Schweser p. 308

Equity Valuation: Concepts and Basic Tools

Enterprise Value Multiples

$$\frac{\text{Enterprise Value (EV)}}{\text{EBITDA}}$$

EV = Market value of common stock
+ market value of debt
– cash and short-term investments

EV represents total market value of firm

EBITDA represents total earnings to both debt and equity investors

 73

LOS 51.i Explain/Demonstrate
CFAI p. 271, Schweser p. 308

Equity Valuation: Concepts and Basic Tools

Enterprise Value Multiples

EV / EBITDA ratios are useful when:

- Firms have different capital structures
- Earnings are negative and P/E ratio cannot be used

 74

LOS 51.i Explain/Demonstrate
CFAI p. 271, Schweser p. 308

Equity Valuation: Concepts and Basic Tools

EV / EBITDA Multiple Example

Stock price	$40.00
Shares outstanding	200,000
Market value of long-term debt	$600,000
Book value of long-term debt	$900,000
Book value of total debt and liabilities	$2,100,000
Cash and marketable securities	$250,000
EBITDA	$1,000,000

 75

LOS 51.i Explain/Demonstrate
CFAI p. 271, Schweser p. 308

Equity Valuation: Concepts and Basic Tools

EV / EBITDA Multiple Example

Step 1: Determine market value of short-term debt and liabilities

- Assume book value = market value for short-term items
- Book value of total debt – book value of long-term debt = $2,100,000 – $900,000 = $1,200,000

 76

LOS 51.i Explain/Demonstrate
CFAI p. 271, Schweser p. 308

Equity Valuation: Concepts and Basic Tools

EV / EBITDA Multiple Example

Step 2: Market value of total debt = market value of long-term debt + short-term debt = \$600,000 + \$1,200,000 = \$1,800,000

Step 3: Market value of equity = stock price × number of shares = \$40 × 200,000 = \$8,000,000

77

LOS 51.i Explain/Demonstrate
CFAI p. 271, Schweser p. 308

Equity Valuation: Concepts and Basic Tools

EV / EBITDA Multiple Example

Step 4: EV = debt + equity – cash = \$1,800,000 + \$8,000,000 – \$250,000 = \$9,550,000

Step 5: EV / EBITDA = \$9,550,000 / \$1,000,000 = 9.6×

Step 6: Compare to competitor or industry average, low values indicate underpriced

78

LOS 51.j Explain/Demonstrate
CFAI p. 273, Schweser p. 309

Equity Valuation: Concepts and Basic Tools

Asset-Based Models

- Equity equals market or fair value of assets minus liabilities
- Analysts usually adjust asset book values to market values
- Asset-based valuation models provide a floor value

79

LOS 51.k Explain
CFAI p. 257, Schweser p. 311

Equity Valuation: Concepts and Basic Tools

Present Value Models

Advantages:

- Theoretically sound
- Widely accepted

Disadvantages:

- Inputs must be estimated
- Valuation can be very sensitive to input values

80

LOS 51.k Explain
CFAI p. 257, Schweser p. 311

Equity Valuation: Concepts and Basic Tools

Multiplier Models

Advantages:

- Widely used, associated with stock returns
- Easily calculated and readily available
- Good for identifying attractive companies in an industry
- Useful for time-series or cross-sectional analysis

Disadvantages:

- Differences in accounting methods reduce comparability
- Multiples for cyclical companies highly variable

81

LOS 51.k Explain
CFAI p. 257, Schweser p. 311

Equity Valuation: Concepts and Basic Tools

Asset-Based Models

Advantages:

- Can provide floor values
- Useful for firm with mostly tangible short-term assets or if firm is to be liquidated

Disadvantages:

- Ongoing firm value may be greater than asset value, does not reflect future cash flows
- Fair values of assets can be difficult to estimate; especially with primarily intangible assets, high inflation environments

82

LOS 51.k Explain
CFAI p. 257, Schweser p. 311

Equity Valuation: Concepts and Basic Tools

Choice of Valuation Model

- Model should be chosen based on available inputs
- Model should be chosen based on the intended use of the valuation
- More complexity is not necessarily better
- Consider values using more than one method
- Consider uncertainty about input values
- Consider uncertainty about the appropriateness of the model

83

Equity Valuation: Concepts and Basic Tools

Stock Valuation – Solution

Acme has an ROE of 18%, EPS of $2.00 for last year, and paid a dividend of $1.20. If the ROE and payout ratio remain the same and the required rate of return is 13%, the value of the stock according to the Gordon Growth Model is *closest* to:

$$18\%\left(1-\frac{1.20}{2.00}\right)=7.2\%=g$$

A. $22.18.

$$\frac{1.20(1.072)}{0.13-0.072}=22.18$$

Equity Valuation: Concepts and Basic Tools

Stock Valuation – Solution

A stock is not expected to pay dividends until three years from now. The dividend is then expected to be $2.00 per share, the dividend payout ratio is expected to be 40%, and the return on equity is expected to be 15%. If the required rate of return is 12%, the value of the stock today is *closest* to:

$$g = 0.15(1 - 0.4) = 0.09$$

B. $53.

$$P_2 = \frac{D_3}{k - g} = \frac{2}{0.12 - 0.09} = 66.67$$

$$P_0 = \frac{66.67}{1.12^2} = \$53.15$$

Study Session 15

Fixed Income: Basic Concepts

Fixed Income: Basic Concepts

52. Features of Debt Securities

Fixed Income Investments

LOS 52.a Explain/Describe
CFAI p. 294, Schweser p. 11

Features of Debt Securities

Bond Indentures

A **bond indenture** specifies all the obligations of the issuer of a fixed income security

Negative covenants – prohibitions on the borrower

- Restrictions on asset sales
- Negative pledge of collateral
- Restrictions on additional borrowings

Affirmative covenants – promises by the borrower

- Maintain financial ratios
- Timely payment of principal and interest

2

LOS 52.b Describe
CFAI p. 295, Schweser p. 12

Features of Debt Securities

Bond Features

- Face value, par value, maturity value
- Coupon rate: Annual % of par value
- Currency denomination
- Redemption: At maturity vs. amortizing

3

LOS 52.b Describe
CFAI p. 295, Schweser p. 12

Features of Debt Securities

Coupon Structures

- **Zero-coupon bonds**
  - Pure discount bonds which pay no coupon
- **Step-up notes**
  - Coupon rate increases over time
- **Deferred coupon**
  - Bond's coupons compound

4

LOS 52.b Describe
CFAI p. 295, Schweser p. 12
Features of Debt Securities

Floating-Rate Securities

- **Coupon formula**
  - Reference rate + margin
  - For example, LIBOR + 1.5%, annualized rates
- **Cap**: Maximum on formula rate
- **Floor**: Minimum on formula rate

 5

LOS 52.c Define
CFAI p. 301, Schweser p. 14
Features of Debt Securities

Accrued Interest

- Paid to a bond seller
- Portion of the next coupon interest payment already earned by the seller
- Full price = clean price + accrued interest

$$AI = \frac{\text{days since last coupon}}{\text{days between coupons}} \times \text{coupon payment}$$

 6

LOS 52.d Explain
CFAI p. 301, Schweser p. 14

Features of Debt Securities

Amortizing and Nonamortizing Bonds

- **Nonamortizing** securities pay only interest until maturity, then the par value is repaid
  - Coupon Treasury bonds
  - Most corporate bonds
- The bond terms may include a **sinking fund** or **call** feature that can accelerate principal repayment
- **Amortizing** securities typically make equal payments over the life of the bond, each consists of interest and principal

7

LOS 52.d Explain
CFAI p. 301, Schweser p. 14

Features of Debt Securities

Call Provisions

- Issuer can repay principal prior to maturity
- Call protection for some period

  Call prices typically decrease over time (e.g., 15-year bond: callable after 5 years @ 102 and callable after 10 years @ par)

8

LOS 52.d Explain
CFAI p. 301, Schweser p. 14

Features of Debt Securities

Refunding

- **Refunding** is calling (redeeming) a bond using the proceeds of a lower-cost issue
- Bond can be **callable but not refundable**

9

LOS 52.d Explain
CFAI p. 301, Schweser p. 14

Features of Debt Securities

Prepayment Option

- On an amortizing security, such as a mortgage
- Prepayments are repayment of principal **in excess of scheduled principal payments**

10

LOS 52.d Explain
CFAI p. 301, Schweser p. 14 Features of Debt Securities

Sinking Fund

- **Sinking fund** redemptions are calls of a portion of an outstanding bond issue, typically at par
- **Premium bonds**: Cash paid to trustee, bonds to be retired chosen by lottery
- **Discount bonds**: Bonds can be purchased and delivered to trustee to be retired

 11

LOS 52.d Explain
CFAI p. 301, Schweser p. 14 Features of Debt Securities

Redemption Prices

- Call prices are regular redemption prices
- Sinking fund redemptions and redemptions under other provisions are special redemption prices

  (e.g., redemptions due to forced asset sales)

 12

LOS 52.e Identify/Explain
CFAI p. 302, Schweser p. 16

Features of Debt Securities

Embedded Options

- Options that **benefit the issuer/borrower** decrease bond values/increase yields
- Options that **benefit the holder/lender** increase bond values/decrease yields

13

LOS 52.e Identify/Explain
CFAI p. 302, Schweser p. 16

Features of Debt Securities

Embedded Options

Option Type	Benefits the...
Call Provision	Issuer/Borrower
Prepayment Option	Issuer/Borrower
Put Provision	Buyer
Conversion Option	Buyer
Caps	Issuer/Borrower
Floors	Buyer

14

LOS 52.f Describe
CFAI p. 308, Schweser p. 17 Features of Debt Securities

Margin Buying and Repurchase Agreements

- **Margin buying:** Borrowing funds to purchase securities. The securities are the collateral for the margin loan
- **Repurchase agreement:** An institution sells a security with a commitment to buy it back at a specified higher price
  - **Repo rate:** The interest rate implied by the two prices
  - **Overnight repo:** Repurchase agreement for one day
  - **Term repo:** Agreement covering a longer period
- Most bond-dealer financing is achieved through repurchase agreements rather than margin loans

 15

Fixed Income: Basic Concepts

53. Risks Associated With Investing in Bonds

Fixed Income Investments

LOS 53.a Explain
CFAI p. 320, Schweser p. 25

Risks Associated With Investing in Bonds

Bond Risks

1. Interest rate risk
2. Call/prepayment risk
3. Yield curve risk
4. Reinvestment risk
5. Credit risk
6. Liquidity risk
7. Exchange-rate risk
8. Volatility risk
9. Inflation risk
10. Event risk

17

LOS 53.b Identify
CFAI p. 320, Schweser p. 27

Risks Associated With Investing in Bonds

Bond Discounts and Premiums

- **Yield = coupon rate** → bond price at par
- **Yield < coupon rate** → bond price over par bond priced at a premium
- **Yield > coupon rate** → bond price under par bond priced at a discount

18

LOS 53.b Identify
CFAI p. 320, Schweser p. 27

Risks Associated With Investing in Bonds

Price/Yield for an 8% Bond

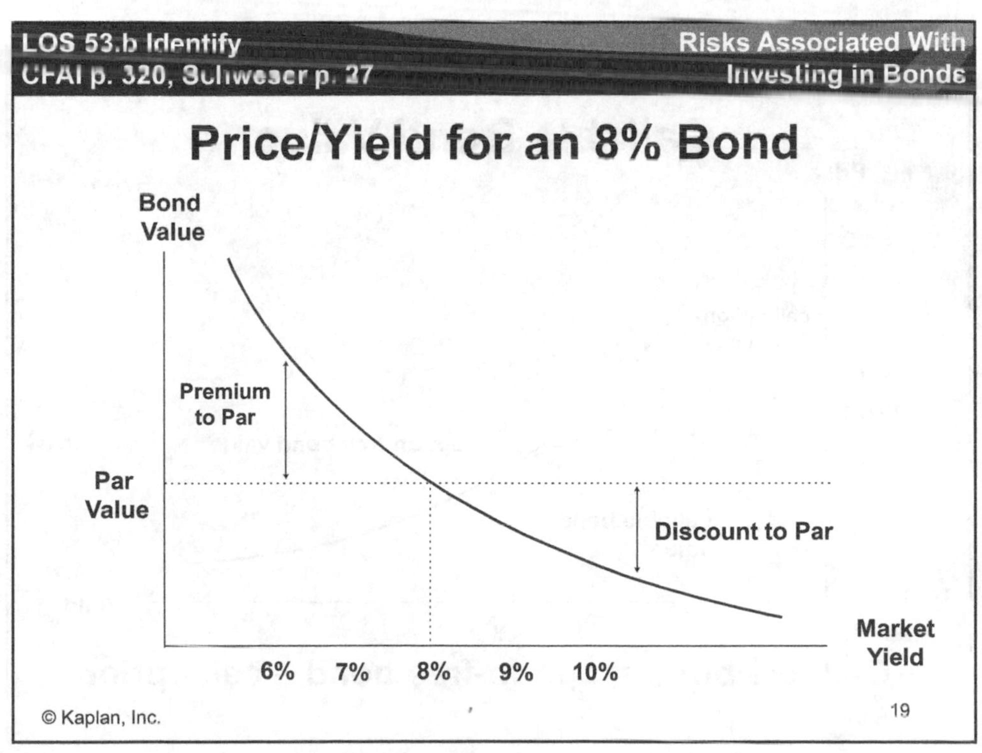

19

LOS 53.c Explain
CFAI p. 322, Schweser p. 27

Risks Associated With Investing in Bonds

Factors Affecting Interest Rate Risk

- Longer maturity → higher interest rate risk
- Higher coupon → lower interest rate risk
- Higher yield → lower interest rate risk
- Call option → lower interest rate risk
- Put option → lower interest rate risk

 20

LOS 53.d Identify
CFAI p. 322, Schweser p. 29

Risks Associated With Investing in Bonds

Callable Bond Value

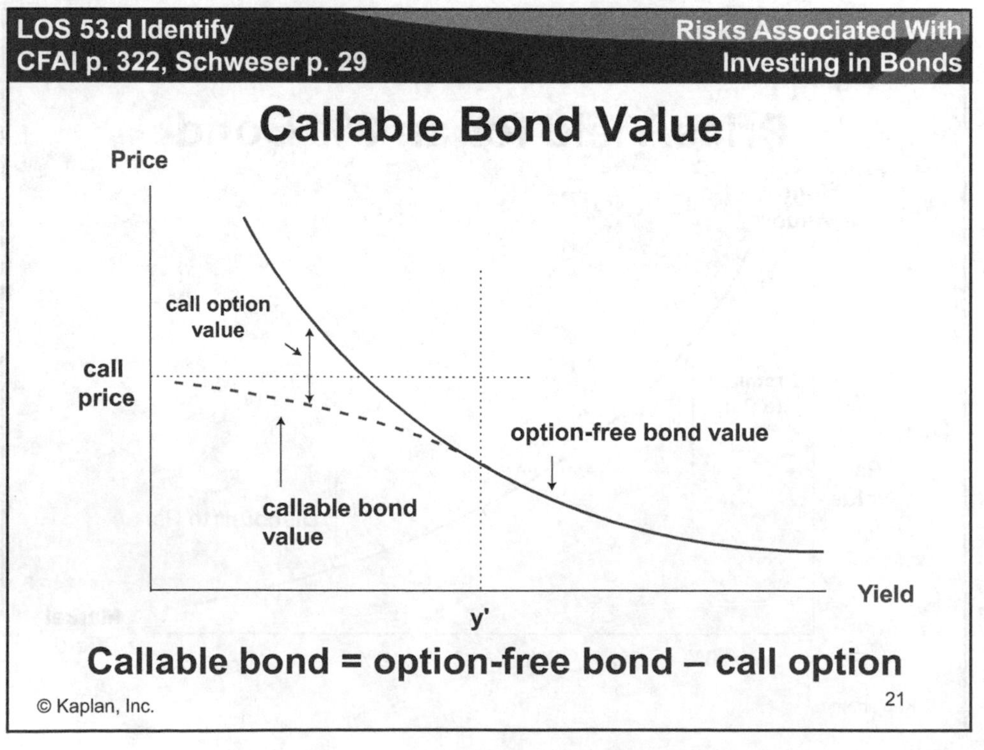

Callable bond = option-free bond – call option

 21

LOS 53.e Explain
CFAI p. 324, Schweser p. 29

Risks Associated With Investing in Bonds

Floating-Rate Securities

- **Coupon is periodically reset** based on a reference rate (plus a fixed margin)
- Has **interest rate risk** between reset dates
- Price may **differ from par at reset** if:
  - Credit quality of issuer changes after issuance
  - Margin over reference rate no longer appropriate

22

Risks Associated With Investing in Bonds

Floating-Rate Securities – Problem

Which of the following regarding floating-rate notes is *false?*

A. The coupon rate is based on a short-term reference rate plus a margin.

B. A cap benefits the issuer (borrower) of a floating rate note.

C. A floating rate note will be valued at par at every coupon (reset) date.

23-2

LOS 53.f Calculate/Interpret
CFAI p. 326, Schweser p. 30

Risks Associated With Investing in Bonds

Measure Interest Rate Risk With Duration

Duration is the approximate percentage price change for a 1% change in yield

$$\text{duration} = \frac{\text{price w/yield decline} - \text{price w/yield increase}}{2 \times \text{initial price} \times \text{decimal change in yield}}$$

If market yield goes up 0.5%, bond price goes from 980 to 960; if yield goes down by 0.5%, price goes to 1,002:

$$\text{duration} = \frac{1{,}002 - 960}{2 \times 980 \times 0.005} = 4.29$$

 24

LOS 53.f Calculate/Interpret
CFAI p. 326, Schweser p. 30

Risks Associated With Investing in Bonds

Price Impact of Yield Changes

Based on the duration of 4.29:

- If the yield goes **up** 0.25%, price goes **down** by **4.29 (0.25%) = 1.0725%**
- For a bond valued at $2.5 million, a yield change of 0.25% leads to an approximate change in value of **1.0725% (2.5 mil) = $26,812.50**
- **Dollar duration** of a bond is approximate change in value for a 1% change in yield: **0.0429 (2.5 mil) = $107,250**

 25

LOS 53.g Describe/Explain
CFAI p. 327, Schweser p. 32

Risks Associated With Investing in Bonds

Duration and Yield Curve Risk

- Portfolio duration is an approximation of the price sensitivity of a portfolio to a **parallel shift** of the yield curve (yields on all the bonds change by the same percent)
- For a **non-parallel shift** in the yield curve, the yields on different bonds in a portfolio can change by different amounts
- **Yield curve risk:** The interest rate risk of a portfolio of bonds that is not captured by the duration measure

26

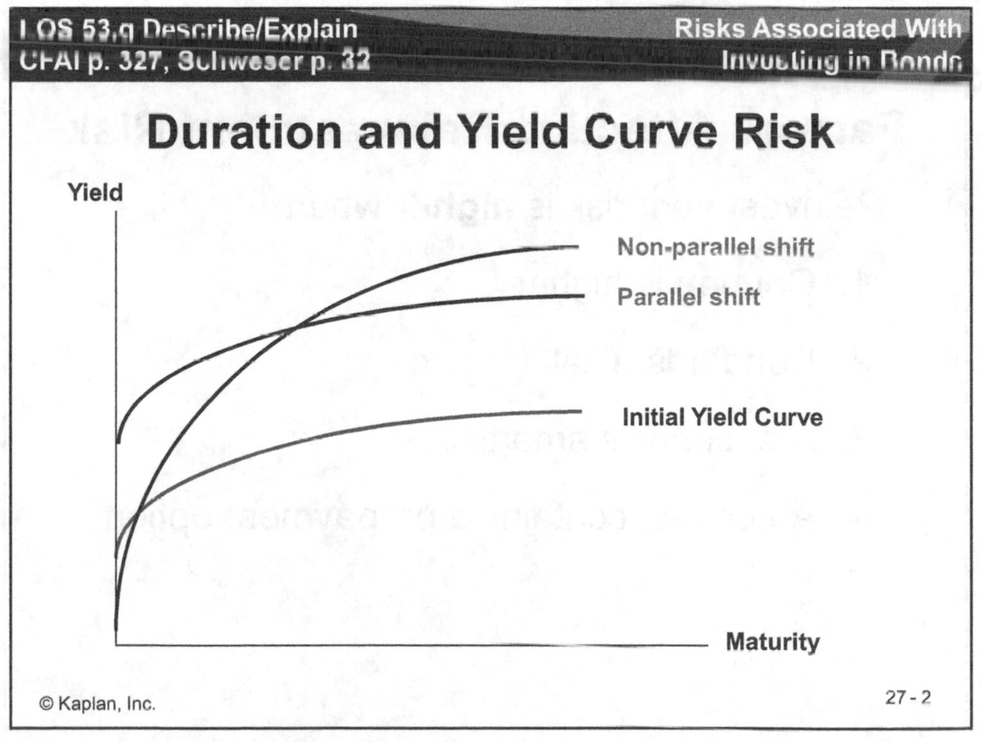

LOS 53.h Explain
CFAI p. 331, Schweser p. 34

Risks Associated With Investing in Bonds

Callable and Prepayable Securities

- Callable securities are likely to be called when interest rates are low
- Principal repayment on prepayable securities is faster when interest rates are low
- Investors must reinvest principal when rates are low

28

LOS 53.i Identify/Explain
CFAI p. 331, Schweser p. 34

Risks Associated With Investing in Bonds

Factors Affecting Reinvestment Risk

Reinvestment risk is **higher** when:

1. Coupon is higher
2. Bond has a call feature
3. A security is amortizing
4. A security contains a prepayment option

29

LOS 53.j Describe
CFAI p. 332, Schweser p. 35

Risks Associated With Investing in Bonds

Forms of Credit Risk

Bond ratings indicate relative probability of default

- **Downgrade risk**: Probability of ratings decrease
- **Default risk**: Probability of default
- **Credit spread risk**: Risk of increase in spread to Treasuries to compensate for given default risk (bond rating)

The higher the rating (e.g., AA vs. A), the lower the market yield

30

LOS 53.k Explain
CFAI p. 336, Schweser p. 36

Risks Associated With Investing in Bonds

Liquidity Risk

- The **bid-ask spread** indicates the liquidity of the market for a security
- A **decrease in liquidity** will increase the bid-ask spread, lead to a lower sale price, and **decrease the returns** on the position
- Even if an investor plans to hold the security until maturity, marking the security prices to market will result in lower returns when liquidity decreases (bids fall)

31

LOS 53.l Describe
CFAI p. 338, Schweser p. 37

Risks Associated With Investing in Bonds

Exchange Rate Risk

If an investor buys a security denominated in a foreign (to the investor) currency

- **Depreciation of the foreign currency** reduces the returns to a dollar-based investor
- **Exchange rate risk:** Actual cash flows from the investment may be worth more or less than was expected when the bond was purchased

32

LOS 53.m Explain
CFAI p. 338, Schweser p. 37

Risks Associated With Investing in Bonds

Inflation Risk

- **Inflation (purchasing power) risk:** Prices of goods and services increase more than expected
- An increasing price level decreases the amount of real goods and services that bond payments will purchase
- When expected inflation increases, nominal yields rise, values of debt securities fall

33

LOS 53.n Explain
CFAI p. 339, Schweser p. 37

Risks Associated With Investing in Bonds

Effects of Yield Volatility

Increase in yield volatility increases option values

Increases value of putable bond =

(option-free bond value + put value ↑)

Decreases value of callable bond =

(option-free bond value – call value ↑)

34

LOS 53.o Describe
CFAI p. 339, Schweser p. 38

Risks Associated With Investing in Bonds

Event Risk

- **Disasters** (e.g., hurricanes, earthquakes, or industrial accidents) can impair the ability of a corporation to meet its debt obligations
- **Corporate restructurings** may result in bond rating downgrades
- **Regulatory issues** may cause large cash expenditures to meet new regulations

  New regulations prohibiting financial institutions from holding a certain type of security can lead to a volume of sales that decreases prices for the whole sector

35

LOS 53.o Describe
CFAI p. 339, Schweser p. 38

Risks Associated With Investing in Bonds

Sovereign Risk

- Sovereign bond credit spread may increase
- Foreign government's credit rating may decline
- Foreign government may default on or repudiate debts
- Origins of sovereign risk are most often low economic growth/tax revenues, high government spending

 36

Risks Associated With Investing in Bonds

Interest Rate Risk – Problem

A bond's interest rate risk will increase with:

A. a put option.

B. shorter maturity.

C. lower coupon.

 37 - 1

Risks Associated With Investing in Bonds

Volatility Risk – Problem

An increase in yield volatility will *most likely:*

A. decrease the value of a callable bond.

B. decrease the value of a putable bond.

C. decrease the values of all option-free bonds.

38 - 1

Fixed Income: Basic Concepts

54. Overview of Bond Sectors and Instruments

Fixed Income Investments

LOS 54.a Describe
CFAI p. 357, Schweser p. 46

Overview of Bond Sectors and Instruments

Government Securities

- **Sovereign debt**: Bonds issued by central governments; domestic, foreign, or Eurobond
  - U.S. Treasury securities considered essentially free of default risk
  - Sovereign debt of other countries considered to have varying degrees of credit risk

40

LOS 54.a Describe
CFAI p. 357, Schweser p. 46

Overview of Bond Sectors and Instruments

Sovereign Debt Issuance Methods

1. **Regular cycle auction—single price:** Highest price (lowest yield) at which the entire issue can be sold awarded to all bidders (e.g., U.S. Treasury debt)
2. **Regular cycle auction—multiple price:** Winning bidders receive the bonds at the prices they bid
3. **Ad hoc auction system:** Government auctions new securities when market conditions are advantageous
4. **Tap system:** Auction of bonds identical to previously issued bonds, periodically, no regular cycle

LOS 54.b Describe/Distinguish
CFAI p. 350, Schweser p. 47

Overview of Bond Sectors and Instruments

U.S. Treasury Securities

- **T-Bills**: Pure discount securities, no coupon, no interest payments, less than one year maturity
- **Notes** and **bonds**: Semi-annual coupon interest, face (par) value at maturity, 2 to 30 years maturity

LOS 54.b Describe/Distinguish
CFAI p. 358, Schweser p. 47

Overview of Bond Sectors and Instruments

U.S. Treasury Securities

Treasury Inflation Protected Securities (TIPS)

- Coupon **rate is fixed**
- Real rate of return
- Par value is **adjusted for inflation**

½ coupon rate × inflation adjusted par value = semiannual payment

LOS 54.b Describe/Distinguish
CFAI p. 358, Schweser p. 47

Overview of Bond Sectors and Instruments

On- and Off-the-Run Treasuries

On-the-run issues

- Most recent auction issues, most liquid, actively traded

Off-the-run issues

- Older issues (replaced by more recent issues)

LOS 54.c Describe/Distinguish
CFAI p. 360, Schweser p. 49

Overview of Bond Sectors and Instruments

Stripped Treasury Securities

A type of zero-coupon bond created from Treasury notes and bonds; the pieces (coupon payments and the principal payment) are separated

- Coupon strips are denoted ci
- Principal strips are denoted pi

STRIPS (zeros) are taxed on implicit interest

LOS 54.d Describe
CFAI p. 363, Schweser p. 49

Overview of Bond Sectors and Instruments

Securities Issued by Federal Agencies

- **Federally related institutions** (e.g., GNMA, TVA)
- **Government-sponsored enterprises** (Sallie Mae, Freddie Mac, Fannie Mae)
- **Agency securities**, very little credit risk
- **Debentures**: Securities not backed by collateral; unsecured bonds

Overview of Bond Sectors and Instruments

TIPS – Problem

U.S. Treasury Inflation Protected Securities (TIPS):

A. have inflation-adjusted coupon rates.

B. have a par value that changes over time.

C. can be worth less than par at maturity.

LOS 54.e Describe/Explain
CFAI p. 364, Schweser p. 50

Overview of Bond Sectors and Instruments

$100,000 30-Year 5.75% Mortgage Monthly Payment = $583.57

Payment	Beginning Principal	Principal Portion	Interest Portion	Remaining Principal
1	$100,000.00	$104.41	$479.16	$99,895.59
2	$99,895.59	$104.90	$478.67	$99,790.69
3	$99,790.69	$105.41	$478.16	$99,685.28
**********	***********	**********	**********	*************
357		$575.52	$11.05	$1,734.07
358	$1,734.07	$575.26	$8.31	$1,158.81
359	$1,158.81	$578.02	$5.55	$580.79
360	$580.79	$580.79	$2.78	0

LOS 54.e Describe/Explain
CFAI p. 364, Schweser p. 50

Overview of Bond Sectors and Instruments

Mortgage-Backed Securities

Mortgage Passthrough Securities

- Backed by pools of mortgages
- Interest, principal payments, prepayments

Collateralized Mortgage Obligations (CMOs)

- Created from mortgage passthroughs
- More complex cash flow claims—tranches

49

LOS 54.e Describe/Explain
CFAI p. 364, Schweser p. 50

Overview of Bond Sectors and Instruments

Mortgage-Backed Securities

CMO Tranche example: Sequential Tranches

Tranche I receives interest on its outstanding principal and **all principal payments** until the tranche is completely paid off

Tranche II receives interest on its outstanding principal and **begins receiving all principal payments** when Tranche I is paid off

Tranche III receives only interest until Tranches I and II are paid off, then receives all remaining principal payments

50

LOS 54.e Describe/Explain
CFAI p. 364, Schweser p. 50

Overview of Bond Sectors and Instruments

Prepayment Risk

- Risk of receiving principal repayment **in excess of scheduled principal payments**
- May lead to more funds to be reinvested when rates for reinvestment are low—reinvestment risk
- When rates increase, prepayments slow
- Rapid prepayment results in gains for PO strips
- Rapid prepayment decreases cash flows from IO strips

 51

LOS 54.f Explain
CFAI p. 369, Schweser p. 52

Overview of Bond Sectors and Instruments

Motivation for Creating a CMO

Alter maturity range and redistribute prepayment risk to make securities attractive to different institutional investors

- Creating a CMO does not alter the *overall* risk of prepayment
- Tranche with less prepayment risk [planned amortization class (PAC)] coupled with tranche with more prepayment risk (support tranche)
- Goal is lower overall cost of funds (always!)

 52

LOS 54.g Describe/Distinguish
CFAI p. 371, Schweser p. 53

Overview of Bond Sectors and Instruments

State and Local Government Issues

- **Municipal securities**, a.k.a. munis, tax-free bonds
  Interest exempt from U.S. income tax and income tax in state of issue, often issued in **serial form**
- **Tax-backed (general obligation) bonds**
  Issued by state, counties, cities, and other political subdivisions; **supported by taxes**
- **Revenue bonds**
  Debt serviced **only with specific project's revenues.** Issued for transportation/airports, housing, port facilities, health care facilities, etc.

 53

LOS 54.g Describe/Distinguish
CFAI p. 371, Schweser p. 53

Overview of Bond Sectors and Instruments

Special Types of Munis

- **Insured bonds**

  Backed by insurance policies in the event of defaults, insured for life of issue, lowers yield, increases liquidity

- **Prerefunded bonds**

  Collateralized with escrow of Treasury securities which will support bond payments

 54

LOS 54.h Describe
CFAI p. 375, Schweser p. 55

Overview of Bond Sectors and Instruments

Corporate Bonds

- **Secured bonds:** First claim against specific collateral (mortgage debt, collateral trust bonds)
- **Debenture bonds:** Unsecured bonds, no specific collateral (debentures)
- **Subordinated debenture bonds:** Lower priority claim

  Bonds have a priority of claims over both preferred and common stockholders in the event of bankruptcy

55

LOS 54.h Describe
CFAI p. 375, Schweser p. 55

Overview of Bond Sectors and Instruments

Corporate Debt Securities

Commercial paper

- 2 to 270 days
- Pure discount
- Not liquid
- Sold through dealers or by the company itself

Medium-Term Notes (MTN)

- Continuously offered by agent
- Buyers can customize
- 9 months to 30+ years
- Fixed, floating, or structured

Structured Notes

- MTN combined with derivative, “rule busters”

56

LOS 54.h Describe
CFAI p. 375, Schweser p. 55

Overview of Bond Sectors and Instruments

Debt Securities Issued by Banks

Negotiable CDs

- Days to 5 years
- Secondary market
- Domestic (U.S.) and Eurodollar
- Issued primarily in London—LIBOR

Bankers acceptances

- Created to guarantee payment for shipped goods
- Short term
- Pure discount
- Few dealers, liquidity risk

LOS 54.i Define/Describe/State
CFAI p. 386, Schweser p. 59

Overview of Bond Sectors and Instruments

Asset-Backed Securities (ABS)

- Debt securities **backed by financial assets** (e.g., mortgages, auto loans, credit card receivables)
- Firm sells assets to **Special Purpose Vehicle**
  Separate entity, bankruptcy remote
- SPV issues securities
  Can have **better rating** (lower yield) than firm's debt
  Reduce funding costs

LOS 54.i Define/Describe/State
CFAI p. 386, Schweser p. 59

Overview of Bond Sectors and Instruments

Asset-Backed Securities (ABS)

External Credit Enhancements

- Corporate guarantees
- Bank letters of credit
- Bond insurance (insurance wrap)

59

LOS 54.j Describe
CFAI p. 388, Schweser p. 60

Overview of Bond Sectors and Instruments

Collateralized Debt Obligations

- **Balance Sheet CDOs**

  To reduce loans on balance sheet (banks)

- **Arbitrage CDOs**

  Profit from cash flow spread

- **Tranches**

  Created based on seniority of claims to cash flows from collateral

  Collateral is a pool of other debt obligations (e.g., business loans, mortgages, asset-backed securities, other CDOs, etc.)

60

LOS 54.k Describe/Distinguish
CFAI p. 389, Schweser p. 61

Overview of Bond Sectors and Instruments

Primary and Secondary Markets

- **Primary market:** Newly created debt securities
  - **Firm commitment:** Investment banker purchases the entire issue and resells it
  - **Best efforts basis:** Investment banker agrees to sell all of the issue that they can
  - **Private placement** (Rule 144A offering): Sold to a small number of investors, issue is **not registered** for sale to the public
- **Secondary market:** Sales of existing securities through exchanges, OTC (dealer) markets, or electronic trading networks

61

Fixed Income: Basic Concepts

55. Understanding Yield Spreads

Fixed Income Investments

LOS 55.a Identify
CFAI p. 408, Schweser p. 69

Understanding Yield Spreads

Interest Rate Policy Tools

- Discount rate
- Open market operations
- Bank reserve requirements

63

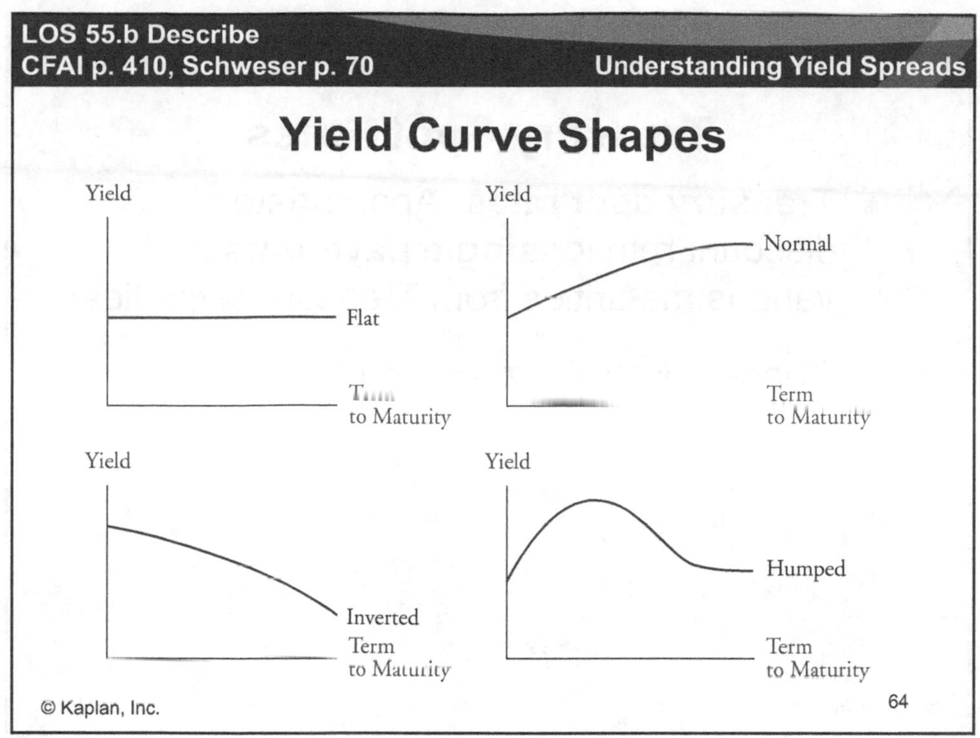

LOS 55.c Explain/Describe
CFAI p. 413, Schweser p. 71

Understanding Yield Spreads

Term Structure Theories

1. **Pure Expectations Theory**

   Yield curve shape determined by expectations about future short-term rates

2. **Liquidity Preference (Premium) Theory**

   Greater premium (yield) required for longer maturities; upward sloping

3. **Market Segmentation Theory**

   Supply and demand for specific maturity *ranges* determines interest rates; any shape

65

LOS 55.d Define
CFAI p. 415, Schweser p. 73 Understanding Yield Spreads

Treasury Spot Rates

- **Treasury spot rates:** Appropriate discount rate for **single payments** of various maturities from Treasury securities
- Conceptually like **zero-coupon** bond rates

 66

LOS 55.e Calculate/Compare
CFAI p. 416, Schweser p. 74 Understanding Yield Spreads

Yield Spread Measures

Absolute spread = Higher yield – Lower yield

$$\text{Relative spread} = \frac{\text{Yield on subject bond}}{\text{Yield on benchmark bond}} - 1$$

$$\text{Yield ratio} = \frac{\text{Yield on subject bond}}{\text{Yield on benchmark bond}}$$

Relative spread preferred because absolute spread is not sensitive to yield levels, only differences

 67

LOS 55.e Calculate/Compare
CFAI p. 416, Schweser p. 74
Understanding Yield Spreads

Yield Spread Calculations

5-year Treasury yields 5%

5-year A-rated corporate yields 6.25%

Absolute spread = 6.25 – 5.0 = 1.25%

Relative spread = $\frac{6.25}{5} - 1 = 1.25 - 1 = 25\%$

Yield ratio = $\frac{6.25}{5} = 1.25$

68

LOS 55.f Describe
CFAI p. 418, Schweser p. 75
Understanding Yield Spreads

Credit Spreads

- Difference between yields of bonds that differ only in credit rating
- Often quoted as a spread to Treasuries
- Credit spreads narrow during expansions and widen during contractions/recessions

69

LOS 55.g Describe
CFAI p. 420, Schweser p. 76 Understanding Yield Spreads

Embedded Options and Spreads

- Including a **put, conversion, or exchange option** with a corporate bond reduces required yield and **decreases yield spread** relative to Treasuries
- Including a **call option** increases required yield and **increases yield spread** relative to Treasuries

 70

LOS 55.h Explain
CFAI p. 422, Schweser p. 76 Understanding Yield Spreads

Liquidity and Yield

- Investors prefer more liquidity so **less liquid** issues have **greater required yields** and **greater yield spreads** relative to Treasuries, which are very liquid
- **Larger issues** typically have **more liquidity** and therefore, lower yields and lower yield spreads than otherwise identical smaller issues

 71

LOS 55.i Calculate
CFAI p. 423, Schweser p. 77

Understanding Yield Spreads

After-Tax and Taxable Equivalent Yields

After-tax yield = Taxable × (1 – Marginal tax rate)

$$\text{Taxable equivalent yield} = \frac{\text{Tax-free yield}}{(1 - \text{Marginal tax rate})}$$

Understanding Yield Spreads

After-Tax Yield – Problem

Tax-free bond yields **4%** **Taxable bond** yields **7%**

Investor marginal **tax rate** is **30%**

Which bond will the investor prefer?

LOS 55.j Define/Explain
CFAI p. 427, Schweser p. 78

Understanding Yield Spreads

LIBOR and Funded Investors

- **London Interbank Offer Rate (LIBOR)**

  Most important reference rate for floating-rate securities

- A **funded investor** borrows short term (typically at LIBOR) to finance an investment position

- **Profits** depend on funding costs

74

Risks Associated With Investing in Bonds

Floating-Rate Securities – Solution

Which of the following regarding floating-rate notes is *false?*

C. A floating rate note will be valued at par at every coupon (reset) date.

Credit rating can change, spread can change, or cap or floor in effect.

Risks Associated With Investing in Bonds

Interest Rate Risk – Solution

A bond's interest rate risk will increase with:

C. lower coupon.

Risks Associated With Investing in Bonds

Volatility Risk – Solution

An increase in yield volatility will *most likely:*

A. decrease the value of a callable bond.

Overview of Bond Sectors and Instruments

TIPS – Solution

U.S. Treasury Inflation Protected Securities (TIPS):

B. have a par value that changes over time.

Understanding Yield Spreads

After-Tax Yield – Solution

Tax-free bond yields **4%** **Taxable bond** yields **7%**

Investor marginal **tax rate** is **30%**

Which bond will the investor prefer?

⇒After-tax yield = 7% × (1 – 0.30) = 4.9%

$$\Rightarrow \text{Tax-equivalent yield} = \frac{4\%}{(1-0.30)} = 5.71\%$$

Either way, we see the taxable is preferred

4.9% > 4% and 5.71% < 7%

Study Session 16

Fixed Income Analysis and Valuation

Fixed Income: Analysis and Valuation

56. Introduction to the Valuation of Debt Securities

Fixed Income Investments

LOS 56.a Explain
CFAI p. 447, Schweser p. 87

Introduction to the Valuation of Debt Securities

3-Step Bond Valuation Process

Bond value = present value of future cash flows, coupons, and principal repayment

1. Estimate cash flows
2. Determine the appropriate discount rate

   The risk factors in Study Session 15 all require increases in yield, including liquidity risk, interest rate risk, call/prepayment risk, credit risk/default risk, etc.
3. Calculate present values of promised cash flows

2

LOS 56.b Describe
CFAI p. 448, Schweser p. 87

Introduction to the Valuation of Debt Securities

Difficulties in Estimating the Cash Flow Stream

- Uncertainty about **timing** of principal cash flows (e.g., call features, put features, prepayment options, and sinking fund provisions)
- Uncertainty about coupon amounts (e.g., floating-rate coupons)
- Uncertainty about cash flows due to **conversion** options or exchange options

3

LOS 56.c Calculate
CFAI p. 449, Schweser p. 88

Introduction to the Valuation of Debt Securities

Valuing an Annual-Pay Bond Using a Single Discount Rate

- Term to maturity = 3 years
- Par = $1,000
- Coupon = 8% annual coupon
- Discount rate 12%

4

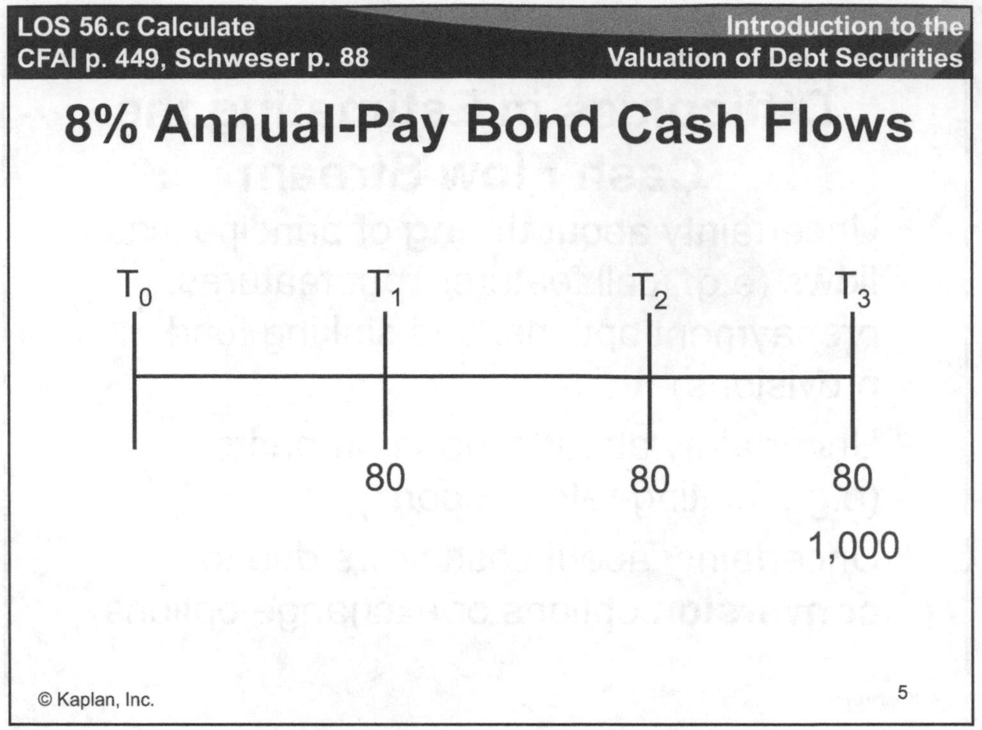

LOS 56.c Calculate
CFAI p. 449, Schweser p. 88

Introduction to the Valuation of Debt Securities

Bond Value: 8% Coupon, 12% Yield

$$\frac{80}{(1.12)^1} + \frac{80}{(1.12)^2} + \frac{80 + 1{,}000}{(1.12)^3} = 903.933$$

N = 3; I/Y = 12; PMT = 80; FV = 1,000;

CPT PV = –$903.93

6 - 2

LOS 56.c Calculate
CFAI p. 449, Schweser p. 88

Introduction to the Valuation of Debt Securities

Same (8% 3-year) Bond With a Semiannual-Pay Coupon

PMT = coupon / 2 = $80 / 2 = $40
N = 2 × # of years to maturity = 3 × 2 = 6
I/Y = discount rate / 2 = 12 / 2 = 6%
FV = par = $1,000

N = 6; I/Y = 6; PMT = 40; FV = 1,000;
CPT PV = –901.65

7 - 2

LOS 56.c Calculate
CFAI p. 449, Schweser p. 88

Introduction to the Valuation of Debt Securities

8% 3-Year Bond With Semiannual Coupon Payments

$$\frac{40}{1.06^1}+\frac{40}{1.06^2}+\frac{40}{1.06^3}+\frac{40}{1.06^4}+\frac{40}{1.06^5}+\frac{1040}{1.06^6}$$

$$=901.65$$

8

LOS 56.c Calculate
CFAI p. 449, Schweser p. 88

Introduction to the Valuation of Debt Securities

Calculate a Zero-Coupon Bond Price

\$1,000 par value zero-coupon bond matures in 3 years and with a discount rate of 8%

TVM Keys:

N = 3 × 2 = 6, PMT = 0, FV = 1,000,

I/Y = 8 / 2 = 4 CPT PV = –790.31

Mathematically: $\frac{1,000}{(1.04)^6} = \$790.31$

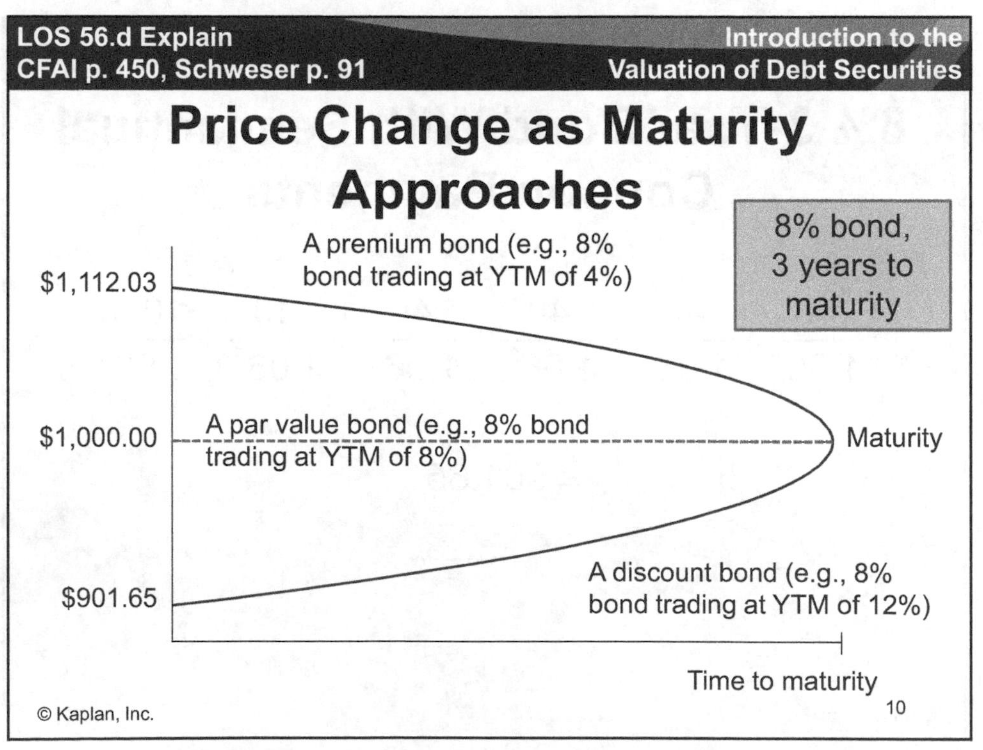

Introduction to the Valuation of Debt Securities

Value Change as Time Passes Problem

A 6%, 10-year semiannual coupon bond has a YTM of 8%

1. What is the price of the bond?
2. What is the value after 1 year if the yield does not change?
3. What is the value after 2 years if the yield does not change?

11 - 3

LOS 56.e Calculate
CFAI p. 450, Schweser p. 92

Introduction to the Valuation of Debt Securities

Price-Yield Relationship Semiannual-Pay 8% 3-year Bond

At 4%: I/Y = 2% N = 6 FV = 1,000 PMT = 40
CPT PV = $1,112.03

At 8%: I/Y = 4% N = 6 FV = 1,000 PMT = 40
CPT PV = $1,000.00

At 12%: I/Y = 6% N = 6 FV = 1,000 PMT = 40
CPT PV = $901.65

12 - 3

LOS 56.f Explain/Demonstrate/Describe
CFAI p. 462, Schweser p. 94

Introduction to the Valuation of Debt Securities

Arbitrage-Free Bond Prices

Dealers can separate a coupon Treasury security into **separate cash flows** (i.e., strip it). If the total value of the individual pieces based on the arbitrage-free rate curve (spot rates) is greater or less than the market price of the bond, there is an opportunity for **arbitrage.**

- The present value of the bond's cash flows (pieces) **calculated with spot rates** is the arbitrage-free value

13

LOS 56.f Explain/Demonstrate/Describe
CFAI p. 462, Schweser p. 94

Introduction to the Valuation of Debt Securities

Arbitrage-Free Pricing Example

Market price of a 1.5-year 6% Treasury note is $984

Value cash flows using (annual) spot rates of 6 months = 5%, 1 year = 6%, 1.5 year = 7%

Maturity	Annual rate	Semiannual rate	Cash flow (per $1,000)
0.5 years	5%	2.5%	$30
1.0 years	6%	3.0%	$30
1.5 years	7%	3.5%	$1030

14

LOS 56.f Explain/Demonstrate/Describe
CFAI p. 462, Schweser p. 94

Introduction to the Valuation of Debt Securities

Valuing the Pieces Using Spot Rates

6 mo. 12 mo. 18 mo.

$$\frac{30}{1.025} + \frac{30}{(1.03)^2} + \frac{1030}{(1.035)^3} = 986.55$$

Buy the bond for $984, strip it, sell the pieces for a total of $986.55, keep the arbitrage profit = $2.55

15

LOS 56.f Explain/Demonstrate/Describe
CFAI p. 462, Schweser p. 94

Introduction to the Valuation of Debt Securities

Arbitrage Process

- Dealers can **strip a T-bond** into its individual cash flows **or combine the individual cash flows** into a bond
- If the bond is priced **less** than the arbitrage free value: Buy the bond, sell the pieces
- If the bond is priced **higher** than the arbitrage-free value: Buy the pieces, make a bond, sell the bond

16

Fixed Income: Analysis and Valuation

57. Yield Measures, Spot Rates, and Forward Rates

Fixed Income Investments

LOS 57.a Describe
CFAI p. 492, Schweser p. 101

Yield Measures, Spot Rates, and Forward Rates

Sources of Bond Return

1. Coupon interest
2. Capital gain or loss when principal is repaid
3. Income from reinvestment of cash flows

18

LOS 57.b Calculate/Interpret/Explain
CFAI p. 493, Schweser p. 101

Yield Measures, Spot Rates, and Forward Rates

Traditional Measures of Yield

Nominal yield (stated coupon rate)

Current yield

Yield to maturity

Yield to call

Yield to refunding

Yield to put

Yield to worst

Cash flow yield

→ IRR-based yields

19

LOS 57.b Calculate/Interpret/Explain
CFAI p. 493, Schweser p. 101

Yield Measures, Spot Rates, and Forward Rates

YTM for an Annual-Pay Bond

Consider a 6%, 3-year, annual-pay bond priced at $943

$$943 = \frac{60}{(1+\text{YTM})} + \frac{60}{(1+\text{YTM})^2} + \frac{1060}{(1+\text{YTM})^3}$$

TVM functions: N = 3; PMT = 60; FV = 1,000;

PV = –943; CPT I/Y = 8.22%

Priced at a discount → YTM > coupon rate

20

LOS 57.b Calculate/Interpret/Explain
CFAI p. 493, Schweser p. 101

Yield Measures, Spot Rates, and Forward Rates

YTM for a Semiannual-Pay Bond

With semiannual coupon payments, YTM is 2 × the semiannual IRR

$$\text{price} = \frac{\text{coupon 1}}{\left(1+\text{YTM}/2\right)} + \frac{\text{coupon 2}}{\left(1+\text{YTM}/2\right)^2} + \ldots + \frac{\text{coupon N + par value}}{\left(1+\text{YTM}/2\right)^N}$$

 21

LOS 57.b Calculate/Interpret/Explain
CFAI p. 493, Schweser p. 101

Yield Measures, Spot Rates, and Forward Rates

Semiannual-Pay YTM Example

A 3-year, 5% Treasury note is priced at $1,028

N = 6; PMT = 25; FV = 1,000; PV = –1,028;

CPT I/Y = 2%; YTM = 2 × 2% = 4%

> The YTM for a semiannual-pay bond is called a Bond Equivalent Yield (BEY)

Note: BEY for short-term securities in Corporate Finance reading is different

 22

Yield Measures, Spot Rates, and Forward Rates

Equivalent Yields – Problem

An annual pay bond has a YTM of 14%.
The BEY for this bond is:

A. 13.54%.
B. 13.86%.
C. 14.49%.

23-2

LOS 57.b Calculate/Interpret/Explain
CFAI p. 403, Schweser p. 101

Yield Measures, Spot Rates, and Forward Rates

Current Yield (Ignores Movement Toward Par Value)

$$\text{Current yield} = \frac{\text{Annual coupon payment}}{\text{Current price}}$$

For an 8%, 3-year (semiannual-pay) bond priced at 901.65

$$\text{Current yield} = \frac{80}{901.65} = 8.873\% \quad \text{YTM} = 12\%$$

24

Yield Measures, Spot Rates, and Forward Rates

Yield Measures – Problem

For a bond trading at a premium, order the coupon (nominal) yield, current yield, and YTM from smallest to largest.

25 - 3

LOS 57.b Calculate/Interpret/Explain
CFAI p. 493, Schweser p. 101

Yield Measures, Spot Rates, and Forward Rates

Yield to First Call or Refunding

- For YTFC, substitute the call price at the first call date for par and number of periods to the first call date for *N*
- Use yield to refunding when bond is currently callable but has refunding protection
- Yield to worst is the lowest of YTM and the YTCs for all the call dates and prices

26

Yield Measures, Spot Rates, and Forward Rates

Yield to Call – Problem

Consider a 10-year, 5% bond priced at $1,028
What is the YTM?

If it is callable in two years at 101, what is the YTC?

27 - 5

LOS 57.b Calculate/Interpret/Explain
CFAI p. 493, Schweser p. 101

Yield Measures, Spot Rates, and Forward Rates

Yield to Put and Cash Flow Yield

- For **YTP,** substitute the **put price** at the first put date **for par** and number of **periods to the put date for *N***
- **Cash flow yield** is a **monthly IRR** based on the expected cash flows of an amortizing (mortgage) security

28

LOS 57.b,c Calculate/Interpret/Explain/Describe
CFAI p. 493, Schweser p. 101

Yield Measures, Spot Rates, and Forward Rates

Assumptions and Limitations of Traditional Yield Measures

1. Assumes held to maturity (call, put, refunding, etc.)
2. Assumes no default
3. Assumes **cash flows can be reinvested at the computed yield**
4. Assumes flat yield curve (term structure)

29

LOS 57.c Describe
CFAI p. 495, Schweser p. 108

Yield Measures, Spot Rates, and Forward Rates

Factors That Affect Reinvestment Risk

Other things being equal, a coupon bond's **reinvestment risk** will *increase* with:

- *Higher coupons*—more cash flow to reinvest
- *Longer maturities*—more of the value of the investment is in the coupon cash flows and interest on coupon cash flows

30

LOS 57.d Calculate/Interpret
CFAI p. 494, Schweser p. 110

Yield Measures, Spot Rates, and Forward Rates

Annual-Pay YTM to Semiannual-Pay YTM

Annual-pay YTM is 8%, what is the equivalent semiannual-pay YTM (i.e., BEY)?

$$\left(\sqrt{1.08}-1\right)\times 2 = 7.846\%$$

31

LOS 57.d Calculate/Interpret
CFAI p. 494, Schweser p. 110

Yield Measures, Spot Rates, and Forward Rates

Semiannual-Pay YTM to Annual-Pay YTM

Semiannual-pay YTM (BEY) is 8%, what is the annual-pay equivalent?

Semiannual yield is 8 / 2 = 4%. Annual-pay equivalent (EAY) is:

$$\left(1+\frac{0.08}{2}\right)^2 - 1 = 8.16\%$$

32

LOS 57.e Describe/Calculate
CFAI p. 508, Schweser p. 111

Yield Measures, Spot Rates, and Forward Rates

Theoretical Treasury Spot Rates

Begin with prices for 6-month, 1-year, and 18-month Treasuries:

6-month T-bill price is 98.30, 6-month discount rate is 1.73% $\frac{1,000}{1.0173} = 983$ BEY = 2 × 1.73 = 3.46%

1-year 4% T-note is priced at 99.50

$$\frac{20}{1.0173} + \frac{1,020}{(1+?)^2} = 995 \quad 995 - \frac{20}{1.0173} = 975.34 = \frac{1,020}{(1+?)^2}$$

$$? = \sqrt{\frac{1,020}{975.34}} - 1 = 2.26\%, \quad \text{BEY} = 2 \times 2.26 = 4.52\%$$

 33

LOS 57.e Describe/Calculate
CFAI p. 508, Schweser p. 111

Yield Measures, Spot Rates, and Forward Rates

Theoretical Treasury Spot Rates

Begin with prices for 6-month, 1-year, and 18-month Treasuries:

1.5-year 4.5% T-note is priced at 98.60

$$\frac{22.5}{1.0173} + \frac{22.5}{(1.0226)^2} + \frac{1,022.5}{(1+?)^3} = 986 \quad 986 - \frac{22.5}{1.0173} - \frac{22.5}{(1.0226)^2} = 942.37 = \frac{1,022.5}{(1+?)^3}$$

$$? = \sqrt[3]{\frac{1,022.5}{942.37}} - 1 = 2.76\%, \quad \text{BEY} = 2 \times 2.76 = 5.52\%$$

By "bootstrapping," we calculated the 1-year spot rate = 4.52% and the 1.5-year spot rate = 5.52%

 34

LOS 57.e Describe/Calculate
CFAI p. 508, Schweser p. 111

Yield Measures, Spot Rates, and Forward Rates

Valuing a Bond With Spot Rates

Use the spot rates we calculated to value a 5% 18-month Treasury note.

$$\frac{25}{1.0173}+\frac{25}{(1.0226)^2}+\frac{1,025}{(1.0276)^3}=993.09$$

35

LOS 57.f Explain
CFAI p. 513, Schweser p. 115

Yield Measures, Spot Rates, and Forward Rates

Nominal and Zero-Volatility Spreads

- **Nominal spreads** are just differences in YTMs
- **Zero-volatility (ZV) spreads** are the (parallel) spread to Treasury spot-rate curve to get PV = market price
- Equal amounts added to each spot rate to get PV = market price

36

LOS 57.f Explain
CFAI p. 513, Schweser p. 115

Yield Measures, Spot Rates, and Forward Rates

Option-Adjusted Spreads

- **Option-adjusted spreads (OAS)** are spreads that take out the effect of embedded options on yield, reflect yield differences for differences in risk and liquidity

Option cost in yield% = ZV spread% – OAS%

Option cost > 0 for callable, < 0 for putable

Must use OAS for debt with embedded options

37

LOS 57.g Explain/Calculate
CFAI p. 520, Schweser p. 118

Yield Measures, Spot Rates, and Forward Rates

Forward Rates

Forward rates are ***N*-period rates** for borrowing/lending at **some date in the future**

Notation for one-period forward rates:

${}_1F_0$ is the current one-period rate S_1

${}_1F_1$ is the one-period rate, one period from now

${}_1F_2$ is the one-period rate, two periods from now

${}_2F_1$ is the two-period rate, one period from now

38

LOS 57.g Explain/Calculate
CFAI p. 520, Schweser p. 118

Yield Measures, Spot Rates, and Forward Rates

Spot Rates and Forward Rates

$$(1+S_3)^3 = (1+S_1)(1+{}_1F_1)(1+{}_1F_2)$$

$$(1+S_3)^3 = (1+S_1)(1+{}_2F_1)^2$$

$$(1+S_3)^3 = (1+S_2)^2(1+{}_1F_2)$$

Cost of borrowing for 3 years at S_3 should equal cost of:

- Borrowing for 1 year at S_1, 1 year at ${}_1F_1$, and 1 year at ${}_1F_2$
- Borrowing for 1 year at S_1 and for 2 years at ${}_2F_1$
- Borrowing for 2 years at S_2 and for 1 year at ${}_1F_2$

LOS 57.g Explain/Calculate
CFAI p. 520, Schweser p. 118

Yield Measures, Spot Rates, and Forward Rates

Forward Rates From Spot Rates

$S_2 = 4\%, S_3 = 5\%$, calculate ${}_1F_2$

$$\frac{(1+S_3)^3}{(1+S_2)^2} - 1 = {}_1F_2 \text{ so, } \frac{(1.05)^3}{(1.04)^2} - 1 = 7.03\%$$

Approximation: 3 × 5% – 2 × 4% = 15% – 8% = 7%

LOS 57.g Explain/Calculate
CFAI p. 520, Schweser p. 118

Yield Measures, Spot Rates, and Forward Rates

Forward Rates From Spot Rates

$S_2 = 4\%,\ S_4 = 5\%$, Calculate ${}_2F_2$

$$\sqrt{\frac{(1+S_4)^4}{(1+S_2)^2}} - 1 = {}_2F_2 \text{ so, } \sqrt{\frac{(1.05)^4}{(1.04)^2}} - 1 = 6.01\%$$

Approximation: 4 × 5% – 2 × 4% = 20% – 8% = 12%

12% / 2 = 6%

${}_2F_2$ is an annual rate, so we take the square root above and divide by two for the approximation

41

LOS 57.g Explain/Calculate
CFAI p. 520, Schweser p. 118

Yield Measures, Spot Rates, and Forward Rates

Spot Rates From Forward Rates

Spot rate is geometric mean of forward rates

$$[(1+S_1)(1+{}_1F_1)(1+{}_1F_2)]^{\frac{1}{3}} - 1 = S_3$$

Example: $S_1 = 4.0\%$, ${}_1F_1 = 5.0\%$, ${}_1F_2 = 5.5\%$

3-period spot rate =

$$[(1.04)(1.05)(1.055)]^{\frac{1}{3}} - 1 = S_3 = 4.8314\%$$

Approximation: $(4+5+5.5)/3 = 4.833$

42

LOS 57.g Explain/Calculate
CFAI p. 520, Schweser p. 118

Yield Measures, Spot Rates, and Forward Rates

Valuing a Bond With Forward Rates

1-year rate is 3.0%; ${}_1F_1$ = 3.5%; ${}_1F_2$ = 4.0%

Value a 4%, 3-year annual-pay bond

$$\frac{40}{1.03}+\frac{40}{(1.03)(1.035)}+\frac{1040}{(1.03)(1.035)(1.04)}=1{,}014.40$$

$1+S_1$ — $(1+S_2)^2$ — $(1+S_3)^3$

 43

Yield Measures, Spot Rates, and Forward Rates

Forward Rates – Problem

Current 1-year spot rate is 6%, 2-year spot rate is 7%, and 3-year spot rate is 6%. The 1-year forward rate for a loan 2 years from now is *closest* to:

A. 6%.

B. 5%.

C. 4%.

 44-3

Fixed Income: Analysis and Valuation

58. Introduction to the Measurement of Interest Rate Risk

Fixed Income Investments

LOS 58.a Distinguish/Explain
CFAI p. 556, Schweser p. 134

Introduction to the Measurement of Interest Rate Risk

Measuring Interest Rate Risk

- **Full valuation approach**: Re-value every bond based on an interest rate change scenario
  - Good valuation models provide precise values
  - Can deal with parallel and non-parallel shifts
  - Time consuming; many different scenarios

- **Duration/convexity approach**: Gives an approximate sensitivity of bond/portfolio values to changes in YTM
  - Limited scenarios (parallel yield curve shifts)
  - Provides a simple summary measure of interest rate risk

46

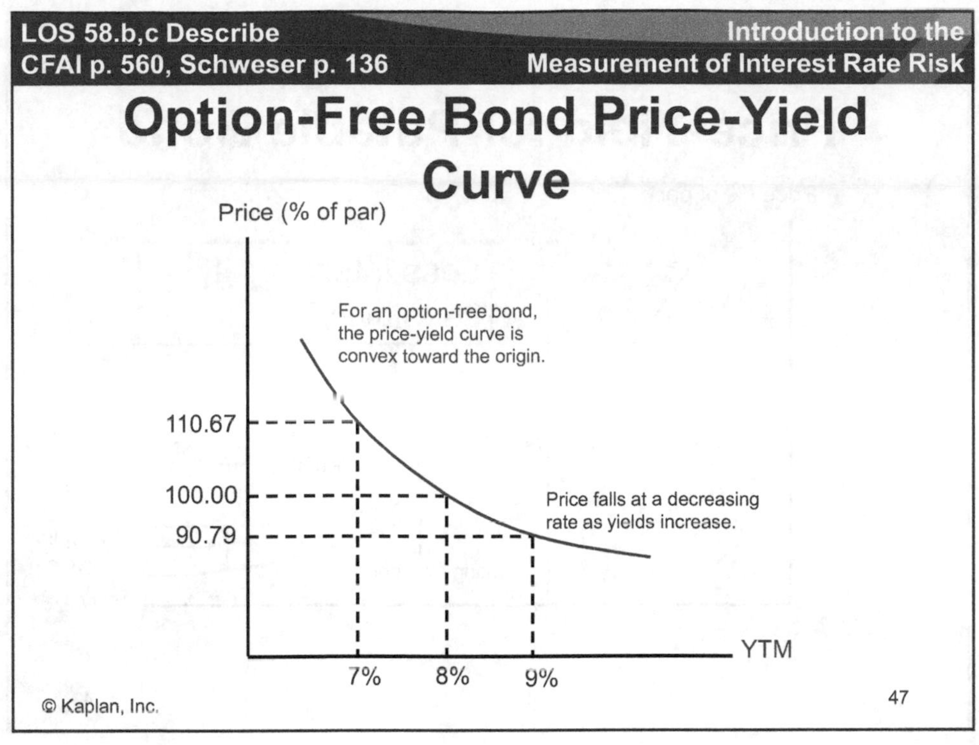
LOS 58.b,c Describe
CFAI p. 560, Schweser p. 136
Introduction to the
Measurement of Interest Rate Risk
Option-Free Bond Price-Yield Curve
Price (% of par)
For an option-free bond, the price-yield curve is convex toward the origin.
110.67
100.00
90.79
Price falls at a decreasing rate as yields increase.
YTM
7%
8%
9%
© Kaplan, Inc.
47

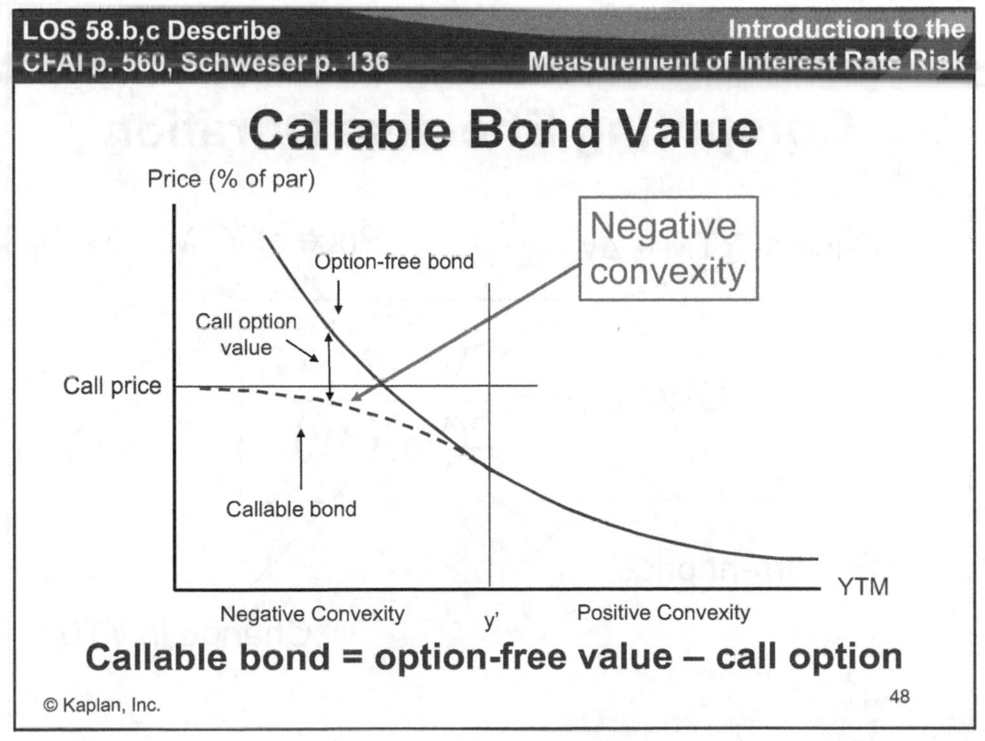
LOS 58.b,c Describe
CFAI p. 560, Schweser p. 136
Introduction to the
Measurement of Interest Rate Risk
Callable Bond Value
Price (% of par)
Negative convexity
Option-free bond
Call option value
Call price
Callable bond
YTM
Negative Convexity
y'
Positive Convexity
Callable bond = option-free value – call option
© Kaplan, Inc.
48

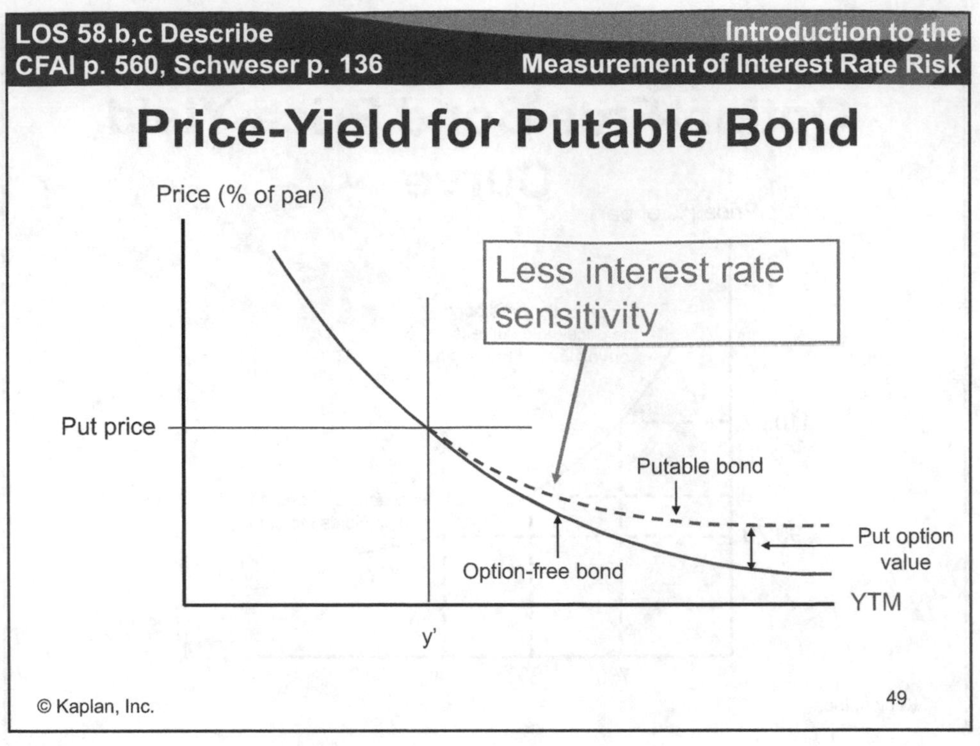
LOS 58.b,c Describe
CFAI p. 560, Schweser p. 136
Introduction to the
Measurement of Interest Rate Risk
Price-Yield for Putable Bond
Price (% of par)
Less interest rate sensitivity
Put price
Putable bond
Put option value
Option-free bond
YTM
y'
© Kaplan, Inc.
49

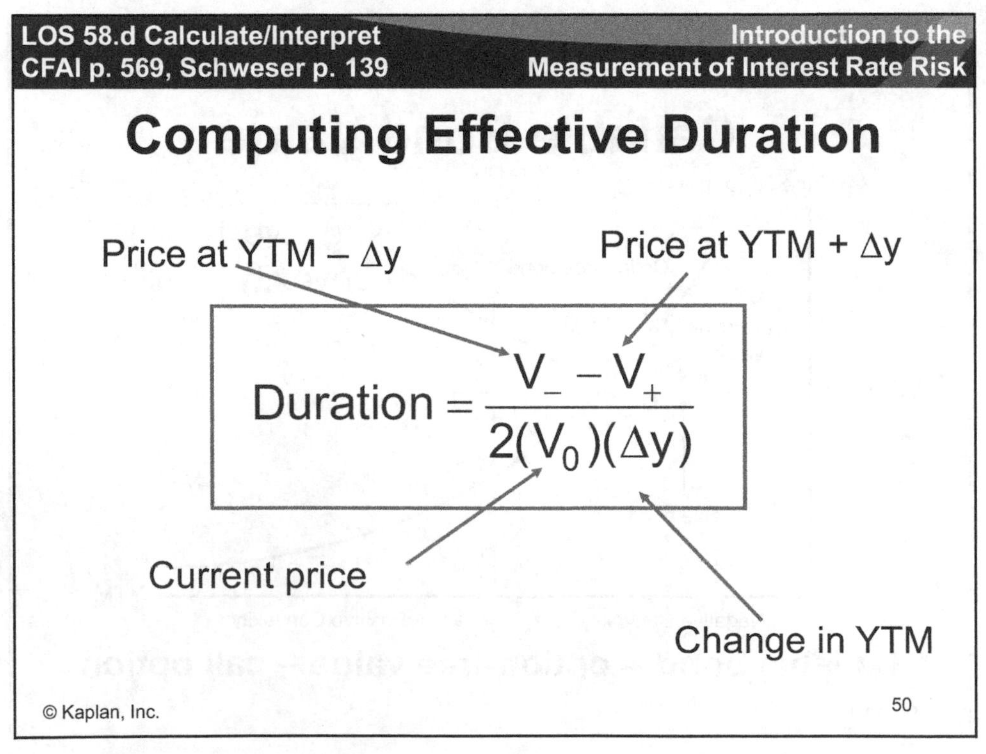
LOS 58.d Calculate/Interpret
CFAI p. 569, Schweser p. 139
Introduction to the
Measurement of Interest Rate Risk
Computing Effective Duration
Price at YTM – Δy
Price at YTM + Δy
$\text{Duration} = \dfrac{V_- - V_+}{2(V_0)(\Delta y)}$
Current price
Change in YTM
© Kaplan, Inc.
50

LOS 58.d Calculate/Interpret
CFAI p. 569, Schweser p. 139

Introduction to the Measurement of Interest Rate Risk

Effective Duration Example

A 15-year, option-free bond, annual 8% coupon, trading at par, 100. Calculate effective duration based on:

Interest rates ↑ 50 bp, new price is 95.848

Interest rates ↓ 50 bp, new price is 104.414

Effective duration is:

$$\frac{104.414 - 95.848}{2 \times 100 \times 0.005} = 8.57$$

V_- (104.414); V_+ (95.848); current price (100); 50 basis points (0.005)

51-2

LOS 58.e Calculate
CFAI p. 570, Schweser p. 141

Introduction to the Measurement of Interest Rate Risk

Using Duration

Our 8%, 15-year par bond has a duration of 8.57

Duration effect = –D × Δy

If YTM *increases* 0.3% or 30 bp, bond price decreases by approximately:

–8.57 × 0.3% = –2.57%

52-1

LOS 58.f Distinguish/Explain
CFAI p. 576, Schweser p. 142

Introduction to the Measurement of Interest Rate Risk

Duration Measures

- **Macaulay duration** is in years
  - Duration of a 5-year, zero-coupon bond is 5
  - 1% change in yield, 5% change in price
- **Modified duration** adjusts Macaulay duration for market yield, yield up → duration down
- **Effective duration** allows for cash flow changes as yield changes, must be used for bonds with embedded options

53

LOS 58.f Distinguish/Explain
CFAI p. 576, Schweser p. 142

Introduction to the Measurement of Interest Rate Risk

Effective Duration

- Both Macaulay duration and modified duration are based on the promised cash flows and ignore call, put, and prepayment options
- **Effective duration** can be calculated using prices from a valuation model that includes the effects of **embedded options** (e.g., call feature)
- For option-free bonds, effective duration is very close to modified duration
- For bonds with **embedded options**, effective duration **must** be used

54

LOS 58.f Distinguish/Explain
CFAI p. 576, Schweser p. 142

Introduction to the
Measurement of Interest Rate Risk

Duration Interpretation

- Present value-weighted average of the number of years until coupon and principal cash flows are to be received
- Slope of the price-yield curve (i.e., first derivative of the price-yield function with respect to yield)
- Approximate percentage price change for a 1% change in YTM: The **best** interpretation!

LOS 58.g Calculate/Explain
CFAI p. 580, Schweser p. 144

Introduction to the
Measurement of Interest Rate Risk

Bond Portfolio Duration

- Duration of a portfolio of bonds is a portfolio value-weighted average of the durations of the individual bonds

$$D_P = W_1D_1 + W_2D_2 + \ldots\ldots + W_nD_n$$

- Problems arise because the YTM does not change equally for every bond in the portfolio

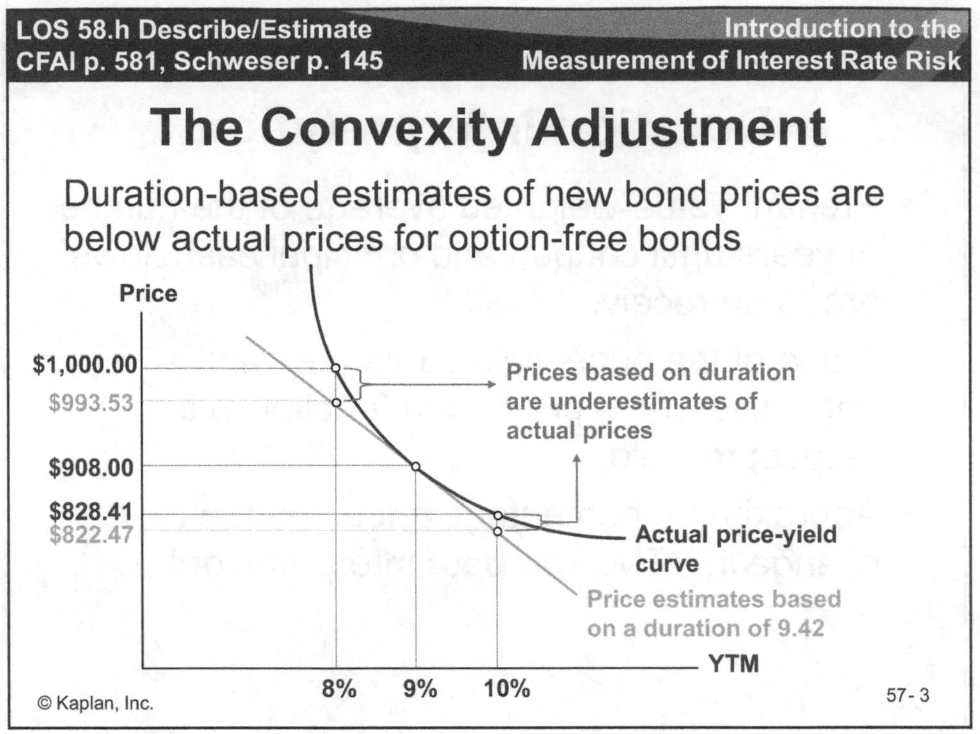

LOS 58.h Describe/Estimate
CFAI p. 581, Schweser p. 145

Introduction to the
Measurement of Interest Rate Risk

Convexity Adjustment

- Recall our 8%, 15-year par bond with duration = 8.57
- For a 50 bp change in yield, price change based on duration is: **8.57 × 0.5% = 4.285%**
- **Actual increase when YTM ↓ 0.5% = 4.457%**
- **Actual decrease when YTM ↑ 0.5% = –4.195%**
- Increase underestimated, decrease overestimated

58

LOS 58.h Describe/Estimate
CFAI p. 581, Schweser p. 145

Introduction to the Measurement of Interest Rate Risk

Convexity Effect

To adjust for the for the curvature of the bond price-yield relation, use the convexity effect:

+ Convexity $(\Delta y)^2$

Assume convexity of the bond = 52.4

Convexity $(\Delta y)^2 = 52.4(0.005)^2 = 0.00131$

$\Delta y = 0.5\%$

So our convexity adjustment is +0.131% for a yield increase **or** for a yield decrease

59

LOS 58.h Describe/Estimate
CFAI p. 581, Schweser p. 145

Introduction to the Measurement of Interest Rate Risk

Duration-Convexity Estimates

For a yield decrease of 0.5%, we have:

$-8.57\ (-0.005) + 52.4\ (-0.005)^2 = +4.416\%$

Duration only = +4.285% **Actual = +4.457%**

For a yield increase of 0.5%, we have:

$-8.57\ (0.005) + 52.4\ (0.005)^2 = -4.154\%$

Duration only = –4.285% **Actual = –4.195%**

Convexity adjustment improved both estimates!

60

LOS 58.i Distinguish
CFAI p. 584, Schweser p. 147

Introduction to the Measurement of Interest Rate Risk

Modified and Effective Convexity

- Like modified duration, **modified convexity** assumes expected cash flows do not change when yield changes
- **Effective convexity** takes into account changes in cash flows due to embedded options, while modified convexity does not
- The difference between modified convexity and effective convexity mirrors the difference between modified duration and effective duration

61

LOS 58.j Calculate/Explain
CFAI p. 584, Schweser p. 147

Introduction to the Measurement of Interest Rate Risk

Price Value of a Basis Point

- A measure of interest rate risk often used with portfolios is the **price value of a basis point**
- PVBP is the change in $ value for a 0.01% change in yield
- Duration × 0.0001 × portfolio value = PVBP

  Example: A bond portfolio has a duration of 5.6 and value of $900,000

  PVBP = 5.6 × 0.0001 × $900,000 = $504

62

LOS 58.k Describe
CFAI p. 585, Schweser p. 148

Introduction to the Measurement of Interest Rate Risk

Impact of Yield Volatility

- Combine **duration** with **yield volatility** to analyze interest rate risk
- Bond with lower duration can have greater price sensitivity to interest rate changes than a bond with higher duration, if its yield volatility is significantly greater
- **Value-at-risk** considers both duration and yield volatility

63

Introduction to the Measurement of Interest Rate Risk

Effective Duration – Problem

If YTM increases by 0.5%, a 5% par bond will decrease in price to 95.5, and if YTM decreases by 0.5% the price will increase to 105.3. The effective duration is:

A. 9.0.

B. 9.8.

C. 4.5.

64 - 2

Introduction to the Measurement of Interest Rate Risk

Duration and Convexity – Problem

Bond has a modified duration of 7.8 and a convexity of 140. If its yield to maturity increases by 80 bp, the approximate change in price is:

A. –6.24%.

B. –7.14%.

C. –5.34%.

65 - 2

Fixed Income: Analysis and Valuation

59. Fundamentals of Credit Analysis

Fixed Income Investments

LOS 59.a Describe
CFAI p. 606, Schweser p. 157

Fundamentals of Credit Analysis

Credit-Related Risks

- **Credit risk:** Risk of losses if borrower fails to pay interest or principal
  - **Default risk:** Probability of default
  - **Loss severity:** Amount or percentage of principal and interest lost if borrower defaults
- **Expected loss = default risk × loss severity**
- **Recovery rate** = 1 – loss severity in %

67

LOS 59.a Describe
CFAI p. 606, Schweser p. 157

Fundamentals of Credit Analysis

Credit-Related Risks

- **Yield spread** (in basis points) quoted relative to default risk-free bond of similar maturity
  - Wider spread → lower price; narrower spread → higher price
- **Spread risk:** Risk of spread widening
  - **Credit migration (downgrade) risk:** Issuer becomes less creditworthy
  - **Market liquidity risk:** Receive less than market value when selling bond

68

LOS 59.b Describe/Explain
CFAI p. 609, Schweser p. 158

Fundamentals of Credit Analysis

Seniority Ranking

- Different bonds from same issuer may have different **seniority** or priority of claims
  - First lien/mortgage > second lien/mortgage
  - Secured > unsecured
  - Senior > junior > subordinated
  - Issues may combine these features
    Example: senior secured > junior secured
- All debt in same category ranks **pari passu** (with same priority of claims)

69

LOS 59.b Describe/Explain
CFAI p. 609, Schweser p. 158

Fundamentals of Credit Analysis

Priority of Claims in Bankruptcy

- Priority of claims is not always followed strictly in bankruptcy
  - Creditors may negotiate different outcome to limit delays and bankruptcy-related costs to issuing firm
  - Bankruptcy court may order different outcome

70

LOS 59.c Distinguish/Describe
CFAI p. 616, Schweser p. 159

Fundamentals of Credit Analysis

Credit Ratings

- **Rating agencies:** Moody's, S&P, Fitch
- **Corporate family rating (CFR):** Issuer credit rating, applies to senior unsecured debt
- **Corporate credit rating (CCR):** Applies to specific debt issue; may be **notched** up or down from CFR

71

LOS 59.c Distinguish/Describe
CFAI p. 616, Schweser p. 159

Fundamentals of Credit Analysis

Credit Ratings

Investment Grade		Non-Investment Grade			
Moody's	**S&P, Fitch**	**Moody's**	**S&P, Fitch**	**Moody's**	**S&P, Fitch**
Aaa	AAA	Ba1	BB+	Caa1	CCC+
Aa1	AA+	Ba2	BB	Caa2	CCC
Aa2	AA	Ba3	BB–	Caa3	CCC–
Aa3	AA–	B1	B+	Ca	CC
A1	A+	B2	B	C	C
A2	A	B3	B–	C	D
A3	A–				
Baa1	BBB+				
Baa2	BBB				
Baa3	BBB–				

In default (C and D)

72

Fundamentals of Credit Analysis

Credit Ratings – Problem

Topper, Inc. has a CFR of Ba2. Topper's subordinated debentures are *least likely* to be rated:

A. Ba1.

B. Ba2.

C. Ba3.

73-2

LOS 59.d Explain
CFAI p. 618, Schweser p. 160

Fundamentals of Credit Analysis

Risks in Relying on Credit Ratings

- Credit rating may change: Downgrade, upgrade
- Rating agencies make mistakes (subprime mortgages)
- Issuer-specific risks may be unpredictable (litigation, natural disasters, leveraged buyouts)
- Prices/spreads adjust faster than credit ratings
  - Ratings assess default risk
  - Spreads reflect expected loss

74

LOS 59.e Explain
CFAI p. 623, Schweser p. 161

Fundamentals of Credit Analysis

Components of Credit Analysis

- **Four Cs: Capacity, Collateral, Covenants, Character**
  - Capacity: Ability to pay on time and in full
  - Collateral: Value of assets
  - Covenants: Legal stipulations of bond issue
  - Character: Management integrity

75

LOS 59.e Explain
CFAI p. 623, Schweser p. 161

Fundamentals of Credit Analysis

Capacity

- **Industry structure**
  - Rivalry, new entrants, substitute products, supplier power, buyer power
- **Industry fundamentals**
  - Growth prospects, cyclicality
- **Company fundamentals**
  - Competitive position, operating history, strategy/execution
  - Leverage and coverage ratios

Also covered in Equity Valuation

76

LOS 59.e Explain
CFAI p. 623, Schweser p. 161

Fundamentals of Credit Analysis

Collateral

- Examine **depreciation expense:** High relative to capital spending may imply insufficient investment, low quality assets
- **Stock price < book value** may also indicate low quality assets
- Intangible assets that **can be sold** (patents, intellectual property) may have value as collateral

77

LOS 59.e Explain
CFAI p. 623, Schweser p. 161

Fundamentals of Credit Analysis

Covenants

- Affirmative: Actions issuer must take (pay interest and principal on time, insure pledged assets, pay taxes)
- Negative: Actions issuer may not take (issue more debt, pledge same assets)
- Goal is to protect bondholders without unduly constraining firm's operations

 78

LOS 59.e Explain
CFAI p. 623, Schweser p. 161

Fundamentals of Credit Analysis

Character

- Management ability to develop sound strategy
- Management's past performance: Bankruptcies, restructurings
- Accounting policies: Aggressiveness, frequent restatements
- Fraud or other legal problems
- Actions that favor equity holders over bondholders (e.g., special dividends)

 79

LOS 59.f Calculate/Interpret
CFAI p. 628, Schweser p. 163

Fundamentals of Credit Analysis

Financial Ratios in Credit Analysis

- Credit analysts focus on **leverage ratios** and **coverage ratios**
- Profit and cash flow metrics:
  - EBITDA, EBIT
  - Funds from operations
  - Free cash flow before/after dividends

80

LOS 59.f Calculate/Interpret
CFAI p. 628, Schweser p. 163

Fundamentals of Credit Analysis

Leverage Ratios

- Higher leverage → higher credit risk
- Adjust debt to include all obligations (underfunded pensions, off-balance-sheet liabilities, DTLs expected to reverse)
- **Debt-to-capital, debt-to-EBITDA:**
  - Higher ratio → higher leverage
  - May adjust capital for writedown of goodwill
- **FFO-to-debt:** Higher ratio → lower leverage

81

LOS 59.f Calculate/Interpret
CFAI p. 628, Schweser p. 163

Fundamentals of Credit Analysis

Coverage Ratios

- Measures earnings relative to interest obligations
- Higher coverage → lower credit risk
  - **EBITDA-to-interest expense**
  - **EBIT-to-interest expense:** More conservative

82

LOS 59.g Evaluate
CFAI p. 631, Schweser p. 167

Fundamentals of Credit Analysis

Example: Credit Quality

	York, Inc.	Zale, Inc.	Industry Average
EBIT	$550	$2,250	$1,400
FFO	$300	$850	$600
Interest expense	$40	$160	$100
Total debt	$1,000	$2,500	$2,400
Total capital	$4,000	$6,500	$6,000

- York has goodwill of $500 and operating lease obligations with a present value of $900
- Zale has a net pension liability of $200 and no operating leases
- Industry averages are goodwill $200, PV of operating leases $200, and no net pension asset or liability

83

LOS 59.g Evaluate
CFAI p. 631, Schweser p. 167

Fundamentals of Credit Analysis

Example: Credit Quality

Recommended analyst adjustments:

- Include operating lease obligations, net pension liabilities in total debt
- Calculate debt-to-capital ratios with and without goodwill

	York, Inc.	Zale, Inc.	Industry Average
EBIT	$550	$1,800	$1,400
FFO	$300	$800	$600
Interest expense	$40	$160	$100
Total debt	$1,900	$2,700	$2,600
Total capital	$4,000 ($3,500)	$6,500	$6,000 ($5,800)

84

LOS 59.g Evaluate
CFAI p. 631, Schweser p. 167

Fundamentals of Credit Analysis

Example: Credit Quality

	York, Inc.	Zale, Inc.	Industry Average
EBIT / interest	13.8×	14.1×	14.0×
FFO / debt	15.8%	29.6%	23.1%
Debt / capital	47.5% (54.3%)	41.5%	43.3% (44.8%)

- York and Zale have interest coverage (EBIT / interest) in line with their industry average
- Adjusting for all obligations, York is more leveraged (lower FFO/debt, higher debt/capital) then Zale and the industry average; Zale is less leveraged than the industry average
- Therefore, Zale appears more creditworthy then York

85

LOS 59.h Describe
CFAI p. 642, Schweser p. 169

Fundamentals of Credit Analysis

Yield Spreads: Level and Volatility

- Yield spread = credit spread + liquidity premium
- Tend to be more volatile for lower-quality bonds than for higher-quality bonds
- Factors affecting yield spreads:
  - Credit cycle
  - Economic conditions
  - Market performance, including equities
  - Broker/dealer capital
  - Supply of new issues

86

LOS 59.i Calculate
CFAI p. 646, Schweser p. 169

Fundamentals of Credit Analysis

Return Impact of Spread Changes

- Return impact = percent change in price
- For option-free bonds:

$$\text{Return impact} \approx -\text{Modified Duration} \times \Delta\text{Spread} + 1/2 \times \text{Convexity} \times (\Delta\text{Spread})^2$$

- Scale convexity based on <u>duration squared</u>
  - Duration = 4, Convexity = 21.8: Okay
  - Duration = 5, Convexity = 0.327: Adjust convexity to 32.7

87

Fundamentals of Credit Analysis

Return Impact – Problem

A bond with a duration of 6.5 has an estimated convexity of 0.634. If the bond's yield spread widens by 50 basis points, the impact on the investor's return is *closest* to:

A. –3.17%.

B. –3.25%.

C. –3.33%.

88-2

LOS 59.j Explain
CFAI p. 650, Schweser p. 172

Fundamentals of Credit Analysis

High Yield Bonds

- Higher default risk than investment grade → Increase focus on <u>loss severity</u>
- Sources of **liquidity:**
  - Balance sheet cash (most reliable)
  - Working capital
  - Cash flow from operations
  - Bank credit
  - Equity issuance
  - Asset sales (least reliable)

89

LOS 59.j Explain
CFAI p. 650, Schweser p. 172

Fundamentals of Credit Analysis

High Yield Bonds

- Project **future earnings and cash flows**, including stress scenarios
- Analyze **debt structure**
  - Estimate leverage, loss severity for each level of seniority
  - Top-heavy capital structure: High proportion of secured bank debt → less ability to increase borrowing in stress scenario → higher default probability, lower recovery rate for unsecured

90

LOS 59.j Explain
CFAI p. 650, Schweser p. 172

Fundamentals of Credit Analysis

High Yield Bonds

- Analyze **corporate structure**
  - Debt may be issued by holding company, intermediate holding companies, subsidiaries
  - **Structural subordination:** Subsidiaries must service own debt before upstreaming dividends to parent → Holding company debt is effectively subordinated to subsidiary debt

91

LOS 59.j Explain
CFAI p. 650, Schweser p. 172

Fundamentals of Credit Analysis

High Yield Bonds

- Analyze **covenants**
  - **Change of control put:** Bondholder may put bond back to issuer if issuer is acquired
  - **Restricted subsidiaries:** Designated to support holding company debt (no structural subordination)
  - **Limitation on liens:** Limits amount of secured debt
  - **Restricted payments** to equity holders

92

LOS 59.j Explain
CFAI p. 650, Schweser p. 172

Fundamentals of Credit Analysis

Sovereign Bonds

- Issued by national governments (sovereigns)
- Analyze **ability** and **willingness** to pay debts
  - Bondholders have no means of forcing an unwilling sovereign to pay its debts
- Bonds may be denominated in **local currency** or **foreign currency**
  - Higher default risk (lower credit rating) for foreign currency debt because government must acquire foreign currency

93

LOS 59.j Explain
CFAI p. 650, Schweser p. 172

Fundamentals of Credit Analysis

Analysis of Sovereign Bonds

- **Institutional effectiveness:** Commitment to repay debts
- **Economic prospects:** Growth rate; per-capita income; demographics
- **International investment position:** Forex reserves, external debt
- **Fiscal flexibility:** Ability, willingness to increase taxes, decrease spending to service debts
- **Monetary flexibility:** Central bank credibility; ability to pursue domestic objectives

94

LOS 59.j Explain
CFAI p. 650, Schweser p. 172

Fundamentals of Credit Analysis

Municipal Bonds

- Issued by governments or agencies below national level (not sovereigns)
- **General obligation:** Full faith and credit of municipality
- **Revenue bonds:** Serviced by revenues from project financed by bonds

95

LOS 59.j Explain
CFAI p. 650, Schweser p. 172

Fundamentals of Credit Analysis

Analysis of Municipal Bonds

- **General obligation bonds**
  - Tax revenue depends on local economy: analyze employment, per-capita income, depth and breadth of tax base
  - Sales taxes, capital gains taxes are cyclical
  - Long-term obligations (e.g., pensions)
  - Inconsistent financial reporting requirements
- **Revenue bonds**: Analyze project
  - Debt service coverage: Revenue / payments

96

Introduction to the Valuation of Debt Securities

Value Change as Time Passes Solution

A 6%, 10-year semiannual coupon bond has a YTM of 8%

1. What is the price of the bond?

   N = 20, PMT = –30, FV = –1,000, I/Y = 4% **PV = 864.10**

2. What is the value after 1 year if the yield does not change?

   N = 18, PMT = –30, FV = –1,000, I/Y = 4% **PV = 873.41**

3. What is the value after 2 years if the yield does not change?

   N = 16, PMT = –30, FV = –1,000, I/Y = 4% **PV = 883.48**

Yield Measures, Spot Rates, and Forward Rates

Equivalent Yields – Solution

An annual pay bond has a YTM of 14%.
The BEY for this bond is:

A. 13.54%.

$$2(\sqrt{1.14}-1)=0.1354$$

Yield Measures, Spot Rates, and Forward Rates

Yield Measures – Solution

For a bond trading at a premium, order the coupon (nominal) yield, current yield, and YTM from smallest to largest.

$$\text{Current yield} = \frac{\text{Annual coupon}}{\text{Bond price}}$$

for premium bond, price > par

Current yield is less than coupon (nominal) yield

YTM is less than current yield for premium bond (movement towards par is negative)

Yield Measures, Spot Rates, and Forward Rates

Yield to Call – Solution

Consider a 10-year, 5% bond priced at $1,028 What is the YTM?

N = 20 PMT = 25 FV = 1,000 PV = –1,028
CPT → I/Y = 2.323% × 2 = **4.646% = YTM**

If it is callable in two years at 101, what is the YTC?

N = 4 PMT = 25 FV = 1,010 PV = –1,028
CPT → I/Y = 2.007% × 2 = **4.014% = YTC**

Yield Measures, Spot Rates, and Forward Rates

Forward Rates – Solution

Current 1-year spot rate is 6%, 2-year spot rate is 7%, and 3-year spot rate is 6%. The 1-year forward rate for a loan 2 years from now is *closest* to:

C. 4%.

$$\frac{1.06^3}{1.07^2} - 1 = 0.04028 = 4.028\%$$

$$3 \times 6 - 2 \times 7 = 18 - 14 = 4$$

Introduction to the Measurement of Interest Rate Risk

Effective Duration – Solution

If YTM increases by 0.5%, a 5% par bond will decrease in price to 95.5, and if YTM decreases by 0.5% the price will increase to 105.3. The effective duration is:

B. 9.8.

$$\frac{105.3-95.5}{2(100)(0.005)}=9.8$$

Introduction to the Measurement of Interest Rate Risk

Duration and Convexity – Solution

Bond has a modified duration of 7.8 and a convexity of 140. If its yield to maturity increases by 80 bp, the approximate change in price is:

C. –5.34%.

$$-7.8(0.0080)+140(0.0080)^2 =$$
$$-0.0624+0.00896=-5.344\%$$

Credit Ratings – Solution

Topper, Inc. has a CFR of Ba2. Topper's subordinated debentures are *least likely* to be rated:

A. Ba1.

CFR reflects senior unsecured debt

If debt with lower seniority is notched, it will be notched downward

Return Impact – Solution

A bond with a duration of 6.5 has an estimated convexity of 0.634. If the bond's yield spread widens by 50 basis points, the impact on the investor's return is *closest* to:

A. –3.17%.

$$-6.5(0.0050) + 1/2\ (63.4)(0.0050)^2 = \mathbf{-3.17\%}$$

Study Session 17

Derivatives

Derivatives

60. Derivative Markets and Instruments

LOS 60.a Define/Distinguish
CFAI p. 5, Schweser p. 191

Derivative Markets and Instruments

Derivatives

- A **derivative security** derives its value from the price of another (underlying) asset or an interest rate
- **Futures and some options** are traded on organized exchanges
- **Forward contracts, swaps, and some options** are custom instruments created by dealers

2

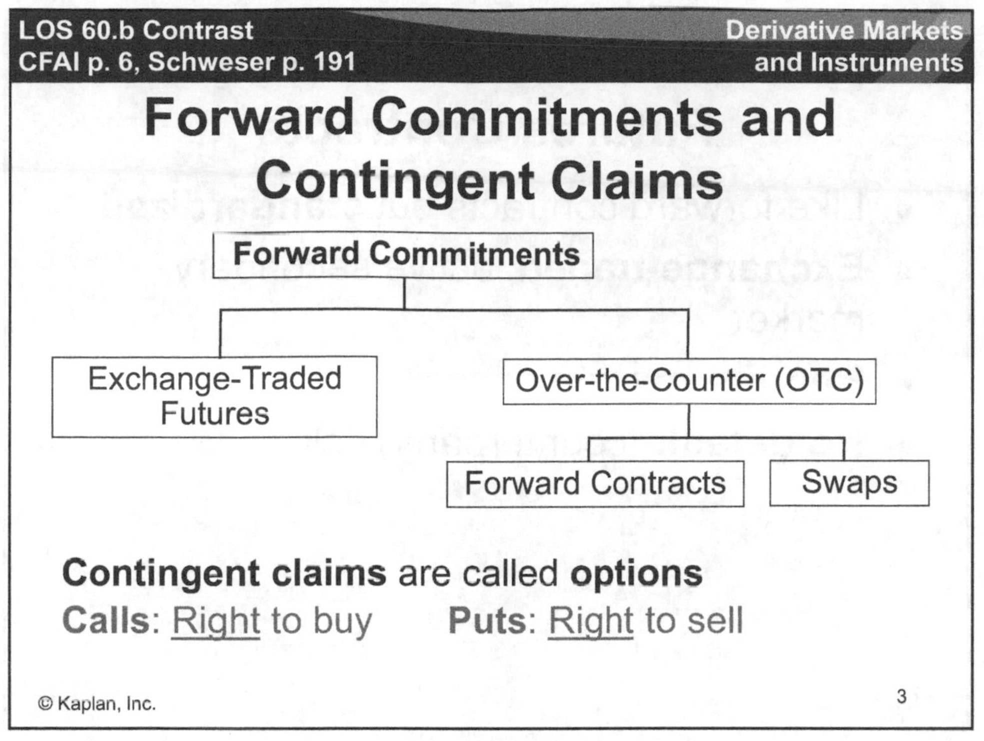

LOS 60.c Define/Compare
CFAI p. 6, Schweser p. 192

Derivative Markets and Instruments

Forward Contracts

- Customized: No active secondary market
- Long obligated to buy; short obligated to sell
- Specified asset (currency, stock, index, bond)
- Specified date in the future
- Long gains if asset price above forward price
- Short gains if asset price below forward price

4

LOS 60.c Define/Compare
CFAI p. 6, Schweser p. 192

Derivative Markets and Instruments

Futures Contracts

- Like forward contracts but **standardized**
- **Exchange-traded**, active secondary market
- **Require margin** deposit
- **No default** (counterparty) risk

5

LOS 60.c Define/Compare
CFAI p. 6, Schweser p. 192

Derivative Markets and Instruments

Swaps

- Equivalent to a series of forward contracts
- Simple interest rate swap
  - One party pays a fixed rate of interest
  - One party pays a variable (floating) rate of interest
- Payments can be based on interest rates or stock/portfolio/index returns
- Can involve two different currencies

6

LOS 60.d Describe
CFAI p. 17, Schweser p. 192

Derivative Markets and Instruments

Purposes and Criticisms of Derivatives

- Derivatives are criticized as being risky and likened to gambling
- Benefits of derivatives markets
  - Provide price information
  - Lower transactions costs
  - Allow the transfer of risk

 7

LOS 60.e Explain
CFAI p. 20, Schweser p. 193

Derivative Markets and Instruments

Role of Arbitrage

- Arbitrage is possible when two securities or portfolios have **identical future payoffs** but **different market prices**
- Trading by arbitrageurs will continue until they affect supply and demand enough to bring asset prices to efficient (no-arbitrage) levels

Arbitrage relations are used to value derivatives

 8

Derivatives

61. Forward Markets and Contracts

Derivatives

LOS 61.a Explain
CFAI p. 28, Schweser p. 197

Forward Markets and Contracts

Forward Contract Positions

Long position (will buy)

The party to the forward contract that agrees to buy the underlying financial or physical asset

Short position (will sell)

The party to the forward contract that agrees to sell/deliver the asset

Neither party pays at contract initiation

10

LOS 61.b Describe
CFAI p. 29, Schweser p. 198 Forward Markets and Contracts

Forward Contract Settlement

- **Delivery**: Short delivers underlying to long for payment of the forward price
- **Cash settlement**: Negative side of contract pays the positive side

 11

LOS 61.b Describe
CFAI p. 29, Schweser p. 198 Forward Markets and Contracts

Early Termination of Forward

1. One party pays the other cash (buys their way out)
2. Enter into an offsetting contract
   - With a different counterparty (default risk still exists)
   - With same (original) counterparty (no default risk)

 12

LOS 61.c Distinguish
CFAI p. 30, Schweser p. 199 Forward Markets and Contracts

Dealers and End Users of Forwards

- A dealer creates a derivative contract and will quote a price to take a long or short position
- An end user is typically a corporation or institution seeking to transfer an existing risk

 13

LOS 61.d Describe
CFAI p. 32, Schweser p. 200 Forward Markets and Contracts

Equity Forward Contract

Can be on a stock, a portfolio, or an equity index

Example: Forward contract to buy 10,000 shares of Acme Industries common stock in 90 days for $128,000 (i.e., $12.80 per share)

An **index contract** payoff is the **notional amount** times the **percentage difference** between the forward index and the actual index value at settlement

 14

Forward Markets and Contracts

Equity Index Forward – Problem

- 90-day S&P 100 forward contract
- Forward contract price = 525.2
- Notional amount = $10 million
- In 90 days, index is at 535.7

What is the payment at settlement and which party receives it?

15 - 1

LOS 61.d Describe
CFAI p. 32, Schweser p. 200 Forward Markets and Contracts

Forward on Zero-Coupon Bond

Example: 100 day, T-bill forward
Underlying: $10 million T-bill
Forward price: $9,945,560 (1.96% discount)

- If interest rates rise, P↓, long loses/short gains
- If interest rates fall, P↑, long gains/short loses

Coupon bonds: Priced at YTM; same principle
Risky bonds: Must provide for default possibility

16

LOS 61.e Describe/Define
CFAI p. 36, Schweser p. 202 Forward Markets and Contracts

LIBOR-Based Loan Example

Loan value = $1.0 million

Term = 30 days

30-day LIBOR = 6%

Interest payment
= $1,000,000 (0.06) (30 / 360) = $5,000

Total payment in 30 days
= $1,000,000 + $5,000 = $1,005,000

 17

LOS 61.f Describe/Calculate
CFAI p. 35, Schweser p. 203 Forward Markets and Contracts

Forward Rate Agreement (FRA)

Exchange fixed-rate for floating-rate payment

- Notional amount
- Fixed rate = forward (contract) rate
- Floating rate (LIBOR) is underlying rate
- Long gains when LIBOR > contract rate

 18

LOS 61.f Describe/Calculate
CFAI p. 35, Schweser p. 203 Forward Markets and Contracts

Forward Rate Agreement (FRA)

- Long position can be viewed as the **obligation to *take* a (hypothetical) loan** at the contract rate (i.e., borrow at the fixed rate); gains when reference rate ↑
- Short position can be viewed as the **obligation to *make* a (hypothetical) loan** at the contract rate (i.e., lend at the contract rate); gains when reference rate ↓

 19

LOS 61.g Calculate/Interpret/Explain
CFAI p. 37, Schweser p. 203 Forward Markets and Contracts

FRA Example

Term = 30 days
Notional amount = $1 million
Underlying rate = 90-day LIBOR
Forward rate = 5%
At t = 30 days, 90-day LIBOR = 6%
Underlying floating rate > fixed rate
→ Long position receives payment

 20

LOS 61.g Calculate/Interpret/Explain
CFAI p. 37, Schweser p. 203 Forward Markets and Contracts

FRA Example: Net Payment

Net payment due to the long 90 days after contract settlement:

$$(0.06-0.05)\times\left(\frac{90}{360}\right)\times 1{,}000{,}000=\$2{,}500$$

Payment at settlement:

$$\frac{\$2{,}500}{1+\left(0.06\times\frac{90}{360}\right)}=\$2{,}463.05$$

PV of interest savings

 21

LOS 61.g Calculate/Interpret/Explain
CFAI p. 37, Schweser p. 203 Forward Markets and Contracts

FRA Settlement Payment to Long

$$\frac{\text{Notional principal}\times(\text{Floating}-\text{Forward})\left(\frac{\text{Days}}{360}\right)}{1+\text{Floating}\left(\frac{\text{Days}}{360}\right)}$$

Days = number of days in floating rate term

 22

LOS 61.h Describe
CFAI p. 38, Schweser p. 205

Forward Markets and Contracts

Currency Forward Contracts

- Currency forward contracts are commitments to buy or sell a certain amount of a foreign currency for a fixed amount of another currency in the future
- As with other forwards, cash settlement is the amount necessary to compensate the party who would be disadvantaged by the actual change in market rates as of the settlement date

23

Derivatives

62. Futures Markets and Contracts

Derivatives

LOS 62.a Describe
CFAI p. 43, Schweser p. 213
Futures Markets and Contracts

Futures Characteristics

- **Contract specifies**: Quality and quantity of good, delivery time, manner of delivery
- **Exchange specifies**: Minimum price fluctuation (tick), daily price limit
- Clearinghouse holds other side of each trade
- Margin posted and marked to market daily
- Margin is a performance guarantee, not a loan
- Long buys and short sells the future

25

LOS 62.b Compare
CFAI p. 43, Schweser p. 213 Futures Markets and Contracts

Forwards vs. Futures

Forwards
- Private contracts
- Unique contracts
- Default risk present
- No margin
- Little regulation

Futures
- Exchange-traded
- Standardized
- Guaranteed by clearinghouse
- Margin required
- Regulated

 26

LOS 62.c Distinguish/Explain
CFAI p. 48, Schweser p. 214 Futures Markets and Contracts

Futures Margin Terms

- **Initial margin**: Deposited before trade occurs
- **Maintenance margin**: Minimum margin that must be maintained in a futures account
- **Variation margin**: Funds needed to restore futures account to initial margin amount
- **Settlement price**: Average of trades during closing period, used to calculate margin

 27

LOS 62.c Distinguish/Explain
CFAI p. 48, Schweser p. 214 Futures Markets and Contracts

A Futures Trade

- July wheat futures call for delivery of 5,000 bu. of wheat in July, futures price is \$2 per bushel. Contract value is 5,000 × \$2 = \$10,000.
- Long **obligated to buy** 5,000 bu. in July at \$2
- Short **obligated to sell** 5,000 bu. in July at \$2
- Both the long and short post same margin amount
- If future price > \$2 long gains, < \$2 short gains

 28

LOS 62.d Describe/Calculate/Interpret
CFAI p. 48, Schweser p. 216 Futures Markets and Contracts

Price Limits

Price limits: Exchange-imposed limits on how much the contract price can change from the previous day's settlement price

- Exchange members prohibited from executing trades at prices outside these limits
- If the new equilibrium price (at which traders would willingly trade) is above the upper limit or below the lower limit, trades cannot take place

 29

LOS 62.d Describe/Calculate/Interpret
CFAI p. 48, Schweser p. 216 Futures Markets and Contracts

Marking-to-Market

- **Marking-to-market** is the process of adjusting margin balance in a futures account **each day** for the change in the futures price (add gains, subtract losses)
- The futures exchanges can require a mark-to-market more frequently (than daily) under extraordinary circumstances (increased volatility)

 30

LOS 62.d Describe/Calculate/Interpret
CFAI p. 48, Schweser p. 216 Futures Markets and Contracts

Margin Calculation Example

- Long five July wheat contracts
- Size = 5,000 bushels
- Futures price = \$2.00/bu
- Initial margin deposit = \$150 per contract
- Maintenance margin = \$100 per contract

Total initial margin = 5 × \$150 = \$750
Total maintenance margin = 5 × \$100 = \$500

 31

LOS 62.d Describe/Calculate/Interpret
CFAI p. 48, Schweser p. 216 Futures Markets and Contracts

Margin Calculation Example (cont.)

- Each **change of $0.01** in the futures price leads to a change of 5,000 × $0.01 = **$50 per contract** in the margin account
- On the **five contracts** in our example, a $0.01 increase in the July wheat futures price will **increase the long's margin by $250** and decrease the margin balance in the short's account by $250

 32

LOS 62.d Describe/Calculate/Interpret
CFAI p. 48, Schweser p. 216 Futures Markets and Contracts

Margin Calculation Example (cont.)

Day	Required Deposit	Price/bu.	Daily Δ	Gain (+) Loss (–)	Balance
0	$750	$2.00		0	$750
1	0	$1.98	–$0.02	–$500	$250
2	$500	$1.99	+$0.01	$250	$1,000
3	0	$1.98	–$0.01	–$250	$750

 33

LOS 62.e Describe
CFAI p. 53, Schweser p. 218 Futures Markets and Contracts

Methods to Terminate a Futures Position at Expiration

- **Reversal** (offsetting trade): Common
- **Delivery of asset** (< 1% of trades)
- **Cash settlement**: May be required
- **Exchange for physicals**: Off exchange

 34

LOS 62.e Describe
CFAI p. 53, Schweser p. 218 Futures Markets and Contracts

Closing a Futures Trade by Offset

- Most futures contracts **closed prior to the expiration** or delivery date
- For example, the long position in July wheat can be **closed out by taking an equal short position** in July wheat
- The futures price when the trade is closed out determines gains or losses on the trade

 35

LOS 62.e Describe
CFAI p. 53, Schweser p. 218 Futures Markets and Contracts

Futures Contract Delivery Options

- T-bond futures
  - **What** to deliver: Which bonds to deliver
  - **When** to deliver: Date during expiration month
- Commodities: **Where** to deliver; location
- Delivery option is valuable to **short**

 36

LOS 62.f Describe
CFAI p. 57, Schweser p. 219 Futures Markets and Contracts

Eurodollar Futures

- Based on 90-day LIBOR
- Add-on yield, rather than a discount yield
- By convention, price quotes are calculated as (100 – annualized LIBOR in percent)
- Contracts settle in cash
- Minimum price change is one "tick," which is a price change of 0.0001 = 0.01%, representing $25 per $1 million contract

 37

LOS 62.f Describe
CFAI p. 57, Schweser p. 219 Futures Markets and Contracts

Treasury Bond Futures

- Traded for Treasury bonds with maturities greater than 15 years
- Deliverable
- Face value of $100,000
- Quoted as a percent and fractions of 1% (measured in 1/32nds) of face value

 38

LOS 62.f Describe
CFAI p. 57, Schweser p. 219 Futures Markets and Contracts

Stock Index Futures

S&P 500 Index Futures:

- Value of a contract is **250 times the level of the index**
- Each index point in the futures price represents a gain or loss of $250 per contract
- A smaller contract is traded on the same index and has a multiplier of 50

Futures contracts covering several other popular indexes are traded as well

 39

LOS 62.f Describe
CFAI p. 57, Schweser p. 219 Futures Markets and Contracts

Currency Futures

- In the United States, currency contracts trade on the euro (EUR), Mexican peso (MXP), and yen (JPY), among others
- Contracts are set in units of the foreign currency, and the price is stated in USD/unit

 40

Derivatives

63. Option Markets and Contracts

Derivatives

LOS 63.a Describe
CFAI p. 72, Schweser p. 226

Option Markets and Contracts

Options Basics

- **Option buyer** (owner, long position)
  Pays a premium to purchase the ***right*** to exercise an option at a future date and price
- **Option seller** (writer, short position)
  Incurs an **obligation** to perform under the option contract terms

42

LOS 63.a Describe
CFAI p. 72, Schweser p. 226 Option Markets and Contracts

Options Basics

- **Call option**: Long has the right to purchase the underlying asset at the exercise (strike) price; short has the obligation to sell/deliver the underlying asset at the exercise price

- **Put option**: Long has the right to sell the underlying asset at the exercise (strike) price; short has the obligation to purchase the underlying asset at the exercise price

 43

LOS 63.b Distinguish
CFAI p. 73, Schweser p. 227 Option Markets and Contracts

Options Terminology

- ***American* options** can be exercised **any time** prior to expiration (early exercise) or at expiration
- ***European* options** can be exercised **only at expiration**
- American options are worth **at least as much** as otherwise identical European options

 44

LOS 63.c Define
CFAI p. 75, Schweser p. 228
Option Markets and Contracts

Moneyness

Call Options

In-the-money	S > X	S – X > 0
At-the-money	S = X	S – X = 0
Out-of-the-money	S < X	S – X < 0

Put Options

In-the-money	S < X	S – X < 0
At-the-money	S = X	S – X = 0
Out-of-the-money	S > X	S – X > 0

45

LOS 63.c Define
CFAI p. 75, Schweser p. 228
Option Markets and Contracts

Call Option Example

- Stock price is $47
- Call with exercise price of $50 is trading at $1.50
  - **Out-of-the-money**: Intrinsic value is zero
  - Time value is $1.50 – 0 = $1.50

- Call with exercise price of $45 is trading at $3.00
  - **In-the-money**: Intrinsic value is $47 – $45 = $2
  - Time value is $3.00 – $2.00 = $1.00

46

LOS 63.c Define
CFAI p. 75, Schweser p. 228 Option Markets and Contracts

Put Option Example

- Stock price is $47
- Put with exercise price of $45 is trading at $1.50
  - **Out-of-the-money**: Intrinsic value is zero
  - Time value is $1.50 – 0 = $1.50
- Put with exercise price of $50 is trading at $4.00
  - In-the-money: Intrinsic value is $50 – $47 = $3
  - Time value is $4.00 – $3.00 = $1.00

 47

LOS 63.d Compare
CFAI p. 76, Schweser p. 229 Option Markets and Contracts

Exchange-Traded vs. OTC Options

- Exchange-traded (listed) options:
  Standardized, regulated, backed by clearinghouse
- Over-the-counter options:
  Customized, unregulated, have counterparty risk

 48

LOS 63.e Identify
CFAI p. 80, Schweser p. 229 Option Markets and Contracts

Types of Options: Underlying Assets

- **Commodity options**: (e.g., call option on 100 ounces of gold at $820 per ounce)
- **Stock options**: Each contract for 100 shares
- **Bond options**: Like stock options, payoff based on bond price and exercise price
- **Index options**: Have a multiplier (e.g., payoff is $250 in cash for every index point the option is in the money at expiration)

 49

LOS 63.e Identify
CFAI p. 80, Schweser p. 229 Option Markets and Contracts

Types of Options: Underlying Assets

Options on futures:

- **Calls** give the option to enter into a futures contract as the **long** at a specific futures price
- **Puts** give the option to enter into a futures contract as the **short** at the indicated futures price

At exercise, futures position is marked to market

 50

LOS 63.f Compare
CFAI p. 81, Schweser p. 230 Option Markets and Contracts

Interest Rate Options

- **Interest rate options**: Payoff based on the difference between a floating rate, such as LIBOR, and the strike rate
- Payoff on a LIBOR-based **interest rate call** is Max[0,(LIBOR – strike rate)] × notional amount **(long gains when rates rise)**
- Payoff on a LIBOR-based **interest rate put** is Max[0,(strike rate – LIBOR)] × notional amount (long gains when rates fall)
  - Payoffs made at the **end of the interest rate term** (after option expiration)

 51

LOS 63.f Compare
CFAI p. 81, Schweser p. 230 Option Markets and Contracts

Two Interest Rate Options = One FRA

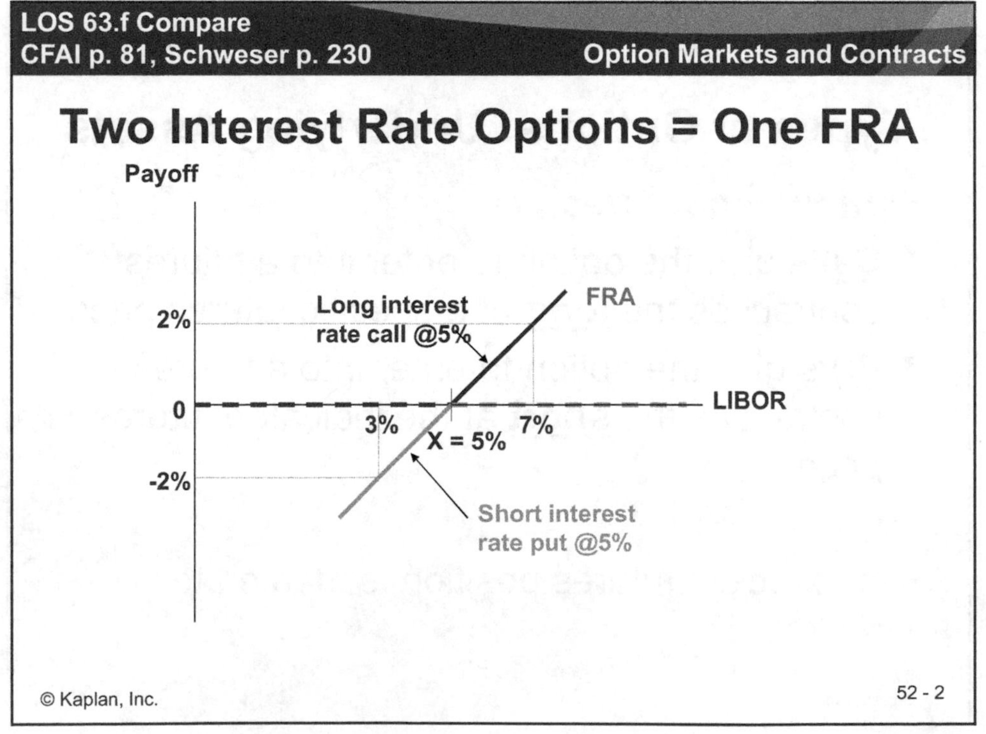

 52 - 2

LOS 63.g Define
CFAI p. 83, Schweser p. 231 Option Markets and Contracts

Interest Rate Caps and Floors

- A **cap** puts a ***maximum*** on an issuer's payments on a floating rate debt
  - Equivalent to series of **long interest rate calls**
  - Makes payments to issuer when floating rate > cap (strike) rate
- A **floor** puts a ***minimum*** on an issuer's payments on a floating rate debt
  - Equivalent to series of **short interest rate puts**
  - Issuer must make payments when floating rate < floor (strike) rate

 53

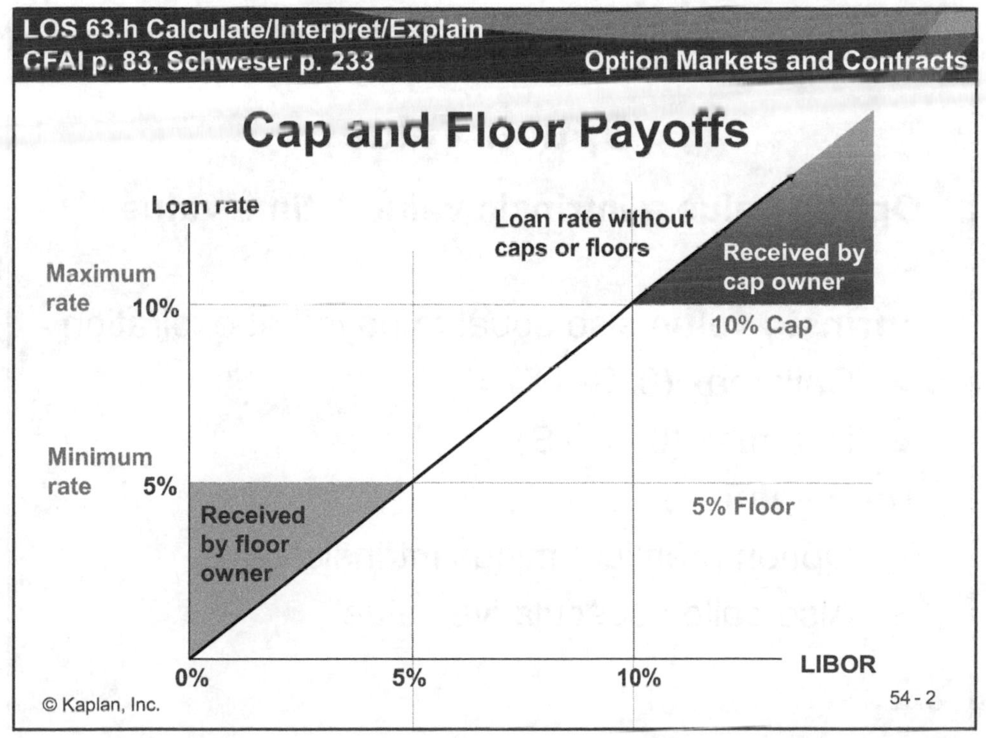

Option Markets and Contracts

Interest Rate Option – Problem

- Long 60-day call on 90-day LIBOR
- Notional amount = $1 million
- Strike rate = 5%
- 90-day LIBOR at expiration (in 60 days) = 6%

What is payoff to long? When is it paid?

55 - 2

LOS 63.i Define/Explain
CFAI p. 88, Schweser p. 234

Option Markets and Contracts

Option Value

Option value = intrinsic value + time value

Intrinsic value also equal to payoff at expiration

- Call: max (0, S – X)
- Put: max (0, X – S)

Time value

- Option premium minus intrinsic value
- Also called speculative value

56

LOS 63.j,k Determine/Calculate/Interpret
CFAI p. 91, Schweser p. 237 Option Markets and Contracts

Options Notation

S_t = price of underlying asset at time t

X = exercise price

T = time to expiration

RFR = risk-free rate

c_t, p_t = European style calls and puts at time = t

C_t, P_t = American style calls and puts at time = t

 57

LOS 63.j,k,n Determine/Calculate/Interpret/Explain
CFAI p. 91, Schweser p. 237 Option Markets and Contracts

Minimum and Maximum Option Values

Minimum	Maximum
$c_t \geq \text{Max}\left[0, S_t - X/(1+\text{RFR})^{T-t}\right]$	S_t
$C_t \geq \text{Max}\left[0, S_t - X/(1+\text{RFR})^{T-t}\right]$	S_t
$p_t \geq \text{Max}\left[0, X/(1+\text{RFR})^{T-t} - S_t\right]$	$X/(1+\text{RFR})^{T-t}$
$P_t \geq \text{Max}\left[0, X - S_t\right]$	X

European puts: No early exercise means lower maximum, PV of X at expiration

 58

LOS 63.l Explain
CFAI p. 96, Schweser p. 242 Option Markets and Contracts

Options That Differ Only By Exercise Price

- Given two **puts** that are identical in all respects except exercise price, the one with the ***higher*** *exercise price* will have **at least as much value** as the one with the lower exercise price
- Given two **calls** that are identical in every respect except exercise price, the one with the ***lower*** *exercise price* will have **at least as much value** as the one with the higher exercise price

LOS 63.m Explain
CFAI p. 98, Schweser p. 243 Option Markets and Contracts

Deriving Put-Call Parity (European Options)

Protective put = stock + put

If $S \leq X$, payoff = $S + (X - S) = X$
If $S \geq X$, payoff = $S + 0 = S$

X
0
X

Fiduciary call = call + $X / (1 + RFR)^T$
(bond that pays X at maturity)

If $S \leq X$, payoff = $0 + X = X$
If $S \geq X$, payoff = $(S - X) + X = S$

Same payoffs means same values by no-arbitrage
Put-call parity: $S + P = C + X / (1 + RFR)^T$

LOS 63.m Explain
CFAI p. 98, Schweser p. 243

Option Markets and Contracts

Parity Conditions and Synthetic Options

$$S + P = C + \frac{X}{(1+RFR)^T} \text{ can be rearranged}$$

$$\text{to get } P = C - S + \frac{X}{(1+RFR)^T}$$

$$\text{and } C = P + S - \frac{X}{(1+RFR)^T}$$

61

Option Markets and Contracts

Put-Call Parity – Problem

- Stock XYZ trades at $75
- Call premium = $4.50
- Expiration = 4 months (T = 0.3333)
- X = $75
- RFR = 5%

What is the price of the 4-month put on XYZ?

62 - 2

LOS 63.l,o Explain/Determine
CFAI p. 96, Schweser p. 242 Option Markets and Contracts

Time, Volatility, RFR, and Strike Price

Longer **time to expiration increases option values**

Except for: Some far out-of-the-money options and European style puts

Greater **price volatility increases option values**

Increase in **RFR** increases call values and decreases put values

For $X_1 < X_2$: call at $X_1 \geq$ call at X_2
put at $X_1 \leq$ put at X_2

 63

LOS 63.n Explain
CFAI p. 104, Schweser p. 245 Option Markets and Contracts

Cash Flows on the Underlying Asset

- If the asset has **positive cash flows** over the period of the option, the cost of the asset is reduced by the present value of the cash flows
- For assets with positive cash flows over the term of the option, we can **substitute this (lower) net cost, S – PVCF,** for S in the lower bound conditions and in all the parity relations

 64

Derivatives

64. Swap Markets and Contracts

Derivatives

LOS 64.a Describe/Explain
CFAI p. 120, Schweser p. 255

Swap Markets and Contracts

Swap Contracts: Overview

- If A loans money to B for a fixed rate of interest and B loans the same amount to A for floating rate of interest, it's an **interest rate swap**
- If one of the returns streams is based on a stock portfolio or index return, it's an **equity swap**
- If the loans are in two different currencies, it's a **currency swap**

66

LOS 64.a Describe/Explain
CFAI p. 120, Schweser p. 255

Swap Markets and Contracts

Characteristics of Swap Contracts

- Custom instruments
- Not traded in any organized secondary market
- Largely unregulated
- Default risk is a concern
- Most participants are large institutions
- Private agreements
- Difficult to alter or terminate

67

LOS 64.a Describe/Explain
CFAI p. 120, Schweser p. 255

Swap Markets and Contracts

Swap Contract Terminology

- **Notional principal**: Amount used to calculate periodic payments
- **Floating rate**: Usually U.S. LIBOR
- **Tenor**: Time period covered by swap
- **Settlement dates**: Payment due dates

68

LOS 64.a Describe/Explain
CFAI p. 120, Schweser p. 255 Swap Markets and Contracts

Terminating a Swap

- Swap can be terminated by:
  - Mutual agreement/payment with counterparty
  - Enter offsetting swap
  - Exercise swaption
  - Sell position with permission of counterparty

 69

LOS 64.b Describe/Calculate/ Interpret
CFAI p. 123, Schweser p. 256 Swap Markets and Contracts

Currency Swap Example

- Assume current exchange rate is \$1.20/euro
- Company A lends \$1.2 million to Company B at 5%/year (USD interest rate)
- Company B lends 1 million euros to Company A at 4%/year (euro interest rate)
- Loans are for two years and interest is paid semiannually

 70

LOS 64.b Describe/Calculate/ Interpret
CFAI p. 123, Schweser p. 256 Swap Markets and Contracts

Currency Swap Cash Flows

At time 0:

Company A lends \$1.2 million to Company B

Company B lends €1 million to Company A

At each semi-annual settlement date (t = 1,2,3,4):

A pays 0.04 / 2 × €1 million = €20,000 to B

B pays 0.05 / 2 × \$1.2 million = \$30,000 to A

 71 - 2

LOS 64.b Describe/Calculate/ Interpret
CFAI p. 123, Schweser p. 256 Swap Markets and Contracts

Currency Swap Cash Flows

At t = 4 settlement date, in addition to the interest payments:

- Company B repays \$1.2 million to Company A
- Company A repays €1 million to Company B
- This is a **fixed-for-fixed** currency swap because both loans carried a fixed rate of interest
- Could be **fixed-for-floating** or **floating-for-floating**

 72 - 1

LOS 64.b Describe/Calculate/ Interpret
CFAI p. 123, Schweser p. 256 Swap Markets and Contracts

Plain Vanilla Interest Rate Swap

- **Fixed interest rate payments are exchanged for floating-rate payments**
- **Notional amount is not exchanged** at the beginning or end of the swap (both loans are in same currency and amount)

 73

LOS 64.b Describe/Calculate/ Interpret
CFAI p. 123, Schweser p. 256 Swap Markets and Contracts

Plain Vanilla Interest Rate Swap

- Interest payments are **netted**
- On settlement dates, both interest payments are calculated and only the difference is paid by the party owing the greater amount
- Floating rate payments are typically made in **arrears**, payment is made at end of period based on beginning-of-period LIBOR

 74

LOS 64.b Describe/Calculate/ Interpret
CFAI p. 123, Schweser p. 256 Swap Markets and Contracts

Plain Vanilla Interest Rate Swap

Fixed rate payment (at time *t*)

$$= (\text{Swap FR} - \text{Libor}_{t-1}) \times \left(\frac{T}{360}\right) \times (\text{NP})$$

FR = fixed rate

T = number of days in settlement period

NP = notional principal

 75

LOS 64.b Describe/Calculate/ Interpret
CFAI p. 123, Schweser p. 256 Swap Markets and Contracts

Fixed-for-Floating Swap Example

Example: 2-year, semiannual-pay, LIBOR, plain vanilla interest rate swap for $10 million with a fixed rate of 6. Semiannual fixed payments are: (0.06 / 2) × $10 million = $300,000

LIBOR t_0 = 5%, t_1 = 5.8%, t_2 = 6.2%, t_3 = 6.6%

First payment:**Fixed-rate payer** pays $50,000 net
(0.06 – **0.05**)(180/360)(10 million) = $50,000

First net payment is known at swap initiation!

 76 - 2

LOS 64.b Describe/Calculate/ Interpret
CFAI p. 123, Schweser p. 256 Swap Markets and Contracts

LIBOR 5% at t_0, 5.8% at t_1, 6.2% at t_2, 6.6% at t_3

Second payment: **Fixed rate payer** pays $10,000 net
(0.06 – **0.058**)(180 / 360)(10 million) = $10,000

Third payment: **Floating rate payer** pays $10,000 net
(0.06 – **0.062**)(180 / 360)(10 million) = –$10,000

Fourth payment: **Floating rate payer** pays $30,000 net
(0.06 – **0.066**)(180 / 360)(10 million) = –$30,000

 77 - 4

LOS 64.b Describe/Calculate/ Interpret
CFAI p. 123, Schweser p. 256 Swap Markets and Contracts

Equity Swaps

Payments based on equity returns are exchanged for fixed-rate or floating-rate payments

Equity return based on:

- Individual stock
- Stock portfolio
- Stock index

Can be *capital appreciation* or *total return* including dividends

 78

LOS 64.b Describe/Calculate/ Interpret
CFAI p. 123, Schweser p. 256 — Swap Markets and Contracts

Equity Swaps

- **Equity return payer**:
  - Receives interest payment
  - Pays any positive equity return
  - Receives any negative equity return
- **Interest payer**:
  - Pays interest payment
  - Receives positive equity return
  - Pays any negative equity return

 79

LOS 64.b Describe/Calculate/ Interpret
CFAI p. 123, Schweser p. 256 — Swap Markets and Contracts

Equity Swap Example

- 2-year, $10 million quarterly-pay equity swap
- Equity return = S&P 500 Index
- Fixed rate = 8%
- Current index level = 986

Q1: S&P 500 = 1030 → Return = 4.46%
Q2: S&P 500 = 968 → Return = –6.02%
Q3: S&P 500 = 989 → Return = 2.17%

Holder of index portfolio + swap gets 2% per quarter (plus dividends) for any index value!

 80

LOS 64.b Describe/Calculate/ Interpret
CFAI p. 123, Schweser p. 256 Swap Markets and Contracts

Equity Swap Example (continued)

Index return payer pays (+) receives (–):

Q1: 4.46% – 2.00% = 2.46%
→ $246,000 net payment

Q2: –6.02% – 2.00% = –8.02%
→ –$802,000 net payment

Q3: 2.17% – 2.00% = 0.17%
→ $17,000 net payment

 81 - 3

Swap Markets and Contracts

Equity Swap – Problem

Acme is the 8% quarterly fixed-rate payer in a $10 million equity swap based on an index (currently 1180) return. If the index is 1140 at the end of the quarter, Acme will:

A. pay $538,983.

B. pay $138,983.

C. receive $338,983.

 82 - 2

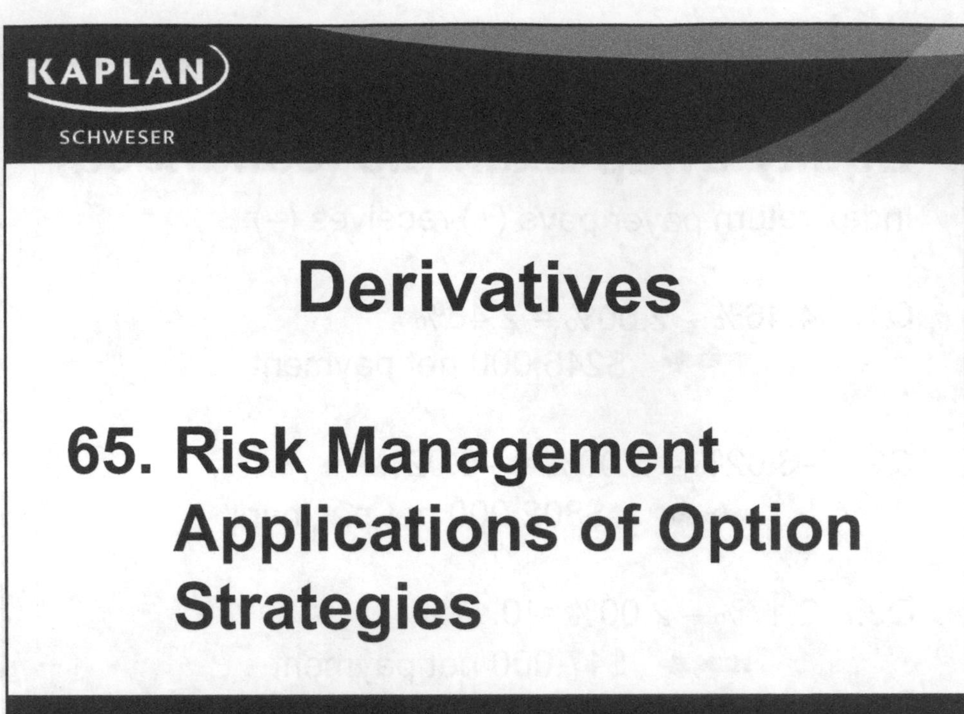
KAPLAN
SCHWESER
Derivatives
65. Risk Management Applications of Option Strategies
Derivatives

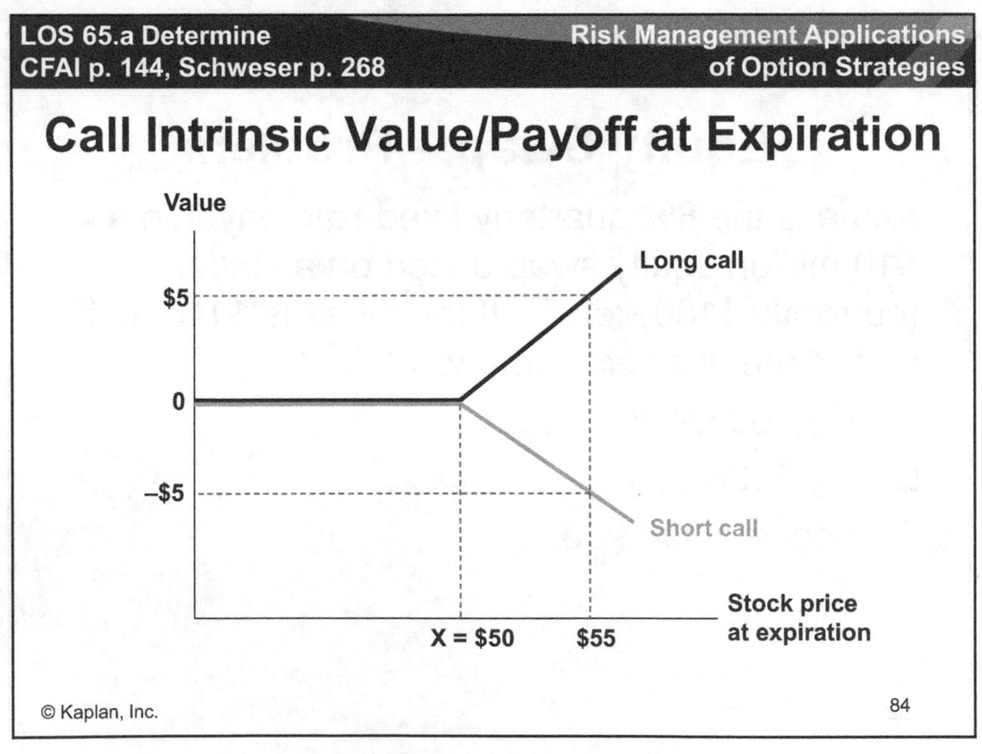
LOS 65.a Determine
CFAI p. 144, Schweser p. 268
Risk Management Applications of Option Strategies
Call Intrinsic Value/Payoff at Expiration
Value
Long call
$5
0
–$5
Short call
Stock price at expiration
X = $50
$55
© Kaplan, Inc.
84

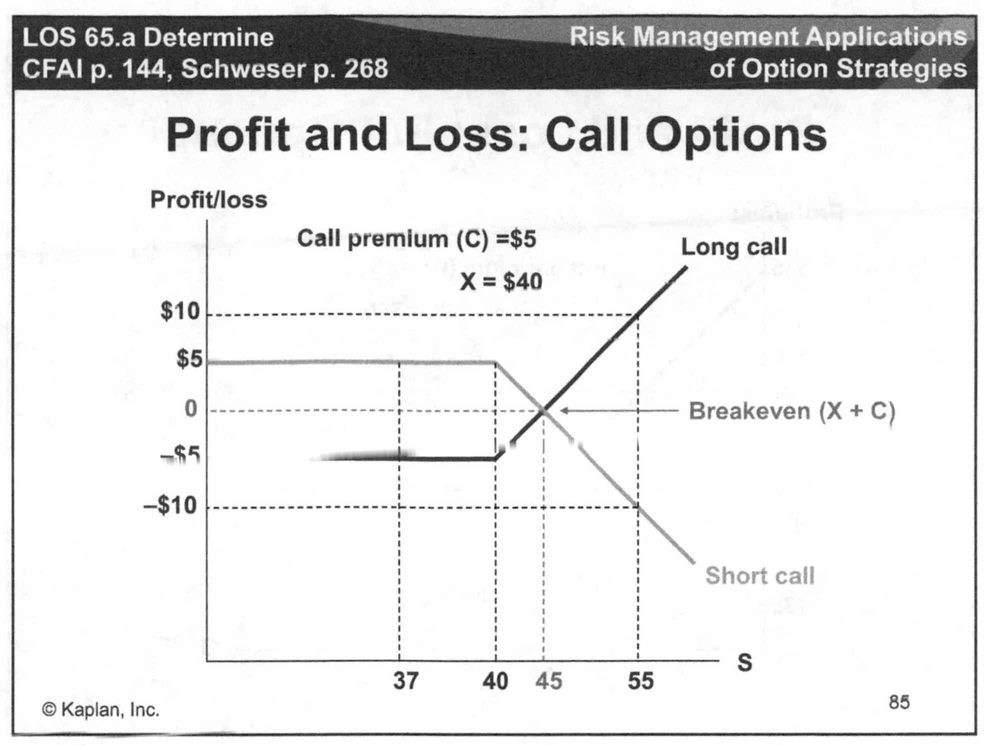
LOS 65.a Determine
CFAI p. 144, Schweser p. 268
Risk Management Applications of Option Strategies
Profit and Loss: Call Options
Profit/loss
Call premium (C) =$5
X = $40
Long call
$10
$5
0
–$5
–$10
Breakeven (X + C)
Short call
37
40
45
55
S
© Kaplan, Inc.
85

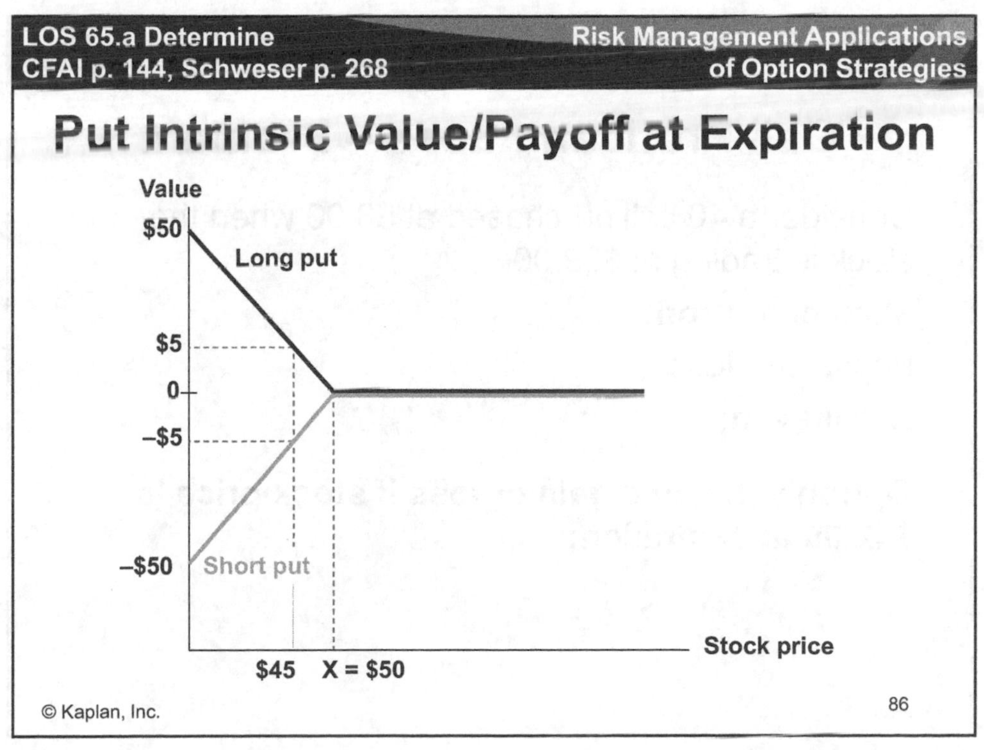
LOS 65.a Determine
CFAI p. 144, Schweser p. 268
Risk Management Applications of Option Strategies
Put Intrinsic Value/Payoff at Expiration
Value
$50
Long put
$5
0
–$5
–$50
Short put
Stock price
$45
X = $50
© Kaplan, Inc.
86

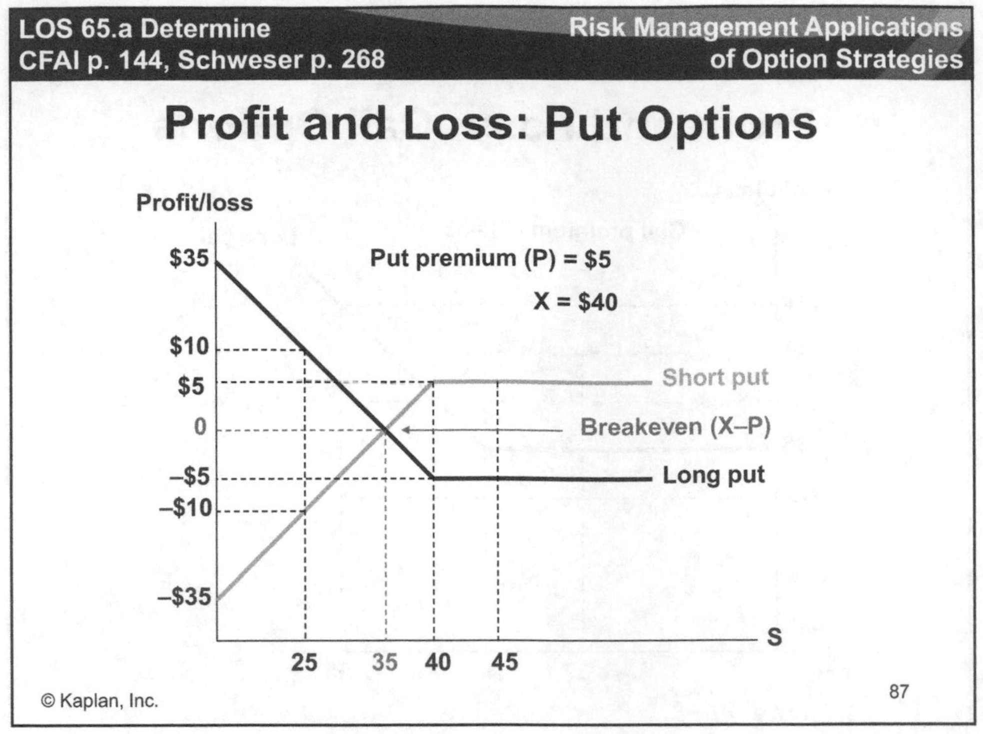

Risk Management Applications of Option Strategies

Call Profit and Loss – Problem

Consider a 40 call purchased at $3.00 when the stock is trading at $39.00

Maximum profit:

Maximum loss:

Breakeven:

Option value and gain or loss if stock price is $42.00 at expiration:

88 - 4

LOS 65.b Determine/Explain
CFAI p. 151, Schweser p. 272

Risk Management Applications of Option Strategies

Covered Call Strategy (Position)

- Writer owns the stock and sells a call
- Any loss will be reduced by premium received
- Writer **trades the stock's upside potential for the option premium**

Risk Management Applications of Option Strategies

Covered Call – Problem

- Buy stock at $39
- Sell a 40 Call at $3
  - **Net cost of *position***:
  - **Breakeven stock price at expiration**:
  - **Maximum gain**:
  - **Maximum loss**:
  - **Profit/loss at stock price of 39**:
  - **Profit/loss at stock price of 32**:

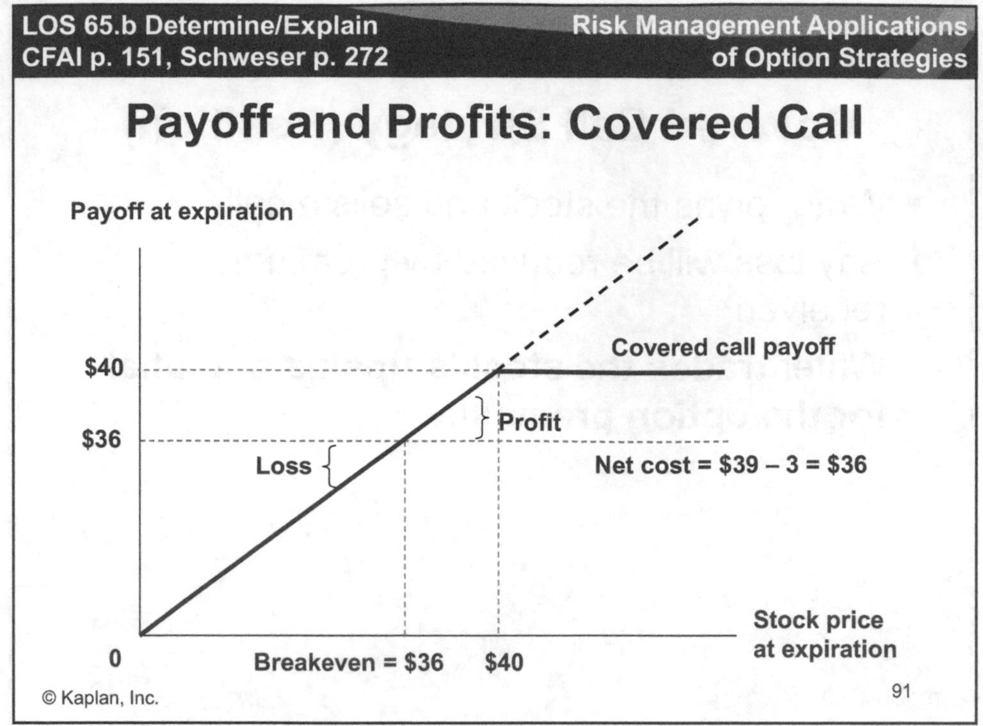

LOS 65.b Determine/Explain
CFAI p. 151, Schweser p. 272

Risk Management Applications of Option Strategies

Protective Put Strategy (Position)

- Long the stock and long a put
- Any gain on the stock will be reduced by premium paid for the put
- Put buyer pays for protection against stock price falling below the strike price

92

LOS 65.b Determine/Explain
CFAI p. 151, Schweser p. 272

Risk Management Applications of Option Strategies

Example: Protective Put

- Buy stock at $41
- Buy a 40 put for $3
- Cost of protective put strategy = 41 + 3 = $44
  - **Breakeven** stock price at expiration = $44
  - **Maximum gain**: Unlimited
  - **Maximum loss**: $4 (if stock price ≤ 40)
    - At stock price of 47 → profit = $3
    - At stock price of 38 → loss = $4

93

LOS 65.b Determine/Explain
CFAI p. 151, Schweser p. 272

Risk Management Applications of Option Strategies

Payoff and Profit: Protective Put

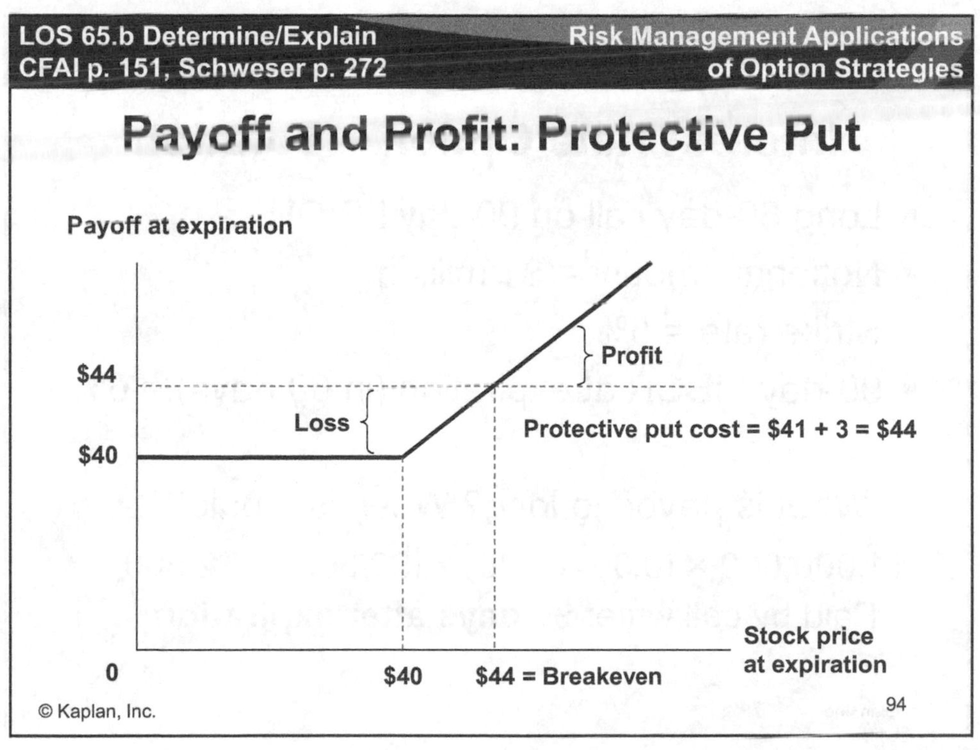

94

Forward Markets and Contracts

Equity Index Forward – Solution

- 90-day S&P 100 forward contract
- Forward contract price = 525.2
- Notional amount = \$10 million
- In 90 days, index is at 535.7

What is the payment at settlement and which party receives it?

Long receives (535.7 – 525.2) / 525.2 × \$10 million = \$200,000 at settlement, paid by the short

Option Markets and Contracts

Interest Rate Option – Solution

- Long 60-day call on 90-day LIBOR
- Notional amount = \$1 million
- Strike rate = 5%
- 90-day LIBOR at expiration (in 60 days) = 6%

What is payoff to long? When is it paid?

\$1,000,000 × (0.06 – 0.05) × (90/360) = \$2,500

Paid by call writer **90 days after expiration**

Option Markets and Contracts

Put-Call Parity – Solution

- Stock XYZ trades at $75
- Call premium = $4.50
- Expiration = 4 months (T = 0.3333)
- X = $75
- RFR = 5%

What is the price of the 4-month put on XYZ?

$$\text{put} = \text{call} - \text{stock} + \frac{X}{(1+\text{RFR})^{T}}$$

$$= 4.50 - 75 + \frac{75}{(1.05)^{.3333}} = \$3.29$$

Swap Markets and Contracts

Equity Swap – Solution

Acme is the 8% quarterly fixed-rate payer in a $10 million equity swap based on an index (currently 1180) return. If the index is 1140 at the end of the quarter, Acme will:

A. pay $538,983.

HPR is negative. Acme must pay 2% fixed, and 3.3898% as the equity return receiver.

Risk Management Applications of Option Strategies

Call Profit and Loss – Solution

Consider a 40 call purchased at $3.00 when the stock is trading at $39.00

Maximum profit: Unlimited

Maximum loss: –$3.00

Breakeven: Stock price at expiration = $43.00

Option value and gain or loss if stock price is $42.00 at expiration:

Value at expiration is $2.00, paid $3.00, so loss is $1.00 (would be gain to call writer)

Risk Management Applications of Option Strategies

Covered Call – Solution

- Buy stock at $39
- Sell a 40 Call at $3
  - **Net cost of *position***:39 – 3 = $36
  - **Breakeven stock price at expiration**:$36
  - **Maximum gain**: 40 – 36 = $4
  - **Maximum loss**:$36 (if stock goes to zero)
  - **Profit/loss at stock price of 39**:$3
  - **Profit/loss at stock price of 32**:–$4

Study Session 18

Alternative Investments

Alternative Investments

66. Introduction to Alternative Investments

Alternative Investments

LOS 66.b Describe
CFAI p. 174, Schweser p. 278

Introduction to Alternative Investments

Categories of Alternative Investments

- Hedge funds
- Private equity
- Real estate
- Commodities
- Others (e.g., collectibles, patents)

2

LOS 66.a Compare
CFAI p. 170, Schweser p. 278

Introduction to Alternative Investments

Alternative vs. Traditional Investments

- Different types of assets held, structure of investment vehicles
- Higher fees (management, incentive)
- Less liquid
- Less regulated, less transparent
- Different tax treatments

3

LOS 66.c Describe
CFAI p. 177, Schweser p. 279

Introduction to Alternative Investments

Benefits of Alternative Investments

- Potential portfolio diversification benefits
  - Low correlation with traditional investment returns
  - Higher average returns than traditional investments
- Return measures biased upward, risk measures biased downward
  - Survivorship bias
  - Backfill bias

4

LOS 66.d,e Describe
CFAI p. 178, Schweser p. 280

Introduction to Alternative Investments

Hedge Funds

- Investment companies structured as limited partnerships
- Use leverage, derivatives, short selling
- Limited to qualified investors
  - Lockup period: Minimum time before investor can withdraw funds
  - Notice period: Days within which a fund must fulfill a redemption request

5

LOS 66.d,e Describe
CFAI p. 178, Schweser p. 280

Introduction to Alternative Investments

Hedge Fund Strategies

1. Event-driven strategies

- Merger arbitrage: Buy shares of firm being acquired, short shares of acquirer
- Distressed/restructuring: Buy if restructuring will increase value
- Activist shareholder: Gain board seats to influence company decisions
- Special situations: Spinoffs, asset sales, security issuance or repurchase

6

LOS 66.d,e Describe
CFAI p. 178, Schweser p. 280

Introduction to Alternative Investments

Hedge Fund Strategies

2. **Relative value strategies**
   - Convertible arbitrage: Convertible bonds versus underlying common stock
   - Asset-backed: ABS, MBS
   - General fixed income
   - Volatility: Trade options based on implied versus expected volatility
   - Multi-strategy: Across asset classes

7

LOS 66.d,e Describe
CFAI p. 178, Schweser p. 280

Introduction to Alternative Investments

Hedge Fund Strategies

3. **Macro strategies**: Trade securities, currencies, commodities based on global economic trends
4. **Equity hedge fund strategies**
   - Market neutral: Equal values in long and short positions
   - Fundamental growth: Identify high-growth companies

8

LOS 66.d,e Describe
CFAI p. 178, Schweser p. 280

Introduction to Alternative Investments

Hedge Fund Strategies

4. **Equity hedge fund strategies, continued**
   - Fundamental value: Identify undervalued companies
   - Quantitative directional: May have net long or short exposure
   - Short bias: Net short exposure

Fund of funds: Invest in multiple hedge funds

LOS 66.d,e Describe
CFAI p. 178, Schweser p. 280

Introduction to Alternative Investments

Hedge Fund Valuation Issues

- Should use bid prices for long positions, ask prices for short positions
- Values of non-traded securities estimated with pricing models
- Illiquid securities
  - Reduce market price to account for illiquidity based on size of position held
  - Trading NAV is adjusted for illiquidity

Hedge Fund Strategies – Problem

A hedge fund manager has taken a large leveraged position long the euro and an equally large leveraged position short the yen. The *most likely* classification of this hedge fund strategy is:

A. market neutral.

B. special situations.

C. macro strategy.

11 - 1

LOS 66.d,e Describe
CFAI p. 178, Schweser p. 280

Introduction to Alternative Investments

Private Equity

- Invest in private companies or take public companies private
- Private equity strategies:
  - Leveraged buyout
  - Venture capital

  (Leveraged buyout and Venture capital: Focus for exam)
  - Developmental capital / minority equity / private investment in public equity (PIPE)
  - Distressed investing

12

LOS 66.d,e Describe
CFAI p. 178, Schweser p. 280

Introduction to Alternative Investments

Leveraged Buyouts

- Most common private equity strategy
- Funded by debt
  - Bank debt, high yield bonds
  - Mezzanine financing: Subordinated debt, includes warrants or conversion to equity
- **Management buyout**: Current managers involved in purchase, remain with company
- **Management buy-in**: Replace managers of acquired company

13

LOS 66.d,e Describe
CFAI p. 178, Schweser p. 280

Introduction to Alternative Investments

Venture Capital

1. **Formative stage**
   - Angel investing: Business plans, market potential
   - Seed stage: Product development, market research
   - Early stage: Begin production and sales
2. **Later stage**: Company expansion
3. **Mezzanine stage**: Prepare for IPO

14

Private Equity Structure and Fees

- Typically structured as limited partnership
- Investors provide **committed capital** which fund managers draw down to invest in portfolio companies
- Management fees typically 1% to 3% of committed capital
- Incentive fees typically 20% of profits
    - Fees paid periodically may exceed 20% over time: Clawback provision requires managers to return excess fees

LOS 66.d,e Describe
CFAI p. 178, Schweser p. 280
Introduction to Alternative Investments

Private Equity Exit Strategies

- **Trade sale**: Sell portfolio company to competitor
- **Secondary sale**: Sell portfolio company to other private equity investors
- **IPO**: Sell portfolio company shares to public
- **Recapitalization**: Issue portfolio company debt to fund dividend payment (to private equity owner)
- **Write-off/liquidation**: Take loss

LOS 66.d,e Describe
CFAI p. 178, Schweser p. 280

Introduction to Alternative Investments

Private Equity Valuation

- Same techniques used to value publicly traded companies are used to value private equity portfolio companies
  - Market/comparables approach
  - Discounted cash flow approach
  - Asset-based approach
- Private companies may require different discount rates or price multiples than publicly traded companies

17

LOS 66.d,e Describe
CFAI p. 178, Schweser p. 280

Introduction to Alternative Investments

Real Estate

- Residential property
- Commercial property
- Mortgages, mortgage-backed securities
- Real Estate Investment Trusts (REITs)
- Farmland, timberland

18

LOS 66.d,e Describe
CFAI p. 178, Schweser p. 280

Introduction to Alternative Investments

Real Estate Valuation

- Comparable sales approach: Recent sales of similar properties
- Income approach
  - Present value of future cash flows from property
  - Net operating income / capitalization rate
- Cost approach: Replacement cost, including land and current costs to rebuild

LOS 66.d,e Describe
CFAI p. 178, Schweser p. 280

Introduction to Alternative Investments

Real Estate Investment Trust Valuation

- Income based: Similar to direct capitalization
  - Funds from operations (FFO)
  - Adjusted funds from operations (AFFO)
  - Capitalization rates
- Asset-based approach to calculating a REIT's NAV: (Market value of total assets – total liabilities) / Number of REIT shares outstanding

LOS 66.d,e Describe
CFAI p. 178, Schweser p. 280

Introduction to Alternative Investments

Commodities

- Commodities exposure most commonly gained through derivatives rather than outright ownership
- Return comes from price changes (no income)
- Hedge against inflation risk

21

LOS 66.d,e Describe
CFAI p. 178, Schweser p. 280

Introduction to Alternative Investments

Commodities

- Commodity ETFs: Available to investors who are restricted to equity shares
- Shares of commodity producers: Less-than-perfect correlation with commodity prices
- Managed futures funds: Active management of commodity investments
- Individual managed accounts
- Commodity sector funds

22

LOS 66.d,e Describe
CFAI p. 178, Schweser p. 280

Introduction to Alternative Investments

Commodities Valuation

Futures price ≈ Spot price × (1 + risk-free rate)
+ Storage costs
– Convenience yield

- Convenience yield: Value of having physical commodity available for use
  - Low convenience yield → **contango**
    Futures prices > spot price
  - High convenience yield → **backwardation**
    Spot price > futures prices

More in "Investing in Commodities"

23

LOS 66.f Describe/Calculate/Interpret
CFAI p. 185, Schweser p. 292

Introduction to Alternative Investments

Hedge Fund Fees

- "2 and 20:" 2% management fee, 20% incentive fee
- Management fee may be calculated on beginning or ending assets
- Incentive fee may be net of management fees or independent of management fees
- Fund of funds typically charges "1 and 10" in addition to fees paid on underlying hedge fund investments

24

LOS 66.f Describe/Calculate/Interpret
CFAI p. 185, Schweser p. 292

Introduction to Alternative Investments

Hedge Fund Fees

- Hard hurdle rate: Incentive fees only on gains above hurdle rate
- Soft hurdle rate: Incentive fees on all gains, but only if return exceeds hurdle rate
- High water mark: Incentive fees only on gains that increase assets above highest previous value

25

LOS 66.f Describe/Calculate/Interpret
CFAI p. 185, Schweser p. 292

Introduction to Alternative Investments

Hedge Fund Fees—Example

Assets under management (before fees) are $110.0 million at initiation, $102.2 million at the end of Year 1, and $118.0 million at the end of Year 2.

Fee structure:

- 2 and 20 based on beginning assets
- Incentive fees net of management fees
- Soft hurdle rate of 5%
- High water mark

26

LOS 66.f Describe/Calculate/Interpret
CFAI p. 185, Schweser p. 292

Introduction to Alternative Investments

Hedge Fund Fees—Example

Year 1

- Management fee = \$110.0 million × 0.02 = \$2.2 million
- Return net of management fee = [(\$102.2 – \$2.2) / \$110.0] – 1 = –9.1%
- No incentive fee: return < hurdle rate
- Total fees = \$2.2 million

27 - 4

LOS 66.f Describe/Calculate/Interpret
CFAI p. 185, Schweser p. 292

Introduction to Alternative Investments

Hedge Fund Fees—Example

Year 2

- Beginning value net of fees = \$102.2 – \$2.2 = \$100.0 million
- Management fee = \$100.0 × 0.02 = \$2.0 million
- Return net of management fee = [(\$118.0 – \$2.0) / \$100] – 1 = 16.0%
- Incentive fee = (\$118.0 – \$2.0 – \$110.0) × 0.20 = \$1.2 million
  High water mark
- Net return to investors = [(\$118.0 – \$2.0 – \$1.2) / \$100.0] – 1 = 14.8%

28 - 5

LOS 66.g Describe
CFAI p. 219, Schweser p. 294

Introduction to Alternative Investments

Risk Management

- Standard deviation is not the most appropriate risk measure
  - Fat tails, negative skewness
  - Returns smoothed by model or appraisal asset valuations
  - Use value-at-risk or Sortino ratio

29

LOS 66.g Describe
CFAI p. 219, Schweser p. 294

Introduction to Alternative Investments

Risk Management

- Risks from use of derivatives (counterparty, liquidity, operational, financial)
- Performance depends on managers' skill
- Lack of transparency
- Illiquidity
- Correlations with traditional investment returns vary over time, may increase during crisis periods

© Kaplan, Inc.

30

Introduction to
Alternative Investments

Risk Management – Problem

Effects of survivorship bias and backfill bias in alternative investment data on the risk and return statistics for this asset class will be:

	Risk	Return
A.	overstated	overstated
B.	overstated	understated
C.	understated	overstated

 31 - 2

Alternatives Investments

67. Investing in Commodities

Alternative Investments

LOS 67.a Explain
CFAI p. 232, Schweser p. 303 Investing in Commodities

Spot Prices and Expected Future Prices

- **Contango**
  Futures price is **above** the spot price
- Long hedgers (users of the commodity) bid up the price of commodity futures—paying a premium for the hedging benefit from taking long futures positions

 33

LOS 67.a Explain
CFAI p. 232, Schweser p. 303 Investing in Commodities

Spot Prices and Expected Future Prices

- **Backwardation**
  Futures price is **below** the spot price
- Dominant traders in a commodity future are **producers hedging** exposure to unexpected **price declines**

 34

LOS 67.b Describe
CFAI p. 234, Schweser p. 304 Investing in Commodities

Sources of Risk and Return

Risk

- Long exposure to a commodity price can be achieved through a derivative investment in forwards or futures
- Some physical commodities cannot be effectively purchased and stored long term, and for others (e.g., precious metals), derivatives may be a more efficient means of gaining long exposure

 35

LOS 67.b Describe
CFAI p. 234, Schweser p. 304

Investing in Commodities

Sources of Risk and Return

Return

The return on a commodity investment includes:

- **Collateral yield**: the return on the collateral posted to satisfy margin requirements
- **Price return**: the gain or loss due to changes in the spot price
- **Roll yield**: the gain or loss resulting from re-establishing positions as contracts expire

  Roll yield is **positive** if the futures market is in **backwardation** and **negative** if the market is in **contango**

LOS 67.c Explain
CFAI p. 239, Schweser p. 305

Investing in Commodities

Commodity Index Investing as an Active Strategy

- A commodity index strategy is considered an active investment because the manager has to decide **which maturities to use** for contracts and determine **when to roll them over** into new contracts
- Active management is also required to **manage portfolio weights** to match those of the benchmark index and to determine the best choice of **securities to post as collateral** and how these should be rolled over as they mature

Investing in Commodities

Commodities – Problem

What is the relationship of futures prices to the spot price if a commodity market is in:

	Contango?	Backwardation?
A.	Futures > spot	Spot > futures
B.	Spot > futures	Futures > spot
C.	Futures > spot	Spot < futures

38 - 1

Investing in Commodities

Roll Yield – Problem

If the dominant demand for hedging using a futures contract are producers of the commodity, the roll yield will *most likely* be:

A. positive.

B. negative.

C. indeterminate.

39 - 2

Hedge Fund Strategies – Solution

A hedge fund manager has taken a large leveraged position long the euro and an equally large leveraged position short the yen. The *most likely* classification of this hedge fund strategy is:

C. macro strategy.

Risk Management – Solution

Effects of survivorship bias and backfill bias in alternative investment data on the risk and return statistics for this asset class will be:

	Risk	Return
C.	**understated**	**overstated**

Surviving firms will be (on average) those that took less risk and those that had higher returns.

Commodities – Solution

What is the relationship of futures prices to the spot price if a commodity market is in:

	Contango?	Backwardation?
A.	**Futures > spot**	**Spot > futures**

Roll Yield – Solution

If the dominant demand for hedging using a futures contract are producers of the commodity, the roll yield will *most likely* be:

A. positive.

Producers hedge by selling futures, driving futures price down, leading to backwardation and a positive roll yield.